Famine and Foreigners: Ethiopia Since Live Aid

Famine and Foreigners: Ethiopia Since Live Aid

Peter Gill

OXFORD
UNIVERSITY PRESS

OXFORD
UNIVERSITY PRESS

Great Clarendon Street, Oxford OX2 6DP

Oxford University Press is a department of the University of Oxford.
It furthers the University's objective of excellence in research, scholarship,
and education by publishing worldwide in

Oxford New York

Auckland Cape Town Dar es Salaam Hong Kong Karachi
Kuala Lumpur Madrid Melbourne Mexico City Nairobi
New Delhi Shanghai Taipei Toronto

With offices in

Argentina Austria Brazil Chile Czech Republic France Greece
Guatemala Hungary Italy Japan Poland Portugal Singapore
South Korea Switzerland Thailand Turkey Ukraine Vietnam

Oxford is a registered trade mark of Oxford University Press
in the UK and in certain other countries

Published in the United States
by Oxford University Press Inc., New York

© Peter Gill 2010

The moral rights of the author have been asserted
Database right Oxford University Press (maker)

First published 2010
First published in paperback 2012

British Library Cataloguing in Publication Data
Data available

Library of Congress Cataloging in Publication Data
Library of Congress Control Number: 2008942646

Typeset by SPI Publisher Services, Pondicherry, India
Printed in Great Britain
on acid-free paper by
Clays Ltd, St Ives Plc

ISBN 978-0-19-956984-7 (Hbk)
978-0-19-964404-9 (Pbk)

1 3 5 7 9 10 8 6 4 2

Contents

Preface   ix
Acknowledgements   xv
Note on the Text   xix
Map of Ethiopia   xx

Introduction: For Richer, for Poorer   1

I.   THEN

   1. Return to Korem   9
   2. The Famine Trail   24
   3. Hunger as a Weapon   45
   4. Rebels with a Cause   63

II. TRANSITIONS

   5. Economic Warfare   79
   6. How to Prevent a Famine   97
   7. Population Matters   120

III. NOW

   8. 2005 and All That   141
   9. Down with Democracy?   161
  10. Free Association   175
  11. Pastoral Affairs   196

IV. PROSPECTS

12. Spoiling the Party   221
13. Enter the Dragon   238
14. Us and Them   255

Select Bibliography   268
Index   271

Preface to the Paperback Edition

Famine has become the F-word in Ethiopia. Ethiopians who care about how the world sees them are troubled by their country's association with hunger and starvation. Some are resentful, a few are outraged. When this book was first published, I encountered only one Ethiopian objection, and that was from officials abroad. It was not about anything in the text, only with a word in the title. I had intended the word 'foreigners' to be pointed, but it was 'famine' that caused offence.

Several times during my researches I was told by Ethiopians that the country's identification with starvation was so great that even the Oxford English Dictionary defined Ethiopia in terms of famine. This connection is a national embarrassment. It is also something of a myth. The full OED entry for Ethiopia does refer to 'repeated famines' during the period of Marxist rule in the 1970s and 1980s, but it also describes Ethiopia as the 'oldest independent country in Africa' and adds that with the downfall of the Marxists 'a multiparty system was adopted.' It is further true that in defining 'famine' as 'extreme scarcity of food' the OED gives this single Ethiopian reference among no fewer than 40 other examples of usage: 'Twenty years after images of starving Ethiopian children shocked the world, famine and drought continue to stalk this African nation.' Zimbabwe and North Korea each gets two examples, India gets one reference, so indeed do Italy and Greece.

In 2011 fresh connections were being made between Ethiopia and severe hunger. The East African food emergency had war-torn Somalia as its epicentre, but the impact of persistent drought extended into northern Kenya, the Somali Region of Ethiopia, and further still into southern Ethiopia. Refugees from starvation and conflict across the Somali frontier added to Ethiopia's burden. As harvests failed, the government in Addis Ababa increased its food aid requirement from around two million people needing help in February, 2011, to 3.2 million in April and 4.6 million in July when a famine was first formally declared in southern Somalia.

That same month the independent online news service *New Business Ethiopia* carried a story presented as a conversation between young Ethiopians in an Addis Ababa cafe. 'Did you guys read about the starvation of over three million people in Ethiopia,' said one. 'I saw the news,' said another, 'but why are you so surprised? The whole world knows us an example of famine thanks to the Oxford English Dictionary.'

The story described how 'many Ethiopians, including those who are successful out of their country, live in humiliation whenever people on the street associate them and their country with hunger and drought.' It quoted one of the group as saying, 'I wonder why feeding ourselves has become so difficult and complicated for us, like a rocket science.'

The OED's definition of the F-word came up again in a national television interview with Meles Zenawi, the Ethiopian Prime Minister. At one point the woman interviewer picked up a copy of the Oxford Advanced Learner's Dictionary and asked him how as an Ethiopian he felt about this linkage. It was a good television gesture, spoilt only by the fact that there had been no reference to Ethiopia and famine in any edition of this dictionary for a decade or more. The Prime Minister took the point head-on, however. He said he felt sad and ashamed about it. It was humiliating. He was determined to play his own role in removing the stigma, but popular perceptions about the country would change only when the situation on the ground changed.

He is surely right, and principal responsibility for combating Ethiopian hunger lies with the Ethiopian government. But there are significant questions raised for the outside world as well, and they are not only about the supply of humanitarian aid during emergencies. There is the western role in the conflict in the Horn of Africa which is an important front in our 'war on terror.' There is also the damaging and one-dimensional image the western world has of Ethiopia and of Africa. It is an image created and sustained by the media and the aid agencies. It has not changed in a quarter of a century, and there is a real danger that we ignore the progress—and thus the potential for progress—made since the dreadful suffering of the 1984 famine when Ethiopian Marxists and Cold Warriors in the West allowed many hundreds of thousands to die of hunger.

The former famine lands of northern Ethiopia are still peopled by poor farmers, still dependent on the rains, but they have seen sustained advances in recent years. There is a sturdiness and stoicism to the Ethiopian peasant, and it is backed by a government and an administration seriously committed to tackling disfiguring poverty. Such is that commitment and the international backing which Ethiopia receives that even as the 2011 crisis unfolded it was possible to predict that there would be a substantial and adequate response to hardship and suffering in the southern borderlands. The cost of getting it wrong would be too great, in human as well as in political terms. The government of Ethiopia, in power for the past 20 years, has seen its predecessors undermined or destroyed by failure to respond to famine. For their part the western democracies can hardly maintain expensive aid programmes around Africa and then fail to prevent widespread death by starvation in a country that has risen right to the top of the priority list of aid recipients.

Another danger in sticking to our pitying images of Africa is that we fail to recognise the bigger economic changes overtaking the continent. Even impoverished Ethiopia has been recording impressive growth rates in recent years, and as for outside players, China's engagement with Africa could well prove more beneficial, more liberating even, than the West's aid and policy prescriptions of the past 50 years. The modern aid movement propounds that social sector services hold the key to more generalised prosperity, and so the West has put its money into education and health. That has not had the desired, transformative effect. We have certainly saved lives and we have improved many people's circumstances, but aid has not created that general economic betterment which 'development' promised. Worse, the suspicion has grown that we are not truly committed to doing so, that we are content to be governed by our pity for Africa.

In an essay first published more than 30 years ago, the Nigerian writer Chinua Achebe referred to the 'dehumanisation of Africa and Africans.'[1] He argued that 'the West seems to suffer deep anxieties about the precariousness of its civilisation and to have a need for constant reassurance by comparison with Africa.' He wondered whether this was changing and went on:

[1] Chinua Achebe, *An Image of Africa: Racism in Conrad's Heart of Darkness*, republished in *Great Ideas*, Penguin Books, 2010.

But as I thought more about the stereotype image, about its grip and pervasiveness, about the wilful tenacity with which the West holds it to its heart; when I thought of the West's television and cinema and newspapers, about books read in its schools and out of school, of churches preaching to empty pews about the need to send help to Africa, I realized that no easy optimism was possible.

As a television and print journalist, I have done quite a bit over the years to draw attention to the impact and the ravages of African food emergencies. Sometimes I have been alongside the aid agencies, on occasions ahead of most of them. I have certainly never witnessed a spectacle more shocking than the huge relief camp at Korem, in the northern highlands of Ethiopia, where famine victims were dying at the rate of 100 a day in October 1984. That recollection has drawn me back several times to find out what happened next.

When I began work on this book in 2008, it was in the expectation that hunger was indeed becoming history in Ethiopia. That would have been the best possible story. My first research trip, at the time of the country's millennium celebrations, coincided with a period of great official optimism. A national renaissance would herald an end to the humiliation of desperate poverty. If not exactly misplaced, such optimism was certainly premature. 2008 turned out to be a bad year and, as Prime Minister Meles Zenawi frankly acknowledged to me, the government had failed in its duty to deal effectively with severe hunger in the South.

Then came, from across the Somali frontier and from within Ethiopia's own borders, the far greater emergency of 2011. My wish to understand the nature of that crisis was not welcomed by some Ethiopian government representatives abroad. I was told that I should not be drawing attention to this. It was an uncomfortable reminder of the distant 1980s, the bad old days under another regime altogether. Circumstances were now quite different. Once again I was likely to make use of the F-word.

I am unapologetic, and 'famine' remains in the title of the book. In another of his early works, Chinua Achebe took on the word *tribe* which had been used in Nigeria's first national anthem, but later dropped. Achebe argued that 'all this self-conscious wish to banish *tribe* has proved largely futile because a word will stay around as long as there is work for it to do.' What goes for the *tribe* surely goes for *famine*. 'Our threatening gestures against it,' Achebe said, 'have been premature, half-hearted or plain deceitful.'[2]

Peter Gill
London, September, 2011

[2] Chinua Achebe, *The Trouble with Nigeria*, republished in *Great Ideas*, Penguin Books, 2010.

Acknowledgements

Several aid agencies made it possible for me to travel into the Ethiopian countryside and meet the people on whose experiences and reflections much of this story is based. In the North I was generously received by Ambassador Tewolde Gebru, director of the Tigray Development Association. Yohannes Seyoum Sahlemariam, head of public relations, was a wonderful travelling companion. With Action Aid I made stimulating trips into the hills around Korem, epicentre of the 1984 famine. It was thanks to Wuletaw Hailemariam, director of the Organisation for the Relief and Development of Amhara, that I spent a week travelling through the highlands of Amhara to the border lowlands and back to the shores of Lake Tana. On the way, I was assisted by the organization's excellent field staff. For two days in Wollo I relied on the expertise of Save the Children Fund UK, which first worked there 70 years ago. In southern Ethiopia I was aided by charities with a strong local presence: the Family Guidance Association of Ethiopia, Community Development Initiative, and the Rift Valley Children and Women Development Association. During my stay in Somali Region, I was looked after by Guled Abdullahi, head of the president's office in Jijiga, and made welcome in Gode by Abdinasir Mohammed, the zonal administrator. I am grateful to them all.

Ambassador Berhanu Kebede in London kindly recommended me to the Ministry of Foreign Affairs in Addis Ababa where Teferi Melesse, head of public diplomacy, went beyond the call of duty in arranging appointments and smoothing my path. Through him I met Bereket Simon, minister for communications, who helped me at key points in my stay, not least in introducing me to Prime Minister Meles Zenawi. Among foreign officials in Addis Ababa, I received help and encouragement from Ken Ohashi, the World Bank's country director, Sukhwinder Singh, the International Monetary Fund's resident representative, and Gavin Cook, at the British embassy. Patrick Gilkes, advisor at the foreign ministry, provided astute guidance, and I am grateful to Irene Beard and members of the London embassy Think Tank for their encouragement. Myles Wickstead, formerly British Ambassador to Ethiopia, introduced me to the group and then supported the book at every step. I also had the support of Professor Stefan Dercon, Dr Sarah Vaughan and Beverley Jones, and all of them took on the additional burden of reviewing the text and preventing me from making too many errors of fact and judgement. Yemeserach Belayneh gave me advice on the population chapter, Stephen Devereux reviewed the chapter on the Somali Region and Wout Soer guided me on matters of food aid and the 'safety net.' None of them has any responsibility for the mistakes and judgements which remain. For contacts with the Ethiopian opposition in exile, I am grateful to Wondimu Mekonnen. Alex de Waal, Keith Bowers, Akbar Noman and John Markakis were generous in sharing their contacts and giving me advice.

This book owes its existence to two commissioning editors at Oxford University Press. My friend Andrew McNeillie introduced me to Sarah Caro who brilliantly steered my proposal through to a commission. Andrew and Sarah have both moved on from OUP, but it is my ambition that their faith in the project should be justified. I have continued to have great support from Aimee Wright and Emma Lambert at OUP and from Sarah's successor Georgia Pinteau.

There were times in my research when I doubted whether I could contribute anything new or worthwhile to an understanding of one of Africa's most complex countries over 25 years of its relationship with the aid-givers. Good friends insisted I keep at it, and I want to thank Roy Head in particular. When the writing was done Ned Campbell brought a grammarian's eye to bear on the text. Ethiopia and this narrative have been my obsession for several years, and I finally thank my wife Nimi for having managed to put up with it all.

Peter Gill
London, January, 2010

Note on the Text

For the sake of simplicity I have not used the Ethiopian forms for Mr/Mrs/Miss, but have nevertheless followed the Ethiopian custom of addressing people by their first names. Thus Prime Minister Meles Zenawi is referred to, for instance, not as Ato Meles or Mr Zenawi, but often simply as Meles. No overfamiliarity is intended. I have used the same approach in the index. I have also kept the alphabet soup of development abbreviations to the bare minimum. A few Ethiopian and international ones remain.

CRDA   Christian Relief and Development Association
CSO   Civil Society Organization
CUD   Coalition for Unity and Democracy (opposition grouping)
EPRDF   Ethiopian People's Revolutionary Democratic Front (ruling coalition)
FGAE   Family Guidance Association of Ethiopia
ONLF   Ogaden National Liberation Front
ORDA   Organization for the Relief and Development of Amhara
TDA   Tigray Development Association
TPLF   Tigrayan People's Liberation Front

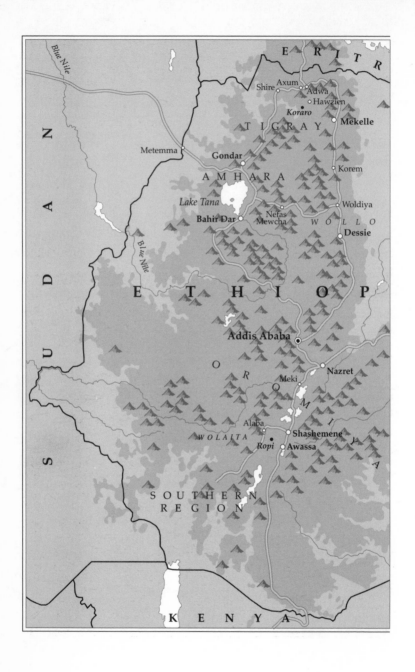

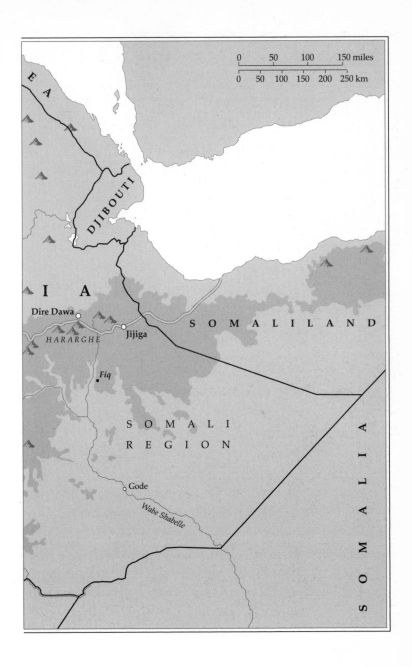

Introduction
For Richer, for Poorer

Ethiopia is one of the richest countries on earth—in its civilization, history, and culture. For as long as Europe has known anything of a wider world, Ethiopia has held our imagination. The story of King Solomon's seduction of the Queen of Sheba and the birth of a boy was the foundation, we are told, of an Ethiopian imperial line which was only extinguished with the murder of Emperor Haile Selassie in 1975.

The Greeks gave Ethiopians their modern name—'burnt faces'—and applied it to anyone living south of Egypt. With the rise of the kingdom of Axum in the century before Christ, Ethiopia became one of the powers of the ancient world. Axum converted to Christianity a few years before Rome and a few centuries before the English. The nurturing of this Christian tradition behind the curtain of Islam enthralled medieval Europe. In the Ethiopian highlands the priest-king Prester John was sought as an ally in the struggle with the Moslems, and it was the Portuguese who eventually found him. Portuguese Jesuits later tried too earnestly to convert the Orthodox Ethiopians to Roman Catholicism, and were expelled for their presumption.

Ethiopia's independence has been sustained to the modern day. A century ago 'Ethiopianism' was the first significant movement to proclaim 'Africa for the Blacks' and even in the development era these tensions have persisted with modern aid-givers. Ethiopia was never colonized, and that was only in part because of its great mountain barriers. At the end of the nineteenth century, an Ethiopian army inflicted on the Italians the most severe defeat Europeans ever suffered at the hands of Africans. Instead of becoming another victim of the imperial scramble for Africa, the Ethiopian emperor extended his own territories southwards.

In 1935 the Italian dictator Mussolini took revenge. His aircraft bombed and gassed Ethiopian civilians and Emperor Haile Selassie fled into exile. He travelled to the League of Nations in Geneva and ended his address, 'God and history will remember your judgement.' The old League did nothing to halt the march of fascism and Ethiopian independence had to be restored through the cataclysm of the Second World War.

Evelyn Waugh, who based his comic novel *Scoop* on press coverage of the Italian invasion, said this was the first foreign war to receive the full modern treatment of press corps, film crews, and propaganda units.

A generation later in 1973 it was a television programme about a famine that played a critical role in the downfall of Emperor Haile Selassie. In 1984 it was a famous television news report which revealed the dimensions of the greatest humanitarian disaster of the late twentieth century. The face of aid was transformed and the face of hunger was Ethiopian.

Over the past twenty-five years it is images of Ethiopian starvation that have held the imagination of the outside world.

Instead of its glorious past and rich culture, we now associate Ethiopia with famine. It has become the iconic poor country.

If we had believed the rich world's rhetoric, we should have banished hunger by now. Fifty years ago in the first 'development decade' US President John F. Kennedy declared, 'We have the ability, as members of the human race, we have the means, we have the capacity to eliminate hunger from the face of the earth in our lifetime. We need only the will.' Ten years later in 1974 US Secretary of State Henry Kissinger brought the deadline much closer. He proclaimed what he called this bold objective, 'That within a decade, no child will go to bed hungry, that no family will fear for its next day's bread and that no human being's future and capacity will be stunted by malnutrition.'

In 1984, the year of the big Ethiopian famine, the World Food Council of the United Nations pronounced, 'Hunger today is largely a man-made phenomenon: human error or neglect creates it, human complacency perpetuates it and human resolve can eradicate it.' Ethiopia 1984 was supposed to be the final turning point. Our expectations and our promises have become grander since then. A new British government set its goal as 'eliminating world poverty'. The successor to Live Aid in 1985 was Make Poverty History in 2005. As the twenty-fifth anniversary approached, the charity Christian Aid was running a 'Poverty Over' publicity campaign which claimed to be more ambitious than what had gone before.

Yet the hunger persists, people still die of starvation, and no country in the world confronts the threat of famine more painfully and more frequently than Ethiopia. For many Ethiopians, their country's association with hunger evokes personal embarrassment and official frustration.

During the years of the big famine Meles Zenawi, who has been in power in Ethiopia since 1991, was a guerrilla commander among the starving peasants of his home region of Tigray. He told me:

> Humiliation can be a very powerful motivation for action and therefore I don't hate the fact that we get humiliated every day so long as it's based on facts, and somebody is not creating a fiction and telling us that we are good for nothing.... If we feel we deserve to be treated like honourable citizens of the world, then we have to remove that source of shame. There is no way round it. For me what has been the most powerful motivation to work daily for economic development is the humiliation of poverty.

When I began researching this book, it was to answer one question. Twenty-five years on from the famine, was hunger becoming history in Ethiopia? My weeks there in 2008 were at a time of optimism shared by Ethiopian officials and the foreign aid-givers. The economy had been growing strongly, harvests were good, a new millennium had dawned in the Ethiopian calendar, and the credit crunch in western banks was someone else's headache.

I returned for several months in 2009 when the world was changing. In the former famine lands of the North there was still progress to be witnessed and achievements to be recognized. But the economy had slowed, the last harvest had been poor, food prices had gone through the roof, and the storm clouds of global recession threatened to burst over the poorest countries in the world. The effectiveness of foreign aid was subject to vehement questioning and the resolve of the aid-givers was in doubt.

World poverty is a burden to be shared, but there is another principle now widely recognized. Poor countries will emerge from poverty only when they take full charge of their own destiny. Ethiopia and its people have never believed otherwise and that led me to further questions. Beyond the challenges of famine forecasting and hunger relief, are there Ethiopian political institutions and policies in place to deliver the transformation known as 'development?'

Over the past twenty-five years extraordinary human dramas have played out in Ethiopia, as vivid as any in its history. Disciplined guerrilla forces overthrew a powerful communist dictatorship and set out to build a new Ethiopia. Democracy has been promised and promoted. It has faltered, although the rhetoric and, perhaps, the aspiration are still in place. The political leadership in power since 1991 states that it will, soon, leave the stage.

In the 1990s Ethiopia laid down a strategy for development which has for the most part been diligently pursued. Yet western perspectives on how to tackle poverty have kept changing while Ethiopia has insisted on retaining a vision of its own. The aid-givers and the aid-receivers have argued fiercely with each other, although almost always courteously.

One of the lessons of Ethiopian history has resonance today—that foreigners with ambitions for the country do not always have Ethiopia's interests at heart. When the Italians were making their advances in the 1880s, their Ethiopian interpreter Petros Gyorgis wrote secretly to his emperor's senior general, 'You may not have read history. But the *faranj* [Europeans] are like an earworm. Earworm is the smallest of worms. But it will eat up and destroy the largest of trees. Likewise, the *faranj* first come in the name of trade; gradually they end up taking over the country. So, hit them now, wipe them out, or your country is lost...You can move a sapling with your toe, but once it is grown, it will require many axes and saws.'[1]

[1] Bahru Zewde, *Pioneers of Change in Ethiopia* (James Currey, 2002).

I

THEN

Chapter 1
Return to Korem

'A horror like this could not occur today without our consent.'

The most remarkable thing about Korem in the Ethiopian highlands is its location on top of an escarpment that lifts the traveller several thousand feet up hairpin bends into the mountains of Tigray. A generation ago, through much of 1984, this road was the final barrier to bringing food to the many thousands of starving people who waited outside Korem for help to arrive—and waited.

I went back to Korem as the twenty-fifth anniversary approached of television's first reports of the famine. There is no disfiguring distress now, but the memory of that time is burned into the consciousness of everyone who was there then and every official with responsibility for the town today.

There is no effort to conceal the awfulness of those events. There are even the stirrings of a famine heritage business so that no one will ever forget Korem's suffering and the role it played in changing the face of aid. Perhaps one day, as in towns and villages in southern Ireland, there will be a visitor centre with special famine displays.

After you negotiate the final hairpin and surmount the edge of the escarpment, a few miles of broken ground give on to the Korem plain and then past fringes of eucalyptus leading into town. It is a thoroughfare, and few travellers stop on their way to the bigger towns of Tigray. Fewer still will see Korem when it is soon comprehensively bypassed by a new Chinese-built highway.

My first stop was in the corrugated iron compound housing the town's administration. Stuck on the outside gate were a number of black and white posters promoting an anniversary symposium on the famine. 'No More Deaths from Hunger', said the headline in English and the local language Tigrinya. In the text I read, 'Never Again, End Hunger'. Around the edges was a border of computer-generated runners drawing attention to a two-kilometre race to publicize the symposium. Along with famine, Ethiopia is also famous for its long distance runners.

The original plan had been to hold the anniversary conference in Addis Ababa, the capital, 400 miles away. Researchers from the university in Makelle, the capital of Tigray, would travel there to share their latest study on the famine. Government officials would present papers on the progress they were making towards eliminating hunger. International experts would join them in the comfort of the big city. But the locals in Korem, epicentre of the worst famine of modern times, were having none of this and forced the authorities to relocate the meeting to the seat of the disaster.

'Korem was known throughout the world as a town of famine, of hunger and of drought,' said the chief administrator. 'So now everyone should realize that Korem is no longer in that condition. It is now a town of development.' We set off in two pick-ups to

Adi Golo, an area of pastureland beneath a church on a hill, at the northern end of the town.

There is a saying in Tigrinya that was constantly quoted to me. 'Better to die than to be buried in Adi Golo.' So undignified, so shaming was the business of dying in the huge relief camp at Adi Golo that it would be better to forgo the chance of survival altogether.

In October 1984 I was the first journalist in months to travel to Korem. The military regime in Addis Ababa was celebrating the tenth anniversary of its coup against the emperor, and it did not want the party spoilt—a too consistent response to exceptional suffering. I had been allowed to go north with a TV documentary crew because we were also investigating why the European Community, blessed with record harvests and a record grain mountain, had not chosen to use some of the surplus to feed the starving.

On the morning we arrived at the relief camp at Korem, the Ethiopian official in charge showed me the little black notebook where he had diligently recorded daily events. For the first time since the camp had opened, there had been more than 100 deaths in the previous twenty-four hours.

Ever since 1984, the very number of the year has been unlucky for the people of this region—except in the Ethiopian calendar, it is not 84, but 77. Ethiopia never adopted the western Gregorian calendar, and remains on the Julian, seven years and eight months behind.

In 1984 the grass land was parched brown and covered in tents. Upwards of 50,000 hungry people had trekked here from the countryside to find food. There were tents for families, communal tents, tents for therapeutic child feeding, and tents for the dying. The warehouse tents for grain were empty, and whenever trucks did come in a plume of dust through the camp there was a mad scramble to pick up every grain that spilled from the sacks—one of the enduring television images of a starving Third World. Today the site of the camp had a flush of green to it, even four months into the dry season, and there were long-horned cattle, sheep, and goats grazing in the sunshine. The area is bisected by the gully of a little river which was flowing that day. Throughout 1984 it was bone dry.

The town's administrator pointed to all the changes there had been in the past twenty-five years. In one corner of the big site there was a primary school. The building that had once been the camp pharmacy was an adult skills centre. The twenty-fifth anniversary of the famine would also be marked by the construction of a hospital for Korem to add to the services of the town's over-stretched clinic. The money was coming from Band Aid, the charity created by Bob Geldof in the weeks after those first famine reports on television.

By his own account, Geldof was 'only a pop singer' and 'by now not a very successful pop singer' when he saw the first television reports of the famine. 'A horror like this could not occur today without our consent,' he wrote in his autobiography *Is That It?* His first idea was to donate the profits of the next Boomtown Rats record to Oxfam, but he knew that would be a pitiful sum. He was trying to promote a new album 'In the Long Grass,' but not getting far. 'We were at our lowest ebb.'

Then Geldof formed Band Aid, which made £5 million for Ethiopia with the record 'Do they know it's Christmas?' As Ethiopians have pointed out ever since, they did of course know it was Christmas because the starving were mainly Christian. The Band Aid venture was matched the next year in America by USA for Africa for which Michael Jackson and Lionel Ritchie wrote

'We are the World'. By July 1985 the overwhelming international response to the Ethiopian famine was symbolized by the Live Aid concerts at Wembley and in Philadelphia.

Geldof had now been joined by Bono, who would become one of the world's biggest rock stars, a status he then used to promote popular and political pressure for aid initiatives in the United States. In 1985 Bono's career was in its infancy and his involvement in the famine cause in Ethiopia certainly helped propel him towards stardom. He had sung on the Band Aid record and his performance at Wembley was one of the highlights. 'All of U2's albums went back into the charts and their status took a huge jump,' said their manager Paul McGuinness. 'Nothing was really quite the same again because everyone knew who Bono was.'[1] Two months after the concert, Bono set off with his wife Alison to visit Ethiopia where they worked for a month in a feeding centre. 'In part it was due to his uneasiness at U2 benefitting commercially from their participation in the historic Live Aid gig.'[2]

Bob Geldof reckoned that Band Aid would be wound up by the end of 1986. It was never to become, he said, 'what I have always most detested—an institution'. But it never did close, just as hunger has never been eliminated. Twenty-five years on, it was still there, although still without staff or an office of its own. When Make Poverty History and Live 8 were conceived for Live Aid's twentieth anniversary in 2005, it made another £10 million.

Two million pounds of that was committed to the new hospital in Korem. When I visited the site at the former famine relief camp, construction work had not yet begun. But there was already a memorial stone dedicated by the UNICEF chief in

[1] U2 and Neil McCormick, *U2 by U2* (HarperCollins, 2006).
[2] Laura Jackson, *Bono, the Biography* (Judy Piatkus, 2001).

Ethiopia. It read 'In Honour of the Children that perished let us build the health of those who follow.'

In the famine of a generation ago it was the children who often died first. Another enduring television image of that era—and of more recent Ethiopian emergencies—was that of the shrunken child corpses, wrapped not in shrouds but in rags, being carried away each morning. Sometimes several children from the same family would have died in the night, and little sibling groups would be taken away.

Where, I wanted to know, had they been buried? My guides gestured in several directions—the Moslems over there, they said, the Christians there near the church at Adi Golo, and then the cholera victims were consigned to a deep communal pit over there—just behind my hotel.

With young locals in the back of the pick-up to guide us, we bumped off across the main road to reach the Moslem graves. We were led on foot across ploughed farmland waiting for the rain to where the famine cemetery was informally fenced off with a line of sticks. There were no memorials, only raised mounds of compacted earth, some with a cactus flowering on top, most just smothered in scrub.

I spoke to Ibrahim, a 45-year-old farmer with a bill hook over his shoulder, walking home from a day in the fields. He had lost an aunt in the '84 famine, he said, but no one in his immediate family, thank God. What did he remember of that time? 'People were very busy burying the dead,' he replied. 'Because the Derg [the communist military regime running Ethiopia] had taken so many people away for resettlement, there was a shortage of labour and some of us were forced to become gravediggers.'

We headed next for the church of St Mary on the wooded hill at Adi Golo where famine graves were much more numerous. Like the Moslem ones, some were just burial mounds, others were piled with black, volcanic clinker for identification. Christian famine victims from the camp were all buried around the bottom of the hill. Local Christians were given the dignity of burial in hallowed ground around the church at the top. Those up on the hill were given proper funerals by the overworked priests. Those at the bottom were given nothing—another distressing indignity for those who died at Adi Golo.

Assefa was coming down from his evening prayers as I was walking up. He was wearing a tattered jacket beneath a shawl whose embroidery had faded to blankness. He was vice-chairman of the local community council.

What did he remember of those bad days? 'I remember the time when 100 were dying every day down there in the camp,' he replied. 'And what was so wrong was that I'd see five or six bodies buried in one hole. The digging was done by day labourers hired by the government, and they were paid for each body they buried. So some of them would just put five or ten bodies in one grave and get paid for each of them.'

I told Assefa that I had heard how the church had disfavoured the dead from the relief camp who were not buried in holy ground around the church. Assefa said it was not discrimination:

It is true that local residents continued to be buried at the top of the hill. But that was because there were so many bodies coming from the relief camp. The only difference I can see is that the locals were always given their own grave. There was hunger and starvation among the locals, too, but we were so much better off, because we didn't get all the diseases that spread in the camp.

Could famine on this scale happen again? 'God alone knows,' Assefa began, but then added that the government was doing its best with credit and fertilizer for farmers. 'All I do know is that famine has been a great lesson to the people. We have learnt about family planning, about modern irrigation and all the assistance government gives to farmers. The sum of these things is that we should prevent famine coming again.'

A generation had grown up in Korem with no memory of the big famine. Younger people relied on their parents for stories of that terrible time. After twenty-five years, surely they could expect to live their lives without fear of catastrophe.

Accompanied by Yohannes, my friend and guide from the Tigray Development Association, which is linked to the government, I walked one afternoon into Korem High School and stood in front of a class of thirty senior students learning English. Such was the pressure on classrooms and teachers that two separate shifts were being taught—one in the mornings and one in the afternoons. Someone banged a truck wheel suspended from a tree branch to signal the start of the afternoon school.

I introduced myself to the class and said that I needed their help to find out what they knew about the famine and what they thought about the future. They all knew about the emergency camp outside the town in 1984 and the separate burial sites for the different communities, including the cholera victims. They all shuddered at the idea of mass graves. 'Better to die than to be buried at Adi Golo' meant nothing to them in English, but they all recognized the saying in Tigrinya.

Most of the students were destined for Ethiopia's fast expanding universities. I asked them which ones, and a bright young man at the front nominated alternatives in southern Ethiopia. Why not one of the universities in Tigray? To the merriment of his classmates, he said he had been told that the food in the residential halls at Makelle, the regional capital, was poor and that students went hungry.

I wrote 'Will Famine become History in Ethiopia?' on the blackboard and risked a show of hands. Who thought it would? About a third of the class slowly raised their hands. Did everyone agree there would be no famines in future? I noticed some discreet head-shaking and a few self-conscious smiles. One brave boy said 'No' and my guide Yohannes asked him whether he even knew the meaning of the word famine. It was plain he did. 'Eighty per cent of our people live in rural areas,' said the student, 'and almost all of them depend on rain-fed agriculture to live. They only have one harvest in a year. So if the rains are bad, then there will be a problem.'

There are two ways of meeting farmers in Ethiopia. One is to go and find them in the fields. The other is to wait for them to come to the weekly market. Thursday is market day in Korem, and as a junction town with a large rural hinterland it has a thriving market.

Yohannes and I pushed our way through the crowds to reach the grain-sellers. Some were gutsy women traders who bought cheap in the countryside and sold at a premium in the town. But there were farmers among them, and I began talking to a brother and sister who had walked 12 miles to market that morning. There is little public transport in rural Ethiopia, even if farmers could afford it, just as there is almost no mechanization on the farms, so farmers must walk to market, just as they must plant and harvest by hand.

The family was selling teff, the fine highland grain that makes the sour pancake which accompanies every highland meal. They had not carried their teff with them, but had kept it under lock and key for the past week in Korem. If they sold it today, they would go home with what they needed from the market and some grubby bank notes in their pocket. If they did not, they would walk the 12 miles home empty-handed, and hope for better luck next week.

Teferi supported his wife and three children on an acre of land. Times were tough at the moment. The last harvest had been poor and the price of food had doubled in two years. But surely the price rise was a good thing because he had grain to sell? 'Yes, it's good for me in one way, but I have to buy other goods from the market and the inflation is pushing everything up far too high.'

I asked Teferi about his family's experience of the famine. He was only 8 in 1984 and like every other farmer's boy in Ethiopia his job was herding animals. When the rains failed again for the third year running there was no grazing and so the family's oxen and goats had to be sold off before they died of thirst and hunger. Then the family's own food reserve dwindled to nothing, and they closed the door on their farm and walked away.

The family split up to improve the chances of survival. Teferi's father took his two older children to relatives in the distant city of Gondar. With her pots and pans on her back, Teferi's mother brought her four younger children over the hills to the feeding camp in Korem.

Teferi had been in the camp for eight months from September 1984 to May 1985. So, when I visited in October 1984, and the daily death toll had exceeded 100 for the first time, the family were just settling in. For an 8-year-old from the starving countryside, the camp represented salvation. It was a place of plenty. 'There was enough food and enough shelter,' he said. 'There was every kind of aid available.'

Did he think there could be another famine? 'We don't know what will come,' he said, 'but there is a saying in the Holy Book that there will be bad years in the future.' He was referring to the 'Sayings of Jesus', part of the literature of Ethiopian Orthodoxy. 'It is a kind of warning,' he said.

During our conversation in the crush of the market, an old woman approached Teferi and from the folds of his jacket he produced something which drew her even closer. There were no words, and the movements were so slight that Yohannes seemed to notice nothing. Could he ask Teferi what the old woman had been doing? Oh, said Yohannes, he's a *keshi*, a priest, and he was offering the old woman his cross. The three swift gestures she had made symbolized the Trinity—a touch of the forehead and then a kiss to the head and foot of the cross.

The next morning I had the help of the charity Action Aid in travelling to Teferi's village of Adi Shumbereket. We made only one stop along the way at a wayside flour mill, always a compelling sight in rural Ethiopia because workers and customers alike are smothered from head to toe in flour dust. We were there just long enough for me to provoke a good-natured argument between the mill owner and a client farmer, both as white as sheets, over God's role in the creation of famine. 'Of course God is our creator,' said the exasperated mill owner finally, 'but this is not about God's anger. We can get out of this bad situation through hard work. That's what required of us.'

The village of Adi Shumbereket appeared to be a model of development. There were some government officials on a visit to conduct consultations with local farmers and my companion from Action Aid went off to see a group of women whom the charity was helping to create small businesses.

I met Rosa, a pretty 22-year-old in pink slacks and a Beyoncé T-shirt, who ran the spotlessly clean health post. This was her first job since graduating from nursing college and she was happy there despite the lack of electricity or any means of getting into town. She said she would like to study more by doing a gynae-cology course, but wanted to come back to use those new skills in the village.

Teferi's farmstead was a couple of miles out of the village and set spectacularly on a bluff above the road. On the top of the hill above the family's mud houses was a huge African fig tree. We picked our way through irrigated land and climbed through dry stony terraces to reach the homes which twenty-five years ago the family had abandoned in the famine. Teferi's father was also a priest—it ran in the family—but he was out of the house for the morning, down at the river washing his clothes.

Teferi's mother greeted us and we retreated from the sun into the home of her eldest son and daughter-in-law. The mother's name was Zenebu and she had total recall of her time in the camp at Korem. 'I remember there was a lady foreign aid worker and she kissed my child. This lady used to dress up in traditional Ethiopian costume and she would dance with the children. I was so grateful to them all. Thanks to them, I didn't have any deaths in my family.' Her face clouded. 'I have lost two of my daughters since they were married.'

We sat and talked in the gloom as Lemlem, the daughter-in-law, handed round a succession of treats for the visitors—barley beer, cups of unsweetened coffee, and roasted grain straight from a pan on the fire. Lemlem had five children but was now on injectable contraceptives from Rosa's health post. 'I told my husband to stop now—although God doesn't allow that,' said the wife who had married into a family of priests.

My companion from Action Aid became earnestly develop-mental. Who brought the water up that steep hill? The wives, of course. 'If the men do it, we will be laughed at,' said the eldest son. 'It is not in our culture.' 'You must condemn this culture,' replied the Action Aid man. He made another sally about the wives doing too much of the work in the fields. 'Let her off the weeding so that she can come home and prepare the food and you can spend time together,' he suggested. 'Otherwise she is working all the time—and much more than you!'

My last objective at Adi Shumbereket was to see Teferi's church a mile away along a hill track, but he was just a deacon and did not have the key. He ran off to get permission for me to visit and assured the parish elder that I was neither a Moslem nor one of those agitating Protestants who might start preaching as soon as I got there. There had been some trouble recently with the Protestants.

It was on the walk back that we met the senior priest, one of eight working in the parish. I had already spotted him below us on the path, dressed in a white turban and pale blue habit, with a fly whisk in his hand and a large wooden cross at his hip. He had now stopped on the track to talk to two men. When we caught them up there was much kissing of crosses. All four of the men were priests and each had to pay his respects to the crosses worn by the others.

Before I left the region to travel southwards, I wanted to track down another Ethiopian of the famine generation. She had been given up for dead in a small relief centre in Tigray, but then became, in the words of Bob Geldof, 'a beacon of hope and inspiration to millions, proof that we can make a difference'. Many other children survived the famine, but the chance attention of the twentieth-century media gave her story a symbolic, global, and lasting impact.

Her name is Birhan Woldu and she was born in a village near the Tigrayan capital. She was 2 when the famine reached its full intensity and her desperate family left their farmland to seek help. They found it, as so many did, with Roman Catholic missionaries. It was at a relief centre run by Irish sisters in October 1984 that the Canadian Broadcasting Corporation filmed a tiny child, on her own, slumped on the ground.

'It looked as though she was dying,' said the CBC reporter Brian Stewart. As an Irish sister scooped up this bundle of rags and took it into the treatment room, the TV crew decided not to follow. 'She was too far gone, she is only going to die,' thought Stewart. 'Let her die in peace.' Birhan revived during the day thanks to the Irish sisters, but it was the original footage, amongst other CBC pictures, which was cut into a sort of pop video, offered to Live Aid, and then introduced on stage at Wembley by David Bowie in July 1985. Among the millions who saw it was Tony Blair, then a young Labour MP.

'PM close to tears as he meets Birhan,' said the *Sun* newspaper twenty years later. 'Blair tells Live Aid girl—you changed my life.' He was in Ethiopia for a meeting of his Africa Commission and Birhan was flown to Addis Ababa to meet him. She had been supported through school by the Canadian journalist who first spotted her and was now studying agriculture. There had been follow-up television programmes in Canada, and now Birhan was on the point of becoming a global celebrity.

When she was asked to travel to London for the Live 8 concert in July 2005, Birhan was asked whether she had heard of any western pop singers. She thought hard and said 'Madonna'. So one of the press pictures of the year was created—the pop star alongside Birhan in traditional Ethiopian dress and a smile so broad that her eyes were almost closed.

At home Birhan is not a celebrity, in fact she is as likely to be recognized walking around London as Makelle. I started my search at the agricultural college where she had studied. There I was told that she was now studying for a nursing degree, and it was through the student mobile telephone network that I established where she was that evening—shopping with girlfriends. We drove off to find her among the 'boutiques' of Makelle's marketplace where scooter rickshaws compete with horses and carts in unlit streets. This famous 'scrap of humanity' was now fashionably thin. She was not traditionally dressed that evening, and wore a denim jacket, jeans, and earrings.

'It is my hope and vision to be a nurse because I want to help children who are affected by disease,' said Birhan. 'It is something connected with my story. When I graduated in agriculture, I thought about the other children who died and I wanted to help them. Many children die because of a lack of professional help.' Why then agriculture in the first place? 'Because my father is a farmer I wanted to study and help in agriculture. And now I have done agriculture and nursing which are my two loves.'

Birhan graduated from nursing college in 2009 and several aid agencies were thinking of employing this well-qualified young woman. The Canadian journalist Brian Stewart had seen to that. Hers was a story which promised a happy ending and Geldof's 'beacon of hope and inspiration' was certainly an encouragement to generous individuals in the West. But too many stories in Ethiopia have not ended like this.

Chapter 2
The Famine Trail

'The only difference now is that a lot of foreigners know about it and are getting excited.'

Professor Mesfin Wolde-Mariam has been a formidable fighter in every cause he has adopted. At the outset of his career it was famine. Then it was human rights. In later life it became outright opposition to the government.

He started out as a geography lecturer and became the head of department at Addis Ababa university. He wrote influential books. He was the founder member of the Ethiopian Human Rights Council. In 2007 he emerged from twenty months in jail for his role in the political opposition. When some Ethiopian opposition leaders went into exile and started calling for the violent overthrow of the government, Prof. Mesfin stuck to political campaigning at home and faced the consequences.

'The simple answer is that I had nowhere else to go,' he said and chuckled. We met in his flat in Addis Ababa in 2009 where he chain-smoked Kent cigarettes for two hours. A few weeks before he had been hit hard by a soldier's rifle butt while protesting at the treatment of a fellow opposition leader. He was then approaching his 79th birthday.

A famine fifty years ago, almost unremarked on by the outside world, started it for Prof. Mesfin. In 1958 he had just married and joined the teaching staff at the university. He told me how he used to visit the home of a classmate whose wealthy mother was also an exceptional philanthropist. 'She was very kind, a lady who if she saw someone ill on the streets would stop the chauffer in her Mercedes and carry that sick person and have him treated.'

The woman's name was Ghenet Wolde-Gabriel. From Roman Catholic nuns she had heard of a terrible famine unfolding in Tigray and she was sending food and clothes through them to the North. Ghenet asked the nuns to bring famine orphans back to her home in Addis Ababa where, in her own yard, she built accommodation and a school building—and then another.

Mesfin went to see the editor of the *Ethiopian Herald*, then as now a government mouthpiece, and urged him to cover this story of great suffering. Not a word appeared. He decided to see for himself what was going on.

He took the bus to Tigray, up those hairpin bends to Korem, beyond them towards the capital Makelle, and further on to the towns where the hunger was at its worst. 'What I saw was horrible, I couldn't take it. The money I'd taken was all depleted when I came back. My wife had to carry me home from the bus. I was starving and shivering. I'd hardly eaten for the last three weeks.'

Prof. Mesfin has since developed a deep antipathy for officialdom, but on this occasion he began to pester 'high official dignitaries' in the imperial government to back his plan for a fund-raising drive. Emperor Haile Selassie was on an official visit to Moscow at the time, and the minister of the interior suggested that a donations committee be set up under the crown prince and that they should approach, as Mesfin put it, 'the duke of so-and-so, and the duke of so-and-so, and His Highness so-and-so, and I told him it would take me a year to get to see these people and by that time the problem would be solved.'

The young lecturer wrote a letter to the emperor and enclosed a few slides he had taken of the suffering. 'A few days later I received a letter from the minister of the pen [on the personal orders of the emperor] telling me that I was to go to Tigray to distribute the grain that His Imperial Majesty had graciously donated—about 20,000 quintals [2,000 tons].'

Only about 500 tons of the grain authorized by the emperor ever got to Tigray, but Mesfin spent another gruelling month in the region face to face with famine. By then some American food was beginning to trickle in, but it was too late for many. One hundred thousand may have died in northern Ethiopia in 1958. 'For me the experience was a nightmare,' said Mesfin. 'A young woman with a baby whom I had befriended was in terrible agony, along with her baby. She was coming in my dreams the whole time. She was haunting me, and it was that which eventually drew me to write about famine.'

Prof. Mesfin published his *Rural Vulnerability to Famine in Ethiopia* almost thirty years later in 1986, in the immediate aftermath of the worst tragedy to befall northern Ethiopia in modern times. In that interval there had been other famines, one of them more severe than the one of 1958. It was this event which undermined and finally sealed the fate of the empire of Haile Selassie.

Mesfin was appointed to chair the commission of inquiry into that 1973 famine, and this was an opportunity to search the files at both national and district level. The very first famine records he found at the Ministry of the Interior were those of 1958. From then on Ethiopia and the outside world had begun fitfully to acknowledge the outrageous human cost of death from starvation and had begun imperfectly to address it.

According to Ethiopia's leading historian, Richard Pankhurst, there have been references to famine in the national literature for almost a thousand years. Between the fifteenth and nineteenth centuries, he found that there was on average one every decade. Towards the end of the nineteenth century Ethiopia was struck by the worst in all its history. This was the Great Famine of 1888 to 1892, known as 'Evil Days'.

Several years of drought had been exacerbated by devastating outbreaks of cattle disease which wiped out most of the national herd. The infection was said to have been introduced by the Italians who had already invoked 'famine abandoned lands' to occupy Eritrea to the north and were now seeking a protectorate over the rest of Ethiopia. The Great Famine that resulted may have killed a third of Ethiopia's population, then put at 12 million.

In his book *Late Victorian Holocausts*, the historian Mike Davis contrasts the cruel indifference of the imperial British towards the millions starving in India in this period with the approach of the Ethiopian emperor. Davis quotes, in a catalogue of similar ob-servations from British rulers, the viceroy Lord Curzon complain-ing about 'humanitarian hysterics' and declared that 'any Government which imperilled the financial position of India in the interests of prodigal philanthropy would be open to serious criticism; but any Government which by indiscriminate alms-giving weakened the fibre and demoralised the self-reliance of the population, would be guilty of a public crime.'

'At the other extreme,' Davis writes, 'was the tragic example of Ethiopia's Menelik II, who struggled heroically but with too few resources to rescue his people from a truly biblical conjugation of natural and man-made plagues.' That struggle related perhaps to imperial concerns for the North, for in the South he was engaged in the brutal extension of empire.

War down the ages had greatly extended the death toll of Ethiopian famines. The observation 'Soldiers eat, peasants provide' was attributed to Emperor Teodoros in the middle of the nineteenth century. The disastrous connection between war and hunger had been noted several centuries earlier by a Portuguese Jesuit. He observed that famines were caused by locusts and 'the marching of the soldiers...which is a plague worse than the locusts because they [the locusts] devour only what they find in the fields, whereas the others [the soldiers] spare not what is laid up in houses'.[1]

In 1973, famine struck in Wollo, which borders Tigray and is linked to the rest of the country by the same north–south road which runs up the country's spine. The 40,000 or more who died of starvation at that time—estimates range from 40,000 to 200,000 and the figures are never exact—brought the attention for the first time of the international media, specifically that of British television.

The journalist Jonathan Dimbleby can never have made a film that had more concrete political impact than *The Unknown Famine*, broadcast in October 1973 as a 'This Week' programme on the ITV network. Earlier that year he had filmed the impact of drought in the Sahel. There he reported on the cattle which were

---

[1] Quoted in Alex de Waal, *Evil Days: 30 Years of War and Famine in Ethiopia* (Human Rights Watch, 1991).

dying and the forced migration of the poor. Now, as he put it in the opening frames of his Ethiopian report, it was people who were dying.

The Unknown Famine would probably not be broadcast in that form today. It has a rawness that makes it nearly unwatchable. There is film of the bodies of children who have died overnight which would almost certainly be banned by modern broadcasters on the grounds that it was too upsetting. The twenty-five minutes comprise relentless images of suffering, a sparse script, and a veiled appeal for assistance. Unusually for a report on suffering in the Third World, there are no white aid officials to explain what the viewer is watching. All the voices and all the faces are Ethiopian. There is nothing 'engaging' or 'accessible', to use modern TV terminology, about *The Unknown Famine*, other than the sheer burden of human distress.

Dimbleby first heard about the unfolding disaster from a friend in Amsterdam who told him that Ethiopian students, alerted to what was happening at home, were trying to get international attention for the crisis. The slow process began of gaining TV access and authorization from the imperial government. The crew was finally allowed to travel to examine 'the problems of drought'.

What soon became apparent was the shocking lack of interest shown by foreign officials towards the unfolding tragedy. This compounded the negligence of the Ethiopian government and was subsequently documented by Jack Shepherd in his *Politics of Starvation*. Shepherd concluded that 'honourable men and women working for honourable institutions refused to jeopardise their jobs or their comfortable relationship with Haile Selassie's government by calling international attention to the Ethiopia's "secret."'

A UNICEF team had travelled to Wollo in August 1973 and put the number of dead at between 50,000 and 100,000. They found 283,000 starving peasants registered at ill-supplied relief camps along the north–south highway. The head of UNICEF in Addis Ababa endorsed the report, but his superior in Geneva 'thought the statistics were unreliable,' according to a US embassy official in Ethiopia quoted by Shepherd. 'The donors buried it.' Shepherd reported that 'U.S. embassy cables to Washington were detailing the famine graphically. So presumably had cables flowing into other major capitals. Yet not one agency or nation—no one—spoke out . . . In Ethiopia, the delays in shipping relief food came not out of bureaucratic foul-up, but from diplomatic choice.'

Dimbleby encountered obstruction in surprising quarters. He recalled a shouting match with the Swedish Red Cross in Wollo which had reached an agreement to open an orphanage in Dessie where the TV crew was filming. 'They were actually telling the local police and local government officials not to allow us to film,' said Dimbleby.

There was clear government resistance to the story emerging. Before UNICEF officials were thwarted by their own senior colleagues in Geneva, they presented their report to imperial officials in Addis Ababa, who rejected it out of hand. 'If we have to describe the situation in the way you have in order to generate international assistance,' the vice-minister of planning told them, 'then we don't want that assistance. The embarrassment of the government isn't worth it. Is that perfectly clear?'

Even after *The Unknown Famine* was shown, the denials continued. 'We've always had localized food shortages in Ethiopia,' the acting chief of the Ethiopian Nutrition Institute told a Swedish aid official. 'This is nothing new. The only difference now is

that a lot of foreigners know about it and are getting excited.'
Dimbleby summed up the United Nations approach to the
humanitarian emergency in 1973 like this: 'The UN took the
government view that until the government acknowledged there
was a problem, there was no problem.'

Domestic agitation over the famine was centred on the university campus in Addis Ababa. When hunger drove a group of
1,500 peasants several hundred miles from the parched hills of
Wollo to the outskirts of the capital, their entry was barred, but
students made contact. Some then travelled to the North and
took photographs which were surreptitiously displayed on campus as part of a geography project on drought. It was this same
student connection that brought Dimbleby to Ethiopia where
winds of protest were now stirring that would soon tear through
the state rooms of the imperial palace.

At this point Mesfin Wolde-Mariam, now professor of geography at the university, re-entered the fray. He was one of three
professors who dared to complain publicly about the government's indifference to suffering in the North. When he described
the emperor's cabinet ministers as willing members of 'a private
company with unlimited benefits and no accountability,' he was
arrested.

In Wollo today, the journalist has to seek out the older generation to hear personal accounts of suffering and survival in the
1973 famine. With the help of Save the Children Fund (SCF) and
the Ethiopian agency ORDA (Organization for the Relief and
Development of Amhara Region) I toured much of Wollo talking
to farmers about modern development efforts. To the surprise of
local agency staff used to horrifying accounts of the 1984 famine,
there was no doubt among the older peasants that the 1973 crisis
was the worst in living memory.

One of the agricultural showpieces of Amhara Region is an irrigation scheme on a great bend in the highway at Jarie which has brought reliable crops and peace of mind to more than 700 households. Even a couple of acres of irrigated land guarantees a family's food for the year and puts cash in their pockets. Many save up to build a modern house with rectangular walls and partitioned rooms to replace their single-roomed mud huts. A gleaming corrugated iron roof denotes substance in rural Wollo. With shared local labour, a new house costs about £700.

When he depended on the rains for his living, Tadesse Mollaw grew sorghum, teff, and maize. If the rains were good, he ate well. If they were poor, he did not. If they failed altogether, he risked starvation. On irrigated land he now grows onions, bananas, cotton, and mangoes as well as maize, and gets more than one crop a year. His livelihood and that of his family is guaranteed. His only complaint was that ORDA and the government had not extended the scheme to more of his neighbours so that they can also benefit from the wonders of irrigation.

Tadesse is in his sixties and had no hesitation in declaring 1973 as the worst year of his life. 'There was no help from the government and no help from outside,' he said. 'People were dying up and down this road. 1984 was also very bad, but we got aid then from Mekanne Yesus [the nearby Protestant church].' In 1973, he said, the family only survived because of modest charity handouts for his two young children. The children's rations kept the whole family alive.

I asked him what else he remembered about 1973. 'During that time it was too bad, just too bad. I can't say more.' There was a long pause. 'I remember this girl on the road on her own. She was going towards Dessie [about 20 miles away]. I wanted to assist her, but what could I do? So many people died on that road. And I never found out what happened to her.'

Did Tadesse believe that emperor Haile Selassie fell because of that famine? 'I agree with that idea,' he replied with emphasis. My guides from ORDA laughed at the bluntness of the reply. Ethiopian peasants are not expected to voice firm political opinions, even on matters of history.

Was it fair that the emperor should have been overthrown? 'It was right and it was correct,' said Tadesse. 'Of course he should have gone.' My companions laughed again, and I was reminded of all the warnings I had received that I would never get honest answers from farmers in the countryside, particularly if my interpreters had connections with the government.

What about the Derg, the military committee that removed the emperor and ruled for seventeen years, how did Tadesse compare the two? 'How could the Derg be better than the emperor? What a question! I have a son who's now 30. If the Derg was still here, he'd be off to the war.'

I risked the contemporary question. Could famine come back again? We both looked down at all the greenery and the water in the irrigation ditches. 'It could happen but I don't think it will be as bad as before.' He had, I thought, neatly summarized thirty-five years of Ethiopia's development history. It was a period which began in a dark rural disaster illuminated for the first time for the world at large to witness.

Ethiopia's authorities did their best to undermine the findings of Jonathan Dimbleby's film. Before he left for home he was summoned to the Ministry of Information and warned off coming to hard conclusions about the extent of the distress or the inadequacy of the response. At other levels, imperial functionaries were as appalled as he was at what was unfolding. A 'minder' from the Ministry was sent north with the TV team, but became so troubled by what he saw that he let them film what they wanted.

When *The Unknown Famine* was shown in Britain in October 1973, the government attempted a counter-attack. Newspapers in London and Washington were approached and notes sent round to other embassies which accused Dimbleby of 'distortion and exaggeration'. But just before transmission, he had received an unexpected endorsement. Tefari Wossen, a senior Ethiopian relief official, had been sent to London for an advance viewing of the film. He watched the cut in silence, and then turned to Dimbleby and said: 'I have been told to say that this is a lie and that you've distorted the truth and created these scenes. Ethiopia has a problem of drought but it is not serious.' Then he added, 'I hope you put this film out untouched.'

The impact of Dimbleby's revelations anticipated the even greater popular response to famine in Ethiopia eleven years later. As well as being transmitted twice on ITV, the film was also shown by the BBC (something else that modern broadcasters would not contemplate) and around Europe. A British appeal was launched and raised £6 million. With responses from Ireland and the rest of Europe, the total rose to £15 million, amounting to some £80 million at 2009 prices.

The international spotlight on Ethiopia's failure to respond to the famine intensified a revolutionary ferment on campus in Addis Ababa. There were daily demonstrations against the government and the growth of an anti-imperial movement which was at first championed, then subverted, and in due course betrayed by the army. This was the 'creeping coup' of 1974, and the Dimbleby film was to be its *coup de grâce*.

Haile Selassie was 80 in July 1972 and birthday celebrations over the following months had played their part in diverting attention from the famine. The inconvenient sideshow of death by starvation was not to obstruct the political agenda. Some who followed these events at the time say the old man was senile by the time the famine took grip. He certainly expressed sorrowful astonishment on his first visit to the region in November 1973. 'I believe Haile Selassie was simply not informed,' Jonathan Dimbleby told me. 'People were too terrified to acknowledge what was happening.'

The Unknown Famine reached a domestic television audience at the Ethiopian New Year in September 1974, ten months after its international screenings. Retitled *The Hidden Hunger*, it was utilized by the coup plotters as the final propaganda blow against the emperor. Ethiopian television cleared its New Year schedules to screen and rescreen the film. As if the pictures of starvation were not instructive enough, the film was re-edited in Addis Ababa to incorporate pictures of a lavish court wedding for which the cake had been flown from Italy. There was footage of the Emperor feeding his pet dogs, and over it all a commentary demanding that he hand over his wealth to the people of Ethiopia.

Few Ethiopians in the capital had television sets, so the army arranged for special showings around town. The Dimbleby film was shown at the Parliament and a huge screen was erected in the city's main market. The target of this assault was ordered to sit in front of a television at the palace and watch it. The New Year scene was thus set for the arrival next morning of an army unit which read out to him the act of dethronement. The emperor was bundled into the back of a Volkswagen Beetle and driven off through the streets to cries of 'thief'. He was taken to a barracks at divisional headquarters and was never seen in public again.

Jonathan Dimbleby's association with Ethiopia continued, and provided a narrative of what happened next to a student revolution hijacked by the army. To begin with, Dimbleby was a hero of the revolution. He had even to resist the renaming of streets in his honour. He was one of the very few western journalists who continued to be allowed into the country as the Derg increased its grip and as Colonel Mengistu Haile-Mariam emerged as the regime's strong man. Dimbleby made five more films in Ethiopia over the next four years and continued to show a zeal for the revolutionary change that *The Unknown Famine* had helped bring about. His sympathy for the cause, he carefully acknowledged later, 'was conveyed with not as much scepticism as in retrospect I should have shown'.

But the love affair between the reporter and the coup makers did not last. Dimbleby was formally banned from Ethiopia in 1978 'as a traitor to the revolution'. Colonel Mengistu had by then begun a sweeping and murderous crackdown on the political parties that grew out of the student movement. For months on end arrests were made by night and bodies were dumped in the streets by morning. This was the 'Red Terror', so styled by the regime itself. Idealistic youngsters fled abroad or to the countryside to avoid such a fate; the Eritrean independence struggle took on fresh life in the North; other regional freedom movements, notably in Tigray, came into existence. The scene was set for Ethiopia's next great humanitarian disaster.

Immodestly but with some justice, the BBC reporter Michael Buerk described his two reports from the famine zone in Tigray in October 1984 as 'by far the most influential pieces of television ever broadcast'. They launched a wave of private giving across the world and forced tardy governments into matching the popular response with increased official funding. They launched an age of celebrity in the aid-giving world where rock stars have done as much, probably more, than politicians, charity workers, and development experts to sustain the West's commitment to the poor.

'Dawn, and as the sun breaks through the piercing chill of night on the plain outside Korem, it lights up a biblical famine, now, in the 20th century.' The opening of Buerk's first report was a model of evocative precision. It also introduced the bold and unblinking camerawork of Mohammed Amin and led into a piece that ran for more than seven minutes, a remarkable length for a foreign news story in that or any other era. A decade after the last famine, it pointed to an enormous scandal in Ethiopia compounded once again of national negligence and international indifference. No wonder rock singers had to come to the rescue.

Unlike the 1973 famine, the unfolding Ethiopian catastrophe of 1984 had been researched by the experts and reported on by the media for months. After a Save the Children Fund report on hunger in northern Ethiopia in early 1983, a television appeal in Britain raised almost £2 million. In July 1984, more than three months before the Buerk reports, ITV had shown a full-length documentary *Seeds of Despair* shot over many weeks as famine tightened its grip. Another public appeal was then launched which raised almost £10 million. Then it had to be opened up all over again in response to the BBC reports.

Ethiopia's own relief authorities had been warning of the scale of the impending disaster since March. That month they issued a formal international appeal asserting that one fifth of the population, some eight million people, would need assistance during the year, and concluded with unusual directness for a government body, 'If those affected do not receive relief assistance, the consequences will be frightening.'

The Relief and Rehabilitation Commission, established with international backing in response to the 1973 famine, calculated that Ethiopia needed 900,000 tons of extra food for the year, a figure which turned out to be remarkably accurate. Far too late, and stretching well into 1985, that was the amount of food aid actually delivered—after all the public outrage over starvation on TV. But the relief commission accepted that the country had big distribution problems and so appealed for only 450,000 tons. This cut was already a fateful concession that would have cost lives, but not as many as the United Nations then managed to squander.

A UN mission from the Food and Agriculture Organization spent a month in Ethiopia in 1984 checking on the relief commission's assessment and the logistics problem. It came to the startling conclusion that an already diminished international appeal for 450,000 tons of food aid should be further slashed to 125,000 tons, a cut of three-quarters. In the *Seeds of Despair* documentary Dr Kenneth King, the most senior UN official in Addis Ababa and a Guyanese, risked censure from his bosses by describing the UN's response to the emergency as 'an exercise in cynicism. People who do not agree with me say that they're being realistic... I'm not talking only figures, what we're talking about are lives... we're condemning by a stroke of the pen 86% of the people who are affected to, if not death, then to a sort of half life, to a life without food over long periods. This I cannot accept.' Predictably this devastating statement did not please the UN in New York—nor its main funder, the US administration of President Reagan—and Dr King was sidelined in the belated UN effort to respond to the famine.

Belying its poignant motto 'A hungry child knows no politics,' the United States responded as poorly as the United Nations. In

April 1984, within days of the first major Ethiopian appeal, the US embassy in Addis Ababa cabled Washington saying that 'a very serious situation could develop in Ethiopia this year and we will be remiss if we are not adequately informed and prepared.' A USAID mission was accordingly sent to Ethiopia and concluded that 'no additional food [should] be offered to the Ethiopian government' on the grounds that it could not be distributed.

As the hunger crisis in the North reached its deadly climax, the Ethiopian government itself stepped in to frustrate any further international attention. Until March, the government press (and there was only the government press in Ethiopia) had reported on the official food appeals. But from then on there was nothing. The Derg had been in power for a decade and was planning a tenth anniversary spectacle in Addis Ababa to be attended by their friends and allies in the Soviet bloc. It would be orchestrated by the North Koreans and would cost $50–100 million. The band would play on despite the famine and foreign journalists would be barred from the North.

Journalists stuck in Addis Ababa for the September celebrations witnessed the inauguration of the Workers' Party of Ethiopia and the unveiling of heroic Soviet-style statuary to the peasants' struggle. Colonel Mengistu delivered a five-hour speech in which he made a passing reference to recurrent drought and famine along with the problems of deforestation and desertification. There was nothing more. Only a month later, long after the last foreign guest had departed, was a journalist allowed north.

The relief commission liked our idea at ITV of trying to shame the European Community into releasing a fraction of its grain mountain to feed the poor of Ethiopia, so they put BBC news second in the queue. After we returned from Korem, I was in fact asked by Ethiopian officials when I thought Michael Buerk's team should be allowed to travel. I said this was their decision, certainly not mine.

The ITV film *Bitter Harvest* played its role in directing attention to official western indifference to the starvation and was broadcast the day after the BBC's first report. In his autobiography *The Road Taken*, Buerk described the reaction in the cutting room after the first viewing of Mohammed Amin's footage. 'People stayed looking at the empty screen. They coughed, cleared their throats, blew their noses. A voice at the back said "fucking hell", just as the man next to me was saying "God Almighty." ' Buerk's story from Korem and the one that followed from Makelle were shown around the world and transformed the aid landscape for a generation.

The government of Margaret Thatcher in Britain came under immediate pressure to respond to the famine. For Thatcher herself, aiding Ethiopia had so far been an anathema. This was a country as far as could be from her principles as the 'Iron Lady'—a wasteful and bureaucratic socialist state in military alliance with the Soviet Union. As her overseas development minister Sir Timothy Raison carefully put it twenty years later, 'It's well known that Mrs Thatcher didn't regard the aid programme as one of her top priorities.'

The British drew a distinction between development aid, which they would not send to Ethiopia, and life-saving humanitarian aid, which they said they did. The distinction had meant little enough in the past when Britain had been reluctant to send aid of any sort to Mengistu's regime. This became apparent a month after the BBC news stories during a Foreign Affairs Committee exchange at the House of Commons between its Conservative chairman, Sir Antony Kershaw, and the Overseas

Director of Save the Children Fund, Colonel Hugh Mackay, who had spent many frustrating weeks in Ethiopia trying to convince British and other officials of the extent of the crisis.

Kershaw appeared to believe that agencies such as SCF had failed in the build-up to the famine to tell British officials what was happening. Mackay insisted they had. 'Did you say that they did not believe you?' Sir Antony demanded. 'I am afraid not at this stage, sir.' The chairman pressed on. 'Can you give me examples of where you predicted a famine and the British government did not take notice?' Mackay replied that the current Ethiopian famine was such an example 'which in our reckoning started two years ago'.

'Did you report it?' 'Yes.'

'Then?'

'They did fuck all, sir.' This last answer appeared in the official record as 'Yes, sir.'[2]

As the famine and the overwhelming public response continued, the prime minister herself was under pressure. In the Commons she was asked why she could not organize relief shipments to Ethiopia in the way she had commandeered troop ships for the Falklands War, and Bob Geldof got the better of her in an exchange about Europe's butter mountain. Mrs Thatcher told Geldof that butter didn't do much good in Africa, and Geldof pointed out that butter oil was an important supplementary food. 'Oh, butter oil, if you can, if you can get it,' Thatcher said.

'But it is a product of butter,' replied Geldof.

Thatcher: 'But look, a lot is going, a lot of food is going. But don't forget...'

Geldof: 'But prime minister there are millions dying and that is the terrible thing.'

---

[2] Starving in Silence: A Report on Famine and Censorship (Article 19, April 1990).

Thatcher: 'Yes, indeed.'

The popular disgust voiced by Geldof at British inaction prompted the main charities to examine their own record. What they found was not reassuring. When I came to write a book about the famine in 1985,[3] I was given a free run of the files at Oxfam and Save the Children. In a more corporate, brand-conscious charity world, that would probably not happen today. What I found, particularly in the case of Oxfam, was that their internal performance assessments were far more critical than I was inclined to be.

Tony Vaux served as an Oxfam field director in India before joining the headquarters disasters team at the end of 1984. His first task was to research what had gone wrong with their response to the Ethiopian famine. For a start, they had not taken the early alarm calls seriously or the urgent requests for help from Ethiopian relief officials. Only with the TV film *Seeds of Despair* in July 1984 did that change. 'Once again it was the media, not the monitoring, that brought awareness,' Vaux wrote in his report.

When I met Vaux in 2009, he recalled the recriminations at Oxfam over these failures and described how Jim Howard, one of the great figures of Oxfam's earlier decades, expressed his disgust at the agency's conduct. He berated team leaders in the field and declared: 'We should all be terribly ashamed.'

Oxfam in the 1980s had been determined to move from relief to development. This was the era of 'Give a man a fish and he can eat. Teach a man to fish and he can make a living'—an inappropriate observation in famine conditions where the rivers have dried up. As Vaux pointed out in his 1991 book *The Selfish Altruist*, Oxfam's trustees had chosen early 1984, when the prospects of famine were

---

[3] Peter Gill, *A Year in the Death of Africa* (Paladin, 1986).

already apparent, to decide that in Ethiopia 'relief projects should be avoided and development projects sought'. Vaux spoke to me of how Ethiopia had cast a long shadow over the charities. The development approach, he said, would now be supplanted by the humanitarian imperative. Oxfam and others would have to go back to basics.

The Vaux report was only one of two self-critical assessments conducted into Oxfam's performance in Ethiopia and the lessons to be learnt. I asked him whether such reports would be conducted in such a spirit today. 'I think not,' he replied.

The popular belief is that one million Ethiopians died in the famine of 1984–5. The United Nations and others have formally adopted this figure, but it has little basis in fact. The true figure is also unknowable because no one was counting in a systematic fashion at the time, and subsequent estimates vary, even if they were made on a scientific basis. The best study produced on the tragedy was *Evil Days* by Alex de Waal for Human Rights Watch in 1991. He described the adoption of the one million figure as 'a trivialisation and dehumanisation of human misery' and concluded from his own researches that a minimum of 400,000 died in the famine.

De Waal looked beyond the drought and the wholesale inadequacy of the relief response to account for more than half these deaths. The burden of his study was that the government of Colonel Mengistu killed them. He argued persuasively that human rights abuses made the famine 'come earlier, strike harder and reach further'. He attributed an additional 50,000 deaths to the centrepiece of the junta's post-famine policy, a programme of mass resettlement from the highlands.

The most eloquent summary of the famine's impact endorsed de Waal's conclusion. It came from the very top of Ethiopia's official relief commission. Dawit Wolde-Giorgis, the commissioner, was an army officer and a member of the politburo. Within two years of witnessing these events he resigned from his post during an official visit to the United States, and wrote an account of his experiences from exile. He revealed that at the end of 1985 the commission had secretly compiled its own famine figures—1.2 million dead, 400,000 refugees outside the country, 2.5 million people internally displaced, and almost 200,000 orphans.[4] 'But the biggest toll of the famine was psychological,' Dawit wrote. 'None of the survivors would ever be the same. The famine left behind a population terrorized by the uncertainties of nature and the ruthlessness of their government.'

---

[4] Dawit Wolde-Giorgis, *Red Tears: War, Famine and Revolution in Ethiopia* (Red Sea Press, 1989).

Chapter 3
Hunger as a Weapon

'Food is a major element in our strategy against the secessionists.'

Within weeks of the television reports of a catastrophic famine, and as foreign aid began to trickle in, Ethiopia's military government launched an anti-hunger expedient of its own. If people were starving in the highlands, then it would pack them off to the lowlands where land was plentiful and productive life could start all over again. It was not a new idea—Ethiopian history is marked out by its southward and westward migrations—but the planned scale of the resettlement programme measured up to Colonel Mengistu's image as the pocket African Stalin, and would be executed in a thoroughly ruthless fashion. Resettlement also served a darker political purpose, and it would be enforced at the barrel of a gun.

There was a war going on in northern Ethiopia in the 1980s, in fact more than one. The Eritrean liberation movement was in fractious alliance with its neighbours the Tigrayan People's Liberation Front to expel and overthrow the military regime. The largest army in Sub-Saharan Africa hit back on the ground and from the air. In the eyes of the government, starving peasants were likely fifth columnists, but thanks to the famine and the international aid effort many were now contained in relief camps and subject to immediate official authority.

Dawit Wolde-Giorgis, the relief commissioner, recalled Mengistu making a speech to the politburo where he invoked the Maoist parallel of fish swimming in the sea to describe the relationship between the northern rebels and the rural people. 'Without the sea there will be no fish,' he said. 'We have to drain the sea, or if we cannot completely drain it, we must bring it to a level where they will lack room to move at will, and their movements will be easily restricted.'[1] For a time Mengistu largely succeeded.

In addition to the relief camps, which they fully controlled, the government set up transit camps in the highlands to accommodate those who had volunteered or been 'volunteered' for resettlement. One settler likened them to rat traps with relief food acting as bait. Once people entered, they were trapped. Guards were posted to stop them getting out and even accompanied them to the latrines. This image of a rat trap came from a series of striking interviews conducted in the 1980s by Alula Pankhurst, academic son of the historian Richard Pankhurst.

The regime's initial resettlement target in October 1984 was to move 300,000 families, about 1.5 million people, out of the highlands. In the course of just fifteen months, more than 500,000 were transported south on trucks, buses, and Antonov cargo planes provided by Mengistu's Soviet allies. Resettlement became a national cause in a country known for taking on big

[1] Dawit Wolde-Giorgis, *Red Tears: War, Famine and Revolution in Ethiopia*.

campaigns. The policy was even enshrined in the Ethiopian constitution. Universities and colleges were closed down, and students and staff dispatched to resettlement areas to help the ruling party set them up.

As well as vacant land, the settlers were promised housing and the means to make a living—seeds, fertilizer, tools, and draught animals. Such assistance may have been intended, but it did not often materialize. The land was in fact never entirely vacant, however sparsely populated, and there was often trouble with local people. Agricultural inputs were in short supply or non-existent. Above all there were diseases in the tropical lowlands to which the highlanders, already weakened by hunger, had no resistance. Insanitary conditions made things worse, and thousands upon thousands died.

In a university thesis which became a book,[2] Dr Pankhurst quoted one settler as saying, 'Disease swept us away like a broomstick' and another on how corpses were taken off for burial 'like sacks of maize'. A Workers' Party cadre told him that since there was no cloth for shrouds—even the empty grain and fertilizer bags had been used up—bodies were buried with a covering of just grass and leaves.

I met a second Addis Ababa academic and authority on resettlement who experienced the programme at first hand when along with other staff and students he was ordered to the far west to help organize a new life for 6,000 settlers. Dr Dessalegn Rahmato was then a university research fellow and has continued to be a critic of resettlement, including a new programme introduced by the Ethiopian government twenty years later. His

[2] Alula Pankhurst, *Resettlement and Famine in Ethiopia* (Manchester University Press, 1992).

experience in the 1980s still made him shudder. 'It was really a tragedy because it was so poorly done. Children were separated from their parents, wives were separated from their husbands, and they went in different directions. A lot died. Some didn't have proper clothing and some were not given any food at all. It was really horrible.'

I asked him what the university team had managed to do. 'We were supposed to help, but I don't know what we could do. We spent most of the time trying to accommodate ourselves.' Dr Dessalegn said that Workers' Party managers at the site barred the university team from meeting the settlers because they might 'subvert' them. 'The settlers wanted to escape but they didn't know where they were. Many died. Some managed to survive on the way home by begging, but many were caught and returned.'

With its huge relief camp, Korem was an immediate resettlement target. As the international relief operation continued through 1985, Oxfam and Save the Children Fund staff recorded the strong-arm tactics used by the regime to persuade people to join the exodus. In one early incident Ethiopian troops surrounded the camp and forced several hundred occupants onto trucks for the journey down the hairpin bends to an airstrip on the plain below.

Later during a second resettlement phase in which Mengistu planned to move a further seven million people out of the highlands, the incidents at Korem became more serious. In January 1988 seven people were killed resisting the press gang and in February 3,000 were forcibly removed after troops shot dead a further twenty. The figures were reported in the previously quoted Human Rights Watch investigation by Alex de Waal who calculated that 50,000 died as a direct consequence of resettlement. He concluded, 'Resettlement certainly killed people at a faster rate than the famine.'

The execution of the resettlement programme around Korem presented a sharp dilemma for foreign relief agencies which had piled in to Ethiopia to help. Should they carry on with their humanitarian work while this went on around them—or should they leave? Should they denounce what they had seen or should they stay silent? The decisions they reached provoked a division within the humanitarian movement which persisted and, if anything, grew wider over the years. On one side were the French, represented by the medical charity Médecins Sans Frontières, and on the other were the British, represented by Oxfam. Ethiopia at this time came to define their differences of approach, and they do not see eye to eye to this day. One senior MSF official described Oxfam to me as 'collaborationist' and a former Oxfam official dismissed MSF as 'the Free French'. I had not invited either to comment directly on the other.

In December 1985 MSF went public with a report that 600 people in Korem had been forced on to resettlement trucks on three occasions in the past two months. They claimed that resettlement had caused the deaths of 100,000. An even more extreme accusation was made later by an MSF director of research who alleged that 6,000 children died in one camp when they were denied help on the grounds that not enough of the adults had agreed to resettlement.[3] The immediate consequence of these public complaints was that MSF was banned from travelling within Ethiopia and thus effectively expelled from the country. This was the first (but not the last) time it happened.

[3] Fiona Terry, *Condemned to Repeat? The Paradox of Humanitarian Action* (Cornell University Press, 2002).

For Dr Rony Brauman, one of the philosopher-kings of Médecins Sans Frontières and at that time its president, their expulsion from Ethiopia was a key moment in the agency's development. It was Brauman who had been prompted into making the first allegations against the resettlement programme at a press conference in Paris, and it was he who then repeated them, also in public, in Addis Ababa. The expulsion followed in ten days. At issue was not resettlement itself, but the way it was being conducted. 'People were taken at gunpoint on trucks and planes for an unknown destination,' Dr Brauman told me. 'It was coercion, intimidation, blackmail.' Even worse, from an international viewpoint, was the use of relief goods to implement the programme. 'Either you accept to volunteer for resettlement and you will receive blankets, food, drugs and everything, or you don't and then you'll die. That was deadly blackmail; that was resettlement.'

Brauman claimed that Oxfam was 'a very strong advocate for resettlement' as co-chair with the Ethiopian Orthodox Church of an official resettlement committee 'that was totally controlled by the Derg'. There had been vigorous exchanges between the two organizations, with Brauman accusing Oxfam of lending its prestige to legitimizing the policy. Almost no public attention was paid at the time to these differences in the humanitarian world. By Christmas 1985 Britain was fatigued by all the compassion it had shown Ethiopia over the past year. Later Tony Vaux, one of the Oxfam staffers who had to grasp the resettlement nettle, offered this defence for staying on: 'Oxfam did not speak out, though it did stop any help for the resettlement programme itself. MSF has adopted the twin objectives of "witness" as well as humanity. But for Oxfam there was just the one objective—the humanitarian one—and it therefore behaved (quite properly, I think) rather differently.'[4]

Rony Brauman would have none of this:

> In Ethiopia it wasn't just *témoignage* [MSF's guiding principle of bearing witness]. It was recognising our position in the political set-up—analysing our situation and looking at the consequences of our work regardless of our intentions. Anyone's intentions are fine. MSF's, Oxfam's, even the Derg's intentions were not to kill people, but to bring more good to the people. It's not a matter of intentions; it's a matter of facts on the ground, what's really happening.

Resettlement divided foreign governments as much as the private agencies. The USA, Britain, and West Germany all opposed it while Italy, Canada, the Soviet Union, and East Germany supported it. MSF was itself divided. When the French arm of the organization was expelled, the Belgian wing stayed on and, said Brauman, 'expressed strong criticism of us'.

A 1990 study on famine and censorship offered one explanation for the decision of Oxfam and others to remain silent in public in the face of the resettlement outrages—money. The anti-censorship campaign group Article 19 argued that this approach had been justified in the early period of the famine when Save the Children Fund and Oxfam were the only agencies in the field. 'However, by 1985–6, the value of this approach was much more questionable. There was now no shortage of either relief or publicity. Oxfam and SCF were no longer alone in northern Ethiopia.'[5] Both agencies had seen their income double in the course of a year as a result of the Ethiopian famine—in Oxfam's

---

[4] Tony Vaux, *The Selfish Altruist* (Earthscan, 2001).
[5] *Starving in Silence: A Report on Famine and Censorship.*

case from £24 million to £51 million; in SCF's case, from £19 million to £45 million. 'If this level of income was to be maintained, it was necessary for relief agencies to remain active in Ethiopia, and therefore not to risk expulsion,' said Article 19. 'The newly-fashionable post-Band Aid humanitarianism demanded action in Ethiopia.'

Wherever I went in Tigray and Wollo I was given accounts of the terrible hardships endured in the Derg's resettlement programme. For hardy Ethiopian peasants, famine is a natural phenomenon, an act of God, even a punishment from God for their sins on earth. By contrast they viewed resettlement as an offence deliberately inflicted on them by their own government.

At the side of an irrigation ditch outside the town of Mersa in northern Wollo, I was engrossed one day in a conversation with an old man about his famine experiences down the decades when a younger man walked up to our party and demanded to be interviewed—not about famines, he said, but about resettlement. We asked him to wait. His name was Tegegne and in 1984 he was in his early twenties. Along with his mother and two sisters he was rounded up and sent off to a resettlement site near the Sudanese frontier. His first complaint was that they were expected to survive on 10 kilograms of rice each per month. They were told in fact to acquire anything else they needed by bartering a proportion of those rations. Worse was to come. One of his two sisters had become detached from the family group on the move south and as far as Tegene knew she was now dead. Then he lost his mother and his other sister to disease. 'I am the only person in my family to survive from that famine.'

With his family gone and to avoid their fate, Tegegne escaped from the resettlement site and fled over the border into Sudan where he was arrested and detained for the day. I had noted that

Tegegne was burly for an Ethiopian farmer and understandably preoccupied with getting enough food to eat. He recalled with precision from twenty-five years ago that the Sudanese police had given him one piece of bread that day. Tegegne made his way in due course to a Tigrayan refugee camp in Sudan where he spent several years and then to a labouring job in Port Sudan. He made it back to Wollo after more than a decade, but the family's land had by then been distributed to others. He was given a tiny parcel in compensation, but now he was married with a child and his wife had inherited a little land. 'We just about manage,' he said.

His experience paralleled what happened to Birhan Woldu, the little girl who nearly died in front of a Canadian television camera in 1984 but was rescued and revived by the Irish Sisters. At around the time her struggle for life was moving the hearts of an international TV audience at Live Aid in 1985, Birhan's family was being swept up in the resettlement dragnet. They too were sent off to the Sudan frontier where Birhan also lost her mother and a sister to the unfamiliar lowland diseases. Rather than risk losing everyone, Birhan's father then walked with his two surviving girls—with Birhan's little sister on his back—several hundred miles back to Tigray.

My research on resettlement took me from the bright and airy highlands to the baking lowlands of the Sudan frontier. I drove one morning from the city of Gondar and its seventeenth-century castles on a highway that drops 3,000 feet through the hills to a dead straight ribbon of asphalt and the border town of Metemma. It was here that the nineteenth-century Emperor Yohannes, the last Tigrayan to occupy the Imperial throne, died in battle against the Sudanese.

I was there to talk to modern settlers who had recently been sent to the scorching plains, but they were not the only settlers there. Not far from the town was a community which had migrated in the time of Haile Selassie. Further afield there were volunteers who had made their way here during the early years of the Derg. Outside the huts which housed the council offices of three settler communities called Villages 6, 7, and 8, I began a series of conversations with people who had recently arrived. I wanted to establish whether they were indeed volunteers.

As usual with foreign visitors I had been given the chair, my companions from the Amhara Development Organization occupied the bench, village councillors found blocks of stone for elevation, and everyone else sat on the ground. We had just started when a woman spoke up in a clear voice from among the faces at the front. She had certainly not come voluntarily, she wanted me to know. There was a hush. Women are not expected to speak out, certainly not on sensitive subjects such as resettlement. No, she had not been a volunteer, she went on, she had been forced to come here.

Mariam was not a new settler. She had come here in 1988 as a girl of 14 along with 7,000 others at the height of the Derg's post-famine resettlement drive. 'The soldiers said we had to volunteer or we would be punished. They said they would beat us until we did volunteer.' Her father was already an old man and he had been too weak to plough the new land in the resettlement area. As soon as the Derg was overthrown, he wanted to return home. He went back in 1992, but died soon afterwards.

By now some of the men were trying to wrest the interview away from Mariam. What *would* the woman say next? But Mariam held her ground and pressed on with her story, even as tears filled her eyes. She was now divorced and had four children aged 7 to 15. They had all dropped out of school because it costs money to send a child to school, even to buy the pencils and paper. The men again shifted uncomfortably beside her. 'We suffer a lot from the weather in this place, but there are bigger problems than that. There is malaria here and kala azar [the biggest parasitic killer after malaria]. People die.' Yes, she would like to return to the highlands where she was born. But that was a hopeless dream. 'It is impossible to transport my family back there. It would cost me so much money and when I got there the government would not give me back the family land.' Mariam finished her story and smiled wearily at me.

I turned to a man on my left wearing a baseball cap. He was also a settler from the Derg years, but his was a story of reasonably good fortune. For him the sickness and death in the famine relief camps of twenty years ago were so bad that he had been glad to make a fresh start. He travelled, he told me, on a large green helicopter. 'Was it Russian?' I asked in the reporter's fashion. 'I don't know,' he replied, 'but it was green.'

His early years of trying to make a living at the resettlement site were a struggle, and he spent some time on the Sudanese side of the frontier in a refugee camp. But now he was cultivating the original hectare of land the government had granted him and renting a further five hectares. He grew sorghum for the family and cotton and sesame as cash crops. He had done well with both in recent years, but he had just brought his cotton crop to market and had been paid only 300 birr [about $30] per quintal [100 kg] for it. Last year he received 600 birr [$60] per quintal. 'Ah,' said the reporter, 'that would be the result of the world economic crisis driving down commodity prices.' 'I have no idea what has caused it,' he replied. 'All I can tell you is that the price has halved in a year.'

The interviews were over and the meeting broke up. I looked around for Mariam, but she had slipped away.

The famine of the mid-1980s lent fresh momentum to the Derg's other decade-old experiments in Soviet communism. The human history of that period can still be unearthed. The physical monuments are fewer and far between. On Churchill Avenue in Addis Ababa, a soaring stone column still stands with its red star and hammer and sickle on top. At its foot are bronze reliefs of soldiers and workers along with victims of the 1973 famine pleading for help from their tyrannical imperial landlords. With fateful irony, the monument was unveiled by Colonel Mengistu in September 1984 as the deaths from starvation in the North finally spiralled out of control. Flanking the monument are photographic memorials to 163 Cuban troops who died fighting the Derg's wars against Somali invaders and northern rebels.

The Russians airlifted 17,000 Cubans to help defend socialist Ethiopia. Soviet arms shipments were worth $9 billion from 1977 to the regime's fall in 1991. In her book on now independent Eritrea, Michela Wrong calculated that in those fourteen years the Russians sent $5,400 worth of weaponry for every Ethiopian man, woman, and child.[6] In the three years which culminated in the catastrophic famine of 1984, Ethiopia imported arms supplies worth $575 million, $975 million, and in the famine year itself $1.2 billion.

Stalinist ventures in the countryside had a direct bearing on peasants' prospects for survival. Vivid parallels have been drawn with the Soviet experimentation in the 1920s and 1930s. In 1977 the Derg established a monopoly Agricultural Marketing Corporation to which farmers had to sell their crops at a price below what they would have received on the open market. The

[6] Michela Wrong, *I Didn't Do It for You* (Fourth Estate, 2005).

consequence was that private transfers from surplus to famine areas were prohibited and farmers consumed as much as they dared of their own food and overall production and trade were diminished.

The showiest of Mengistu's rural initiatives were the 'villagization' programme and the state farms. One contemporary American estimate put the number of Ethiopians forced into collectivized villages at between 12 and 15 million.[7] The justification was that this would provide them with better services; the wretched reality was that farmers had to tear down their own homes and re-erect them at government-designated locations. They would have to travel further to their fields, they were prohibited from staying outside the villages at night, and places of worship were banned.

Paul Henze was first sent as a US national security adviser to Ethiopia in 1977 where he made fruitless efforts to divert Colonel Mengistu from the Soviet course. Henze then became a regular visitor and travelled with remarkable freedom in the countryside. Having been a witness to the early impact of communist agricultural schemes, he was later able to chart their collapse. On one rural tour in 1990 'it proved impossible to find some of the villages I had been taken by Derg escorts to "admire" a few years before,' he wrote. 'They had literally disappeared without a trace. People had dismantled their houses and returned to their original home sites . . . "Killed" towns were being rebuilt.'

Evidence of the old state farms can be found more easily. Outside the town of Gode, in one of the furthest flung corners of the Somali Region, I was taken to see a great irrigation scheme on the banks of the Wabe Shabelle which rushes in a muddy

[7] Paul B. Henze, *Ethiopia in Mengistu's Final Years* (Shama Books, 2007).

torrent through hundreds of miles of waterless scrub and desert towards the Kenyan border. I had an early morning appointment with managers and engineers at their sprawling headquarters compound near the river.

At first sight there was nothing surprising about the place at all. It was what you would expect from a government institution in a distant corner of a remote and troubled region in the Third World—shabby single-storey office blocks, underused engineering sheds, and a very large quantity of rusting equipment. The history of the compound emerged only on inspection and inquiry. It had begun life under Haile Selassie as the headquarters of an imperial research farm on the banks of the river. With the arrival of the Derg, it was nationalized and became a state cotton farm. Now it was run by the Somali regional government and its several thousand acres of well-watered land had been parcelled up as smallholdings for the local landless, many of them pastoralists whose herds and flocks had been wiped out by recent droughts. Around us in the compound was the engineering archaeology of that twentieth-century evolution.

A Land Rover, a Jeep, and a Fiat truck—all of them from the imperial era when Ethiopia looked to the West—were almost submerged in the undergrowth. The contemporary outlook has also been broadly western and I had seen the brand new Perkins diesel pumps installed at the river to extend irrigation capacity. For the most part, though, the compound was occupied by rank upon rank of Soviet bloc farm machinery—all disused, some of it cannibalized decades ago and much of it tyre-less and wheel-less. I asked my guides which countries it had all come from. They pointed to the sun-bleached blue tractors which were East German and the tall orange tractor-trailers which were from Belarus.

When the Derg nationalized the emperor's research farm and converted it to cotton production, they looked to settlers from the North to work it. In all, some 3,000 farmers and their families were relocated from Wollo to the far south-east. With the overthrow of the military regime in 1991, the worm turned once again and they were all thrown out. The new government of Meles Zenawi introduced a federal constitution based on Ethiopia's ethnic identities, and there was less of a welcome for Amharic-speaking northerners. In a second immense upheaval of their lives, almost all the 3,000 sent here from the North were told to start all over again in the uncultivated lands along the Sudanese border. They were resettled around Metemma.

Only one small group remained, and I met some of them outside the engineering sheds. They had been invited to stay on or, as they put it more pointedly, 'the regional government selected us to stay.' They were all engineers from the North who after some perfunctory training from the military had originally been sent as plant operators and mechanics on the new state farm. They were still bitter about the way they had been uprooted.

'They brought us from Wollo by force,' said one of the managers who had trained in East Berlin. 'They took us first to a military camp in Addis Ababa and then to the war front. They gave us some training, and then brought us here to Gode.' There was fighting then, as there is now in the region, between central government forces and Somali rebels, so the engineers found themselves working with farm machinery by day and with guns by night. 'Our duty at night was to defend our surroundings,' said the manager without emotion. 'We had the sickle in one hand and the gun in the other. That was the Russian principle.'

In the group in front of me sat a studious figure with a notebook. He was preparing to tell his own story. He wanted me to know that he was not from Wollo at all, but from Tigray. His name was Equar and he was from a town in the Hawzien district north-west of the capital Makelle. He was a man of precision. He had written in his notebook that as well as the 3,035 original settlers from Wollo, there had been 108 Tigrayans.

Equar said that Derg officials had cheated to get him to come to Gode thirty years ago. They had first offered him fifteen days of training and a promise that he would return home. Equar then had a wife and child at home, but the marriage foundered long ago and they both now have other partners. Wives and children had been allowed to join their menfolk, but only after a gap of seven years. The bachelors among them were never trusted to go home and look for wives. The Derg brought prospective brides to them.

For Equar, the biggest injustice remained the way he was duped into travelling in the first place. The promise of a fortnight's training turned into another month in a military camp in Addis Ababa, then another month of agricultural training. Finally officials told the Tigrayans that they would never go home. Equar protested as loudly as he dared. Finally an exasperated official told him: 'Give up the dream of ever going back to your country. The hyenas in Harar make exactly the same sound as the hyenas in Tigray.' Harar is Ethiopia's great Moslem city in the South-East. Even as the crow flies it is still some 300 miles short of Gode where Equar ended up.

In Tigray and Eritrea, the Derg intensified its military operations throughout the 1980s. In his *Evil Days* study, Alex de Waal detailed the dates and the targets of the numerous offensives against the rebels and concluded that they were deliberately aimed at hampering food production and the food trade. Much of the aerial bombing was directed at market towns on market days. Towns were hit again and again, a campaign that culminated in the virtual obliteration of Hawzien in June 1988. The attack cost 1,800 dead from daylong bombing and strafing.

The Derg did not always make much of an effort to deny the purpose of its tactics against the rebels. Even some private aid agency officials concluded that the relief operation may have helped sustain the regime. First the famine had emptied rural areas because the hungry had to find food in the shelters. Now that relief was flowing, the Derg's hands were free to prosecute the war. When the US chargé d'affaires, David Korn, called on the acting foreign minister, Tibebu Bekele, in December 1984, he was told 'probably with more candour than he intended that "food is a major element in our strategy against the secessionists." '[8]

But the world was changing, the Cold War was coming to an end, and the Derg would be left high and dry. Six months after Mengistu established his Workers' Party of Ethiopia—the last such group to be formed anywhere in the world—Mikhail Gorbachev became general secretary of the Soviet Communist Party. Disengagement from a disastrous and unwinnable war in Afghanistan was a priority, but there was also dwindling enthusiasm for expensive military embroilment in Africa. Kremlin-watchers noted this Soviet commentary in *Asia and Africa Today* in 1987, 'It is immoral to throw hundreds of millions of dollars into the development of homicide when millions starve and are devoid of everyday necessities.'[9]

For a time Mengistu held to the faith. For several years the newspapers were formally banned from using the terms *glasnost*

[8] David Korn, *Ethiopia, the U.S. and the Soviet Union* (Croom Helm, 1986).
[9] Quoted in Michela Wrong, *I Didn't Do It for You.*

and *perestroika*. But in 1988 even he got the message when he returned empty-handed from a mission to Moscow to acquire more arms. There were belated second thoughts about a rigidly controlled economy, support was withdrawn from the collectives in rural areas, and the Workers' Party was renamed the Democratic Unity Party. But it was all too late. Guerrilla forces in the North were in the ascendant and had won back the territory and the towns lost during the Derg's post-famine offensive. Their disastrous experiments at the expense of the poor were to end in ignominious flight.

Chapter 4
Rebels with a Cause

'We had an even higher objective than just keeping people alive.'

Romance is not a word much associated with Africa's guerrilla wars and Meles Zenawi, head of government in Ethiopia for nineteen years and a guerrilla commander for the sixteen years before that, is not a romantic. In interview, he comes across as courteous (a word he likes), precise, and professorial. He has no small talk when there are interesting issues to be addressed. Any trace of sentiment quickly gives way to analysis and he is dry-eyed in discussing the death and destruction of Ethiopia's recent wars and famines. Yet in answer to my questions about the Tigrayan origins of the ruling Ethiopian People's Revolutionary Democratic Front (EPRDF) he used the word 'romantic' or 'romanticization' five times.

In order to review what EPRDF ministers call the 'years of struggle' against the Derg, I spoke to two leaders of the Tigrayan People's Liberation Front (TPLF), forerunner and core component of the ruling party. One was Meles himself, who commanded

Tigray's central region, a swathe of territory running north and south from his home town of Adwa. The second was Lieutenant-General (Retd.) Tsadkan Gebre-Tensae, who commanded the eastern region. After Mengistu's fall, Tsadkan became Chief of Staff of the new Ethiopian army and remained in command for more than a decade before being dismissed by Meles. The issue that divided them, the general said, was the pace of democratization in Ethiopia—or the lack of it. Not everyone would accept such a cut-and-dried account of the intricate struggles within the government. Tsadkan claimed there was a fearfulness in Meles's heart—and thus at the heart of government—that did not allow him to relax the regime's control. The general now runs a think tank with offices near Addis Ababa airport.

Meles and Tsadkan were friends and student contemporaries in the capital as the tide of protest and revolt rose and overwhelmed the empire. Tsadkan had thought of joining Meles to read medicine, but chose to study chemistry and biology instead. Neither completed his course. As the military moved to take over the apparatus of government in Ethiopia, the two Tigrayan activists left university in their second year and joined others in the North in a disparate underground movement.

Revolutionary student nationalism was one thing. Survival in the harsh Tigrayan countryside was another. Most of the young Tigrayans who wanted to fight were from the towns, some of them from landowning families used to treating peasants as serfs. For Meles, there was immediate recognition that the movement's survival depended on the peasantry. 'If they gave us food, we would have enough to eat. If they didn't, we would go hungry.'

'We had to learn to love our people, our peasantry, and to respect them—it is not difficult to respect somebody who has full control over your very existence—and that took us a few years. It was not as difficult as it could have been because of this romanticization.' He spoke of the 'quasi-romantic ideas' held about the peasants by town-based students who had read all there was to read about the revolutionary revolts of Mao Tse-tung, Fidel Castro, and Ho Chi Minh.

General Tsadkan said the breakthrough in their relations with rural Tigray came with the TPLF's decision to distribute land in the liberated areas. 'Land to the Tiller' had been the cry of urban activists against the empire's feudal landlords, and the Derg had quickly introduced a sweeping land nationalization measure of its own. But in Tigray it was the TPLF who confronted the landlords on the peasants' behalf and gave them security of tenure, although they did not grant them outright ownership, nor have they since. Land in Ethiopia has remained government owned.

'The Right was against land distribution, it was against the empowering of the peasant,' said General Tsadkan. 'They were the people of the past. We had to fight the Right militarily, politically, economically and socially. At the Third Congress [of the TPLF] there was a decision to act for the peasants and to mobilize them on the basis of their own interests. After that they began to flow to our position.'

The TPLF needed peasant support against rival leftist groups as well as the landlords' party. Differences among anti-Derg groups were resolved with 'ruthless determination' as the TPLF attacked their fellow revolutionaries and executed some of their leaders.[1] Further challenges had to be faced with Mengistu's 'Red Terror' in the towns and cities. 'There was no subsequent supply from urban areas,' said Meles. 'Our urban structures had been crushed.' In a single incident in Abi Adi in central Tigray, the

[1] John Markakis, *National and Class Conflict in the Horn of Africa* (Zed Books, 1990).

Derg executed some 178 people in the town square 'undoubtedly because of TPLF support in the area'.[2] 'The [TPLF] movement became essentially a peasant movement with a trickle of semi-urban intelligentsia here and there,' Meles said. 'So there was a transformation—an urban transplant surviving in a peasant environment.'

The personal attitudes of the TPLF's leadership were also transformed. 'Those who had their origins in urban areas began over time to think like the average peasant,' said Meles, 'so when the rains come most urbanites would feel uncomfortable. "I'm getting wet" is uppermost in your mind, but when you begin to feel like a peasant and it rains, you think "Ah, my land is going to get watered" so you are very happy, even if you do get wet.'

This process was the wellspring of EPRDF policy once in power: a concentration on the welfare of rural areas where 85 per cent of the people lived and greater emphasis on agriculture than on commerce and industry. 'If we can mobilize the labour of the peasants, we can improve production and productivity, and that could push industrialization,' was the Meles formulation for an approach that became a political principle. Rural areas were often the first to benefit from improvements to the education network and the health system.

Tigrayan guerrillas lived down Emperor Teodoros's dictum that 'Soldiers eat; peasants provide.' Most accounts, including of course those of Prime Minister Meles and General Tsadkan, testify to an authentic bond between rebel and peasant. In addition to land distribution, the TPLF began agricultural extension work, created the still-respected relief agency REST (Relief Society

---

[2] John Young, *Peasant Revolution in Ethiopia* (Cambridge University Press, 1997).

of Tigray) and established what Meles described as a 'participatory governance structure' of local councils known as *baidos*.

The TPLF continued to march on its stomach, and in the good years marched very well. Tsadkan came from Raya, one of the richest areas in Tigray, and fought there against the Derg. 'We were being fed by the peasants with lavish food, if I can call it that. We used to get yoghourt, milk, meat, all this food from, say, 1979 right up to the hunger of 1984.' Then came the desperate lean years.

'Suddenly there were people whom we knew with hundreds of cows—with 150 or 200 cows—suddenly all of them were left with nothing, they were begging from us. They were the same very generous people who had been feeding us, giving us everything, and they were now at the mercy of our organization.' The TPLF had begun receiving relief supplies from across the border with Sudan, and that was passed on. Whenever government positions were overrun, said the general, the TPLF let their peasant supporters loot the money and the food while the guerrillas took the weapons—and the communist textbooks.

Meles described the famine years as the worst time of his life. 'I don't think I've had as bad and as nightmarish a time as that,' he said. As people died from starvation and the survivors fled, the guerrillas found themselves moving through empty villages.

You'd see the odd stray dog. The dogs could eat the carcasses, but eventually the hunger even caught up with them. So when you got to a village, what you'd find is an abandoned, eerie silence. . . . Normally you'd go for water and there would be kids to fetch it for you. Now there were no kids. Normally, there would be an old grandmother who'd be very kind and say 'Are you tired? Come and sit here and I'll get you something.' All of these had gone. It was literally as if they'd been pulled out of the womb.

As famine deaths behind their lines multiplied, the TPLF decided on a mass civilian evacuation across the border into Sudan. Some 200,000 people trekked up to 300 miles escorted by guerrillas and strafed by government warplanes. The exodus was arranged in part to counter the grim alternatives offered to the people of Tigray by the Derg—either stay with the guerrillas and starve or go to government relief camps and be forcibly resettled. It also had the effect of making sure that international aid-givers recognized the extent of the suffering in guerrilla-held territory.

The Sudan lifeline was to have long-term political implications both for governments and the relief agencies. In modern controversies over the boundaries of humanitarian interventions in the poor world, there are strong echoes of issues raised first during the Ethiopian civil war.

In 1981 European church groups had established an Emergency Relief Desk (ERD) in the Sudanese capital Khartoum to link up with Eritrean and Tigrayan guerrillas and to channel emergency food into liberated areas. The local agencies that took delivery were the relief wings of the rebel movements, and no realistic distinction could be made between food that fed guerrillas and food that fed civilians. Indeed when the war was over, the victorious guerrillas thanked the Emergency Relief Desk not specifically for aiding their civilians as 'for helping their struggle'.[3] The ERD became the largest humanitarian operation ever undertaken by church agencies, said its chairman Jacques Willemse, of Dutch Interchurch Aid, in the foreword to the book just quoted. 'Protestant church agencies, which formed the basis of ERD, and the humanitarian

[3] Mark Duffield and John Prendergast, *Without Troops and Tanks: Humanitarian Intervention in Ethiopia and Eritrea* (Red Sea Press, 1994).

arms of liberation movements are not natural allies.' Not everyone was as surprised as he was by the link.

There was instinctive sympathy between radical charities and church groups in the West and liberation groups fighting a thuggish military dictatorship, but for a long time official western donors fought shy of contributing to the relief effort in rebel territory. The Mengistu regime was still the legally recognized authority in Ethiopia, even if it was a Cold War ally of the Soviet Union. Yet that principle of national sovereignty was soon overlooked after the TV coverage of the famine and the worldwide clamour for action. Both the European Community and the United States government mounted food operations across the border, although neither was to have any formal contact with the rebels until 1990.

Professor Mark Duffield was at that time Oxfam's country representative in Khartoum and a close observer of the cross-border operation. His experience inspired a career-long focus on the relationship between humanitarian agencies and governments in the developing world, including an account of the history of the Emergency Relief Desk referred to here. He later became professor of development politics at Bristol University and a provocative critic of the humanitarian agencies by which he was once employed.

When we met in Bristol, Prof. Duffield described the 1984–5 famine in Ethiopia as a milestone in the breakdown of what he called the Cold War model of humanitarian intervention in which Third World states formally invited big donors to assist them in dealing with an emergency. After the famine, western governments came to rely on NGOs (Non-Governmental Organizations) to deliver aid, and the NGOs themselves grew into major institutions. Duffield wrote in his 1994 study of the cross-border operation, 'The shape of Western humanitarian politics has been increasingly influenced by a weakening of the principle of sovereignty and a propensity towards more direct forms of intervention.'

As we shall see later, Duffield's scepticism about the role of the NGOs is shared and endorsed by Meles Zenawi and the government of Ethiopia, but it has found little favour at home, and very little indeed among his students. 'Development is a new religion,' he told me. 'Trying to take a critical view of NGOs is like trying to tell people that God doesn't exist.' His students were sometimes upset at his strictures on the NGOs because many hoped to pursue careers with them. 'We're dealing with a widely held perception that the NGOs can do no harm, that they exist only to do good,' Prof. Duffield said. There was a belief that NGOs were above politics, that they were on the margins always doing good. 'I know the humanitarian agencies keep people alive. I'm trying to get a critical perspective across without throwing the lot out.'

For Meles and the TPLF, the overriding objective in the mid-1980s was not to keep every starving peasant alive, but to win the war, and that provoked differences with the charities. 'Obviously we wanted to keep our people alive because if they died the objective of the cause died at the same time,' he said. 'But we felt that in keeping them alive we had to transform their circumstances, and in order to transform their circumstances we had to remove the Mengistu regime. So we felt we had an even higher objective than just keeping people alive.'

In spring 1985 with the prospect of rains in the highlands, the TPLF wanted farmers whom they had escorted on the long trek out of Ethiopia to return and prepare for the next crop. There is a

Tigrayan proverb which goes 'Lose one June [the planting season] and you lose the next seven.' So they asked for volunteers among the several hundred thousand refugees in Sudan, and there were many. They advised farmers to leave their wives and children behind, but they did want the able-bodied men to return. Most of the relief agencies operating near the border were appalled at the idea of civilians returning to a war zone in the middle of a famine and refused to help in the repatriation. They argued strenuously against the move and would not even provide transport as far as the border. So the farmers had to walk the whole way home.

'We felt yes, this was a war zone, but the only way round it was to win the war,' Meles responded. 'This was also going to be a hunger period, but if they don't plant now they're going to be displaced permanently, they would become permanent refugees. So the choice was between being uprooted permanently and taking the risk of returning to a war zone.'

Most of the women and children remained behind in the refugee camps, but not all of them. Meles recalled that some of the men said, 'I can't cook, so my wife will come,' and then, 'If my wife is coming with me, who is going to take care of my children?' The argument was settled in favour of a mass return and once again, in small matters as in large, Ethiopians had exercised independent judgement over their own affairs.

Ever since the guerrilla war ended in 1991, there has been debate over whether it was prolonged or shortened by the famine and the world's response. For some, such as Paul Henze who wrote from his experience on the ground about the Derg's decline and fall, the famine was 'the beginning of the end' for Mengistu and his government. The regime had been exposed as 'dishonest and unprincipled' and had demonstrated to Ethiopians that 'the world had not forgotten them'.[4] Since the Derg lasted for seven years after the famine and behaved with increasing ferocity and desperation during that time, this seems an optimistic account. The more widely held view is that the famine and the relief operation served to prolong the conflict. Alex de Waal, already quoted in his study for Human Rights Watch, came to this blunt conclusion: 'The humanitarian effort prolonged the war, and with it, human suffering.'[5]

My interviews with the prime minister and his former chief of staff tended to confirm de Waal's view, certainly in relation to the effects of the famine. 'When the hunger came this was a setback,' said General Tsadkan, and paused to reflect. 'This was a big setback, a very huge setback...looking back on it, if there had been another bad year, it would have been extremely difficult for us, but 1985 was a very good harvest.'

In his analytical fashion, Meles provided a more elaborate account of the impact which the famine and its aftermath had on the course of the war, but he too concluded that it had delayed a rebel victory. 'In the end the Mengistu regime benefited more than we did because in 1984–5 the villages became phantom villages and the struggle effectively stopped for some time. For the villages to be full of life again took several years. That's how much the struggle lost. A couple of years were added to the conflict.'

After television reported the famine, 'the international community demanded certain things such as access to the poor and the hungry,' as Meles put it. 'That was more important [to them] than the cause of the war and the prosecution of the war.' Both

[4] Paul Henze, *Ethiopia in Mengistu's Final Years.*
[5] Alex de Waal, *Famine Crimes* (James Currey, 1997).

sides in the conflict on the ground 'needed on the one hand to accommodate such demands and on the other hand make sure that militarily this does not disadvantage them.'

The Derg intensified military operations against the TPLF at the same time as relief supplies began finally to reach the hungry in quantity. Their eighth offensive was launched in February 1985 and lasted until May.[6] Some relief food certainly went to feed government militias—as it also found its way to TPLF fighters—and since the regime was getting the lion's share of the assistance its forces probably benefited disproportionately. Yet Meles, still the analyst, also underlined the damage done to the government. 'The famine did indicate that the Derg's policies were a shambles, a failure, and that after what happened to the Emperor it also discredited them in the eyes of the Ethiopian people as a whole. To that extent it shortened the life of the Mengistu regime.'

Two major battles finally did for the Derg's position in northern Ethiopia. In March 1988 the Eritrean People's Liberation Front (EPLF) inflicted a humiliating defeat on the regime around the town of Afabet, and in February 1989 the TPLF delivered a body blow to the government in Tigray by capturing the town of Shire. This battle was fought on both sides with Soviet armour supplied to or captured from government forces, and when the EPLF sent a force to help the Tigrayans, that too deployed in captured Soviet armour.[7] The traveller in northern Tigray today can clamber over the burnt-out hulks of tanks and armoured personnel carriers rusting by the side of highways or in defensive positions on hilltops.

---

[6] Alex de Waal, *Evil Days*.
[7] Paul Henze, *Ethiopia in Mengistu's Final Years*.

Shire is not far from where the TPLF was raised in 1975 and where its foundation is marked each year. I was there in February 2008 when the occasion assumed extra importance because of the Ethiopian millennium. At the parade in the morning everyone waved their red and yellow TPLF pennants. In the afternoon Prime Minister Meles spent several hours handing out medals, cups, and certificates to 200 farmers as reward for their 'model' feats of productivity and profit. This was not the only 'Farmers' Festival' I attended in Ethiopia where Meles gave away the prizes live on TV. The support of the peasantry—and the romance of the association—remained at the TPLF's core.

After the defeat at Shire, the Derg abandoned all of Tigray to the rebels, and the EPRDF's expanding guerrilla alliance started the military and political manoeuvres that would end in the takeover of Addis Ababa two years later. The Soviet bloc was close to casting Mengistu adrift. No belated acts of liberalization would save him. For his part Meles Zenawi, barely known outside Tigray, began introducing himself to a wider world.

An early encounter with the western press led to an observation that has dogged him ever since. He told an interviewer at the end of 1989 that the Soviet Union and other eastern bloc countries had never been truly socialist and added, 'The nearest any country comes to being socialist as far as we are concerned is Albania.'[8] As Meles set off in 1990 on his first venture to the United States, his aspiration to the mantle of Enver Hoxha and to run Ethiopia on Albanian lines did not inspire much confidence.

In Washington he met the veteran Ethiopia-watcher Paul Henze. Henze was as impressed by Meles as many foreigners

[8] Richard Dowden, 'Tigrayans Home in on Ethiopia's Lifeline', *The Independent*, London, 28 November 1989.

have been in the years since, and he made detailed notes after two long conversations. Meles had to deal first with the Albanian connection. 'I have never been to Albania,' Meles told Henze. 'We do not have any Albanian contacts. We are not trying to imitate in Tigray anything the Albanians have done.'

Meles was equally keen to reject the Marxist tag. 'We are not a Marxist–Leninist movement,' he said. 'We do have Marxists in our movement. I acknowledge that. I myself was a convinced Marxist when I was a student at [Addis Ababa University] in the early 1970s, and our movement was inspired by Marxism. But we learned that Marxism was not a good formula for resistance to the Derg and our fight for the future of Ethiopia.'

As the EPRDF moved out of the countryside to take over the towns and the cities, it emerged into a post-communist world, and a rapid political make-over was needed. 'When we entered Addis Ababa, the whole Marxist–Leninist structure was being disgraced,' said General Tsadkan. 'We had to rationalize in terms of the existing political order . . . capitalism had become the order of the day. If we continued with our socialist ideas, we could only continue to breed poverty.'

In his Washington conversations in 1990, Meles was impatient with the emphasis that politicians and press placed on the delivery of aid to the exclusion of what had led to famine. The TPLF was not stopping the food getting through to people in the liberated areas. It was the Derg. 'Why can't people here in Washington understand that?' he asked Paul Henze. 'The way to get famine relief to people who are starving is to put more pressure on the Derg—and then to see that the Derg is replaced so there is a government in Ethiopia that all the people can support. Then there will be no more famines.'

Meles and the EPRDF would have their opportunity and his undertaking to end famine would be put to the test. In May 1991 Mengistu fled into exile in Zimbabwe to become a guest of Robert Mugabe. The next day the Derg's 200,000 strong army in Eritrea surrendered to Eritrean guerrillas. Derg forces defending the capital 'evaporated like dew under a hot sun,' according to a statement issued by the Supreme Council of the EPRDF,[9] and there was almost no resistance in the city when their forces finally entered Addis Ababa.

[9] Quoted in Sarah Vaughan, 'Ethnicity and Power in Ethiopia', Ph.D. thesis, 2003, Edinburgh.

II

TRANSITIONS

Chapter 5
Economic Warfare

'Sometimes pain is necessary, but it is not a virtue in its own right.'

The formal education of Meles Zenawi was interrupted when he was a second-year medical student aged 19. It was resumed when the guerrilla war ended and he became president of a transitional government in Addis Ababa at the age of 36. Meles adopted the unusual course for a head of state of signing up for a degree at the Open University in Britain and he instructed his cabinet ministers and fellow guerrilla fighters to do the same.

After four years of study Meles acquired a first class master's degree in business administration which the university said was one of the best in its history. His education did not finish there. By now prime minister, he embarked on a master's degree in economics at Erasmus University in Rotterdam. This pursuit was interrupted once again by war. He set aside his studies for the duration of the conflict with independent Eritrea from 1998 to 2000, and was awarded his M.Sc. in 2004.

When it came to the subject matter for his final thesis, Meles did not deliberate for long. He described the paper to me as 'my attempt to academically vindicate our already existing policies. In a sense it was an articulation of the policy of the EPRDF in academic terms. It was primarily intended for our own local consumption to see if our policies could stand up to the rigour of some academic scrutiny.' The thesis took on a life of its own. He worked further at it, gave it the title 'African Development: Dead Ends and New Beginnings' and then posted fifty pages of excerpts online. It is, redundantly, headed 'Not for Quotation' and has this odd disclaimer on the front page, 'The author is the Prime Minister of Ethiopia. The views expressed are personal and do not necessarily reflect the official position of the Government.' There is a bibliography running to eight pages which is marked, alarmingly, 'to be completed'.

Even his bitterest critics do not deny Meles's brilliance. Those who have worked with him testify to a remarkable intellect. One commendation came from Lord Stern, a former chief economist at the World Bank and director of policy and research for Tony Blair's 2005 Africa Commission on which Meles also sat. He had worked with three Nobel Prize-winning economists, Professor Stern said, and Meles could hold his own with any of them. Clare Short, Britain's first secretary of state for international development, described him to me as 'the most intelligent politician I've met anywhere in the world'.

On a Saturday morning in February 2008, the prime minister subjected his thesis—'a paper I wrote a while back'—to further scrutiny. He gave a public lecture at the United Nations conference centre in Addis Ababa on the theme of the 'developmental state'. His lecture lasted an hour, and then for two more hours he took questions from an audience of several hundred—members of the Ethiopian Economics Association and foreigners. The burden of the lecture was that the West's faith in the market had been an economic dead end for Africa. In his answers to questions, he ranged from the fortunes of Taiwanese peasants under the Kuomintang to the harshness of the English enclosure movement. Ken Ohashi, the World Bank chief in Ethiopia, asked a question about Japan as a 'developmental state' and its failures in the fascist era and during the economic stagnation of the 1980s. Meles's long reply touched at one point on Japan's regard in the 1930s for a Prussian style of leadership which in turn, he said, may have owed something to that of Napoleon III.

What stood out most was his summary of Ethiopian resistance to the reconstruction of its economy along free market lines. 'We in Ethiopia very nicely and politely have rejected a number of neoliberal prescriptions given to us, and we have lived to tell the story.' Time and again he invoked the name of Professor Joseph Stiglitz, winner of the 2001 Nobel Prize for economics and former chief economist at the World Bank, and his work on the efficiency or otherwise of markets.

Ethiopia had a direct and formative influence on the course— and the achievements—of Joe Stiglitz's three years as chief economist at the World Bank. An academic economist by background, he had risen to prominence in Washington as chair of President Clinton's Council of Economic Advisers. He moved to the Bank in 1997 and Ethiopia became an immediate preoccupation. The lessons he learnt on the ground there—and then chose so vividly to pass on—told us more than we had ever known of the workings of the global financial institutions and their determination to tell poor countries how to run their affairs.

Ethiopia became a key battleground in a broiling Washington war between the World Bank and the International Monetary

Fund, the two great institutions of post-war global finance. The country provided an eloquent case study of what developing world critics had long identified as the IMF's high-handed and ideological commitment to the merits of modern capitalism. More significant still, thanks to Stiglitz, this institutional conflict remained neither behind closed doors nor confined to high economics. It provided a defining early chapter 'Broken Promises' in his most famous book *Globalization and its Discontents*.[1] It was a battle in which the IMF was badly worsted. Even in 2009, more than a decade later and in a world where the deficiencies of markets were almost universally acknowledged, the IMF remained instinctively uncommunicative on the subject.

Barely a month after he moved to the World Bank, Joe Stiglitz set off on his first visit to Ethiopia where, as he put it in his book, 'I became fully immersed in the astonishing world of IMF politics and arithmetic.' The International Monetary Fund and the government of Meles Zenawi were involved in a series of disputes over economic management, and the IMF had just suspended disbursements under an arrangement worth 88 million SDRs— the IMF's Special Drawing Rights convertible into international currency. More important than the sum involved was the formal notice the suspension gave to the World Bank and other western donors that Ethiopia was an unreliable partner, a bad bet.

When he came to write about this period, Stiglitz concluded that the basic problem was the IMF's insistence on playing a central role in shaping economic policy and not being content with giving advice. 'And it could do this,' he wrote, 'because its position was based on an ideology—market fundamentalism—that required

---

[1] Joseph Stiglitz, *Globalization and its Discontents* (Penguin Books, 2002).

little, if any, consideration of a country's particular circumstances and immediate problems.'

There were a number of sticking points between the government and the IMF which brought about the breakdown—one was the Ethiopian budget, another was the early repayment of foreign bank loans. Stiglitz plunged into both battles. On the budget, the IMF complained that Ethiopia was relying more on foreign aid than on taxes and that aid flows could well go down. So expenditure should be financed out of domestic revenue. On the contrary, argued Stiglitz, aid was a more stable source of income than tax, and it needed to be spent as the funders intended—on the many priorities of development. 'To me, the IMF's position made no sense, and not just because of its absurd implications,' Stiglitz wrote, and quoted Prime Minister Meles as having told him that 'he had not fought so hard for seventeen years to be instructed by some international bureaucrat that he could not build schools and clinics for his people once he had succeeded in convincing donors to pay for them'.

When I spoke to Prof. Stiglitz in September 2009, he was focused on his role at the United Nations Commission on the international financial system which he had chaired since the global financial collapse of 2008, but in our interview he turned his attention back to Ethiopia in the 1990s and to the arguments over the status and reliability of aid. He said there had since been academic studies in this area, including into why aid had not promoted more growth in poor countries. 'One of the reasons is that particularly in Africa foreign aid goes disproportionately into reserves,' Stiglitz said, 'and not surprisingly really, if it can't be spent because of IMF strictures (which is the model they were pursuing in Ethiopia) it's not going to help with development.' Prime Minister Meles had argued that aid money should be wholly committed to aid projects because if it dried up the projects could always be halted. 'They [the IMF] were never able to answer that and it did provoke a lot of thinking on their part—and in the end a softening of their position, but never fully reformed.'

Another sticking point was Ethiopia's early repayment of American bank loans taken out by the Derg to buy two aircraft for Ethiopian Airlines. These loans involved high interest charges and other arduous conditions. For instance, even if the Ethiopians paid back the loan on one aircraft, lenders would still retain a charge on the plane because the entire debt had not been settled. Ethiopian Airlines wanted to pay off the whole loan, Ethiopian state banks had the foreign exchange available, and so the government authorized the settlement. Simple? No. The IMF complained that Ethiopia had not told them of the transaction and that their reserves should not have been used to pay off such loans. But, as the government pointed out, the IMF had just suspended its lending arrangements with Ethiopia, 'so there is no agreement in force to stop us being helpful to the airline'.

I was told all this by Newai Gebre-Ab, chief economic adviser to the prime minister, who hinted at a darker reason for IMF (and American) objections to early repayment. 'The IMF didn't openly say you shouldn't have repaid the banks, but it's possible the banks would have preferred the loan to be completed on schedule rather than terminate it early,' said Newai. Arduous loan conditions for Ethiopia of course meant benefits for foreign banks. 'It left a sour taste in the mouth. Our relations with the IMF reached their lowest point.'

Stiglitz once again backed the Ethiopians, as he was to do with extraordinary consistency in this and other areas. 'The transaction made perfect *economic* sense,' he wrote in *Globalization and its Discontents*. 'I, too, would have advised them to repay . . . why should a sovereign country ask permission of the IMF for every action which it undertakes?'

There was an ideological chasm between the IMF and the government of Ethiopia. One side favoured opening up Ethiopia's financial markets to western competition; allowing foreign exchange and interest rates to float free; and privatizing industry and the utility companies. The other side favoured only cautious moves into the marketplace; only modest relaxation of government control over the economic levers of power; and only partial privatization. 'Our argument has been that the neoliberal model does not work in Africa,' Prime Minister Meles told me in 2009. 'In developed countries it is a perfectly legitimate alternative (or it was—it needs serious modification now). In the case of underdeveloped economies without the push of the state, an effective developmental state, it is very unlikely that the markets that do exist now are going to function efficiently and push the country forward.'

It was a wrangle over the exchange rate which led finally to the IMF suspending its loan arrangements with Ethiopia. When the EPRDF came to power, it inherited an exchange rate unchanged from the days of empire which had ridiculously overvalued the currency. It had to be devalued—that much was common ground between the IMF and the government—but how was it be fixed, indeed was it to be fixed at all?

I was taken through the process by the prime minister's adviser Newai Gebre-Ab. 'The way the IMF negotiates,' he explained, 'is to come up with maximum demands, find out whether they are acceptable or not, and if they are not, then work for a negotiated

position that at least satisfies some of their basic requirements.'
So the tortuous process began.

'First they wanted to see if we would agree to float the currency,
and of course we didn't agree to that. The reason's quite simple—if
it was to be floated, it would be subject to speculative attack and
that would have dire consequences on inflation.' Then there would
be 'a vicious circle' of inflation, depreciation, and devaluation.
Such consequences were soon to be witnessed in the East Asian
and other currency crises around the world. 'I think they saw early
on that this was a non-starter for us,' said Newai.

After eighteen months and three rounds of negotiation, the
two sides settled on what Newai called a 'semi-managed system of
regulating the exchange rate' which would bring the official and
black market rates more into line. IMF and Ethiopian officials
all appeared satisfied, and the first three-year loan agreement
(or 'Structural Adjustment Facility', as the IMF called it) valued
at 50 million Special Drawing Rights was fully honoured. 'The
important lesson really for us was that if you didn't negotiate you
could end up agreeing to the maximum demands—that's the real
story behind it,' said Newai.

But the IMF was not finished yet. When negotiations began
for an 'Enhanced Structural Adjustment Facility', their demands
for relaxation in the foreign exchange regime resurfaced. First, the
IMF wanted the exchange rate to be determined by buying and
selling among the banks. 'We agreed to all that,' said Newai.
Then there was the question of how individuals would sell or
acquire their foreign exchange, and the Ethiopians thought they
should come into a bank, state-owned of course, and use the
foreign exchange bureaux there. 'I recall what [the IMF] wanted
instead was foreign exchange bureaux outside the bank. We
didn't like that. It would have meant opening up the markets to

any foreign operator . . . effectively they were looking for the legalizing of the parallel [black] market, and that's what we didn't want.'

According to Newai, the IMF accepted Ethiopian concerns and agreed to the bank arrangement. 'We thought at least they agreed. At the end of every year, the IMF sends a mission and they came up with a new formulation. They considered setting up bureaux within the banking system was "non-effective implementation." Well, we said, that's your interpretation, but that's what we agreed.'

In the IMF canon, 'non-effective implementation' is serious. 'They were a bit aggrieved over that, I must say,' said Newai. The 'Enhanced Structural Adjustment Facility' was suspended with only two of its six payments made and it lapsed altogether in 1999.

But, I asked Newai, did these dismal economic intricacies actually matter to the poor farmers of Ethiopia on whose behalf the government was supposed to be acting? He made a persuasive case that they did.

If the 85 per cent of Ethiopians dependent on agriculture were to increase their production, they would need such basic inputs as fertilizer and that in turn would mean gaining access to credit at affordably low rates of interest. Newai argued that breaking up the banks, allowing in foreign operators, and abandoning all exchange controls—as the IMF wanted—would lead to higher interest rates and the interests of these farmers being overlooked. 'The consequences for our development strategy would have been extremely negative. You can't be saying you will be tackling rural poverty and not link it in to your macro policy on foreign exchange markets and financial market liberalization. They are inter-related.'

Joe Stiglitz, whose arrival in Ethiopia coincided with the breakdown in relations between the IMF and the government, was withering in his characterization of the IMF's approach:

> Soaring interest rates might, today, lead to starvation, but market efficiency requires free markets, and eventually efficiency leads to growth, and growth benefits all. Suffering and pain became part of the process of redemption, evidence that a country was on the right track. To me, sometimes pain *is* necessary, but it is not a virtue in its own right. Well-designed policies can often avoid much of the pain. . . .[2]

Stiglitz took the fight back to Washington where he mounted what he called a campaign of 'intellectual lobbying' to persuade his World Bank colleagues and the IMF that Ethiopia deserved to be supported, not shunned. He trundled out the biggest guns in his armoury, including Clinton administration officials and America's own representative at the Fund, to try and shift the battle in Ethiopia's favour. Ethiopia figured regularly at breakfast meetings between the president of the World Bank and the managing director of the IMF. Stiglitz began to gain ground.

His big achievement was to ensure that the World Bank did not follow the IMF's lead in cold-shouldering the Ethiopians. Bank lending to Ethiopia in fact trebled in the years ahead. The de-linking of the two institutional programmes was the key. 'I don't know whether it was historically unprecedented, but it was certainly unusual when we went ahead with lending when the IMF suspended,' he told me. 'It's a precedent that's not been followed as much as I would have liked, so I can't say it revolutionized the pattern of behaviour, but it did set an important precedent.'

---

[2] Joseph Stiglitz, *Globalization and its Discontents.*

The IMF also changed course, but its own 'structural adjustment' took much longer. There was a gap of several years between the suspension of its programme in Ethiopia for 'non-effective implementation' and its final resumption in 2001. Stiglitz had left the Bank by then. He told me he believed his campaign had 'raised fundamental issues that the IMF gradually began to try to come to terms with, but never really got hold of'.

It is not surprising that World Bank staff should find it easier than their IMF colleagues to talk about this period. For the Fund to be reminded of their former selves may have been unwelcome in 2009 when it was centre-stage in efforts to rebuild the international financial order after the 2008 crisis—a crisis of the markets whose virtues the Fund had for so long promoted.

I was courteously received in the IMF office in Addis Ababa, but received little help from the press office in Washington, certainly nothing as useful as a formal interview. Two months after they were alerted to my interest and after a number of explanatory emails and reminders from me, I received two short documents written in response to Prof. Stiglitz's book seven years before. Neither of them was enlightening. My follow-up inquiries to the press office were ignored.

However disdainful of criticism the IMF remained, its rhetoric was certainly changing. Gone for instance are the 'Structural Adjustment Facilities' and the 'Enhanced Structural Adjustment Facilities' of the 1990s. The lending arrangement that Ethiopia entered into for the new century went by the far cosier name 'Poverty Reduction and Growth Facility'. IMF and government officials in Addis Ababa both declared in 2009 that relations were now good.

With the backing of Stiglitz and others Ethiopia's leadership won most of their arguments against the free-market enthusiasts for whom time was finally called in the crash of 2008. 'Meles: Vindicated?' was the front page headline in the Addis Ababa weekly newspaper *Fortune* in April 2009 on a flattering account of his wisdom and foresight. But one of the poorest countries in Africa had paid a heavy price for failing to do the bidding of the International Monetary Fund.

Officials catalogued the fall-out—the loss of the IMF loan facility, the delay at least in World Bank lending, the downgrading of Ethiopia's status as an aid recipient, the consequent loss of donor assistance, and most damagingly of all, a delay of some years in the country benefiting from HIPC, the Heavily Indebted Poor Countries initiative set up by the IMF and the World Bank in response to a popular tide of western objections to the burden of debt in the Third World.

According to former World Bank staff, the IMF fought to the last moment to prevent Ethiopian entry into the debt relief scheme. Since its programme there had been suspended, the Fund argued that Ethiopia should have to wait and then maintain an unbroken three-year record before it could finally qualify. 'In the end the huge international support—the Jubilee Campaign and all the rest—just about allowed us to sneak through,' Prime Minister Meles told me. 'The debt had become so obnoxious in the eyes of so many people in the West that . . . if word sneaked out that the IMF was playing politics and stopping a country that deserves debt reductions for ideological reasons, this would not be seen favourably . . . so this gave us the room to sneak through. But it was very tough, but we just made it, just made it in time.'

The alliance that Meles and Prof. Stiglitz formed against the International Monetary Fund in 1997 raised Ethiopia's profile in the corridors of Washington, a valuable advantage for a poor country. It meant that both the World Bank's country office and the Ethiopian prime minister could bring the influence of the Bank's chief economist and its president James Wolfensohn to bear on important national issues. 'We could call on Joe when the Fund was being difficult, we could call out the big guns,' said Oey Meesook, the World Bank's country director for Ethiopia at the time. 'The prime minister would not hesitate to call up Wolfensohn and Stiglitz.'

The most celebrated economist of the era and the former guerrilla leader also formed a strong personal bond. Meles utilized Stiglitz's arguments in support of his account of 'the developmental state' and for his part Stiglitz wrote that Meles 'demonstrated a knowledge of economics—and indeed a creativity—that would have put him at the head of any of my university classes'. This meeting of minds, commented Oey Meesook, 'made Meles even more stubborn, you could say, because he thought he had Stiglitz behind him.'

Stiglitz made his first and last official trips as chief economist to Ethiopia, and made others in between. It was that first meeting with Meles at the height of the IMF crisis in 1997 which led to their most memorable encounter, a two-day 'retreat' in an imperial summer palace south of Addis Ababa. Meles brought his entire economics team and Stiglitz was accompanied by senior World Bank staff. The subject for discussion was the economics of development. 'It was an absolutely incredible experience,' said Ms Meesook. 'Just talking, talking, talking straight through meals. I was there at high table in the evening with Meles and Stiglitz and we did not get up from the table until after midnight.'

When I asked Prof. Stiglitz about this 'retreat' he made one passing reference to being 'very struck at the level of insight [Meles] showed on macro-economic structures,' and then went straight on to recall the detail of discussions they had on privatization and land reform, two of the most significant issues facing Ethiopia at that time, as they are now and will be in future.

In a 2005 country report, the IMF complained that privatization was 'slow and targets were frequently missed'. Only about half of the state-owned enterprises that the government inherited from the Derg had been privatized. The Fund objected to the ruling party's dubious links with 'foundation' companies which enjoyed an unfair advantage over their commercial rivals. The World Bank was similarly frustrated. Oey Meesook said the drive for privatization had made no progress at all during her years as country director and she had threatened to wind up the Bank's own 'private sector development team' in Addis Ababa because it had achieved so little.

A perennial focus was—and would continue to be—the archaic state of the government-owned telecommunications industry. As a traveller without access to good communications, I shared my own frustrations with Newai Gebre-Ab. 'The management is quite inadequate,' he replied. 'Everybody including us complains about the service, so the point is well-taken.' He said the government planned to modernize the service before 'offering it out', but appeared to be in little real hurry.

Stiglitz, who had studied privatization initiatives around the world, showed surprising sympathy for the government's caution in selling off Ethiopian Telecommunications. He complained again that 'the IMF focused on the ideological position of the private sector always being more efficient than the public sector,' but also complimented the prime minister on identifying other privatization pitfalls. '[Meles] was aware that international companies would not offer the fair value—that has been the experience. If you look around the world at IMF-sponsored privatizations or even non-IMF-sponsored privatizations, they have been the source of enormous accumulations of private wealth, simply money that has been given away in many societies and led to inequality.'

Land tenure has been the most vexed issue of all ever since the feudal system was first seriously challenged by students in the 1960s. With a peasant culture rooted in the soil, failure to liberate farmers' productive capacity risks stagnation and more hunger. But overstepping the mark in a zeal for reform risks something worse—dispossession and destitution. Many Ethiopians and many foreign development experts have strong views about the buying and selling of land. Views of course come cheap—lives are expensive. The government of Ethiopia has had the terrifying responsibility of getting it right, and for the EPRDF the matter was settled long ago.

As the prime minister told the story, the World Bank and the IMF urged private landownership on the new government soon after it had put an end to the Sovietized system of the Derg. 'We told them this is going to be a bombshell—politically, socially, and economically,' he said.

Meles argued that there was no conflict between state owner-ship of land and the capitalist development of agriculture 'as the latest experience in China and Vietnam has also begun to prove'. To force it on the country would be particularly hazardous in southern Ethiopia, still seen by many of its peoples as 'conquered lands' from Ethiopia's own imperialist expansion at the end of the nineteenth century. The danger lay in the likely return of the old feudal landlords, now often city-dwellers or living abroad, to reclaim their inheritance.

'We finally settled it in the constitution,' said Meles. Govern-ment ownership of land is part of Ethiopia's basic law and one of the most difficult provisions to amend. 'You know the game of chicken, with the two cars coming at each other? The best way to play it if you don't want to "blink" is to remove the steering wheel and throw it out of the window.' That is what they wanted to do with the land issue. 'I think they [the international financial institutions] recognized that the issue was dead.'

Ethiopia saw off the World Bank and the IMF at the time, but the land reform issue was still not settled. Some in the development agencies with long experience of Ethiopia are convinced that official resistance to buying and selling is based less on eliminating poverty than on an autocratic desire for control. These experts argue that the risk to poor farmers of selling up in the bad times, moving to the towns, and ending up destitute has to be accepted. Only that process can lead to more economic farms in the hands of progressive farmers. When I argued the point with one knowledgeable development worker, he responded with this question: 'Do you hold back the winners because you fear for the losers?'

Ethiopian opposition figures have also argued for wholesale land reform. Prof. Mesfin Wolde-Mariam, whose remarkable early studies of famine I have described, concluded at one point that hunger in Ethiopia had little to do with the land question. 'Let us first dismiss the simple notion that land tenure is the cause of famine. The relationship between ownership of land and famine is very insignificant.'[3] But as he moved from the academic world to human rights campaigning and then to party political activism, the professor appeared to shift his stance dramatically. 'For me it was absolutely clear,' he told me. 'Unless the peasants were free, unless the peasants were their own agents, it would be impossible, absolutely impossible, to eradicate famine from Ethiopia.'

---

[3] Mesfin Wolde-Mariam, *Rural Vulnerability to Famine in Ethiopia 1958–1977* (Intermediate Technology, 1986).

One of the few institutions to have asked the farmers themselves what they thought about the land question was the Ethiopian Economic Association. The research was conducted in 2002 when the head of the association was Dr Berhanu Nega, an American-trained economist who later emerged as the country's most charismatic opposition leader before becoming the protagonist in a life and death political drama. He was first elected to office, then arrested and charged with treason. He was released and went into exile in the United States. In 2009 he was charged, convicted, and condemned to death in his absence for masterminding an assassination and sabotage plot.

The research Dr Berhanu commissioned was based on a survey of 8,500 farm households and painted a vivid statistical picture of poverty in the countryside.[4] A third of these households lived off the produce of an acre or less of land. One in ten of them had no land at all. More than 60 per cent of households failed to reach the government's own astonishingly low national poverty line—around £80 per household per year, amounting to barely 20p a day. Even adding non-farm income to these earnings, more than 50 per cent of households remained below the line. 'This clearly shows,' the research paper concluded mildly, 'that the poverty situation in rural Ethiopia has reached rather desperate levels.'

Also unexceptional was the paper's observation that, 'As sensitive as land policy issues are, the country cannot afford to ignore the problem and hope that the problem will go away.' But as to what the farmers wanted to happen, the research appeared to point to the merits of the status quo. Sixty-one per cent viewed

[4] 'Land Tenure and Agricultural Development in Ethiopia', Ethiopian Economic Association/Ethiopian Policy Research Institute, Addis Ababa, 2002.

the current land system favourably compared with 38 per cent who saw it negatively. When asked about alternative forms of tenure, 46 per cent said they preferred public ownership compared with 38 per cent favouring private. Support for the present system was as high as 78 per cent in the densely populated southern region and above 50 per cent in the country's other main regions.

Yet almost all these farmers knew that the government owned the land they cultivated, and three out of four of them did not feel secure enough to believe it would be theirs in five years' time. Only 4.5 per cent of households said they would sell their land if they had the chance, with more than 90 per cent saying they would neither sell all nor part of it.

For a further judgement on the Ethiopian land issue, I returned to Prof. Stiglitz, Nobel Laureate and scourge of 'free market fundamentalism'. I was no longer surprised that there should be a strong identity of view between him and Prime Minister Meles. Stiglitz said he too feared the return of the old feudal landlords; he too worried about the creation of rural destitution in the towns; and he too pointed to China's accomplishments with very limited land reform. He had written a paper on land privatization and efficiency, he said, showing that 'the argument that efficiency required landownership in the world we lived in was wrong'.

Was there anything at all, I asked Prof. Stiglitz, on which he had had big differences with Meles—where there had been robust arguments between them? His reply perhaps explained the basis of his battles with the IMF over Ethiopia in the 1990s. 'My own style in different countries', he said, 'is more of a diagnostician than to tell people what to do.'

Chapter 6
How to Prevent a Famine

'The most extensive drought in the country's modern history passed without a measurable increase in child mortality.'

At the beginning of 2003 Ethiopia faced another famine. The rains had failed in the South and then more widely. The government's Disaster Prevention and Preparedness Agency had based a series of steadily more alarming appeals on the number it considered being at risk from starvation. In January 2002 it put the figure at 3.6 million; in August at 5.7 million; by autumn it was 6.3 million. But if there was no harvest in store by now for the hungry months of 2003, the crisis was only just beginning. In January 2003 the government said that 14.3 million people were at risk from starvation, one in five of the population.[1]

Ethiopian relief officials provided me with figures for 'affected population' and 'food requirement' stretching back to the days of

---

[1] Figures from Sue Lautze, Angela Raven-Roberts, and Teshome Erkineh, 'Humanitarian Governance in the New Millennium: An Ethiopian Case Study', Overseas Development Institute, 2009.

empire. They appear to show that no food at all reached the starving in the early months of the 1973 famine, underlining why the first television pictures of famine in Ethiopia were so grim, even in comparison with what came later. In the terrible two-year build-up to the 1984 famine, when the world displayed such indifference to the suffering, five million people were going hungry. By the time publicity broke the dam, the number had reached 7.9 million. Twenty years on that figure was dwarfed, with a final calculation for 2003 of 13.2 million in need and an emergency appeal for 1.4 million tonnes of food aid. The number affected and the size of the appeal were the largest in the country's history.

On this occasion, for a change, the government was alert, so were the donors, and their joint systems had been improved. As early as July 2002 the government's disaster prevention agency organized a rural tour for western ambassadors to show them the state of the crops. 'Everyone knew it was going to be far worse in 2003,' said Teshome Erkineh, who was then head of the agency's early warning system,

> so we began a massive mobilization of resources in December and January 2003 instead of waiting as we usually do until April or May. Then the donors said to us 'Why does the government always launch appeals and not do much more themselves?' So the prime minister mobilized domestic resources [the government made a major commitment of its own towards grain purchases] and so the international community responded.

With Ethiopia and the aid-givers gearing up to prevent a loss of life on the scale of previous famines, the journalist Jonathan Dimbleby approached ITV in London with a proposal to make another film. His documentary *The Unknown Famine* for the same network three decades earlier had for the first time brought Ethiopian hunger to popular international attention. ITV later contributed to public exposure of the 1984 catastrophe with documentaries shot before the BBC's news reports from northern Ethiopia.

Dimbleby was by now a senior broadcaster with his own politics show on ITV and he took his proposal for a special half-hour *Tonight* programme to the top. With Ethiopia facing the largest humanitarian disaster in its history, he wanted to establish whether a better early warning system and better distribution would mean that another tragedy could be avoided. 'How many skeletons will there be in the film?' the senior ITV executive asked him. 'Well, I hope there will be none,' said Dimbleby and explained the premise of the film. The executive said he would consider the idea and get back to him. Dimbleby heard no more. The film was never commissioned.

Jonathan Dimbleby was right in his surmise that Ethiopia in 2003 would avoid the horrors of the televised famines of the late twentieth century. In 1984 7.9 million had faced starvation, and more than 600,000 died. By contrast in 2003 13.2 million faced the prospect of a famine and only 300 died.

Neither set of statistics is entirely reliable, it should be stressed. However scientifically gathered, they are based on surveys and samples rather than head and body counts. In the case of famine deaths, precision is further clouded by the fact that far too many Ethiopians die of starvation or hunger-related disease in a 'good' or 'normal' year. The statisticians have thus come up with the notion of 'excess mortality' to establish the difference between those who die as a consequence of crisis and those who would have died anyway. Yet there is little doubt that the outcome of the 2003 emergency was something of a triumph for the Ethiopian government and the aid donors.

In their joint conclusion at the end of the year, government and donors declared, 'Collective action and an unprecedented donor and public response throughout 2003 prevented widespread famine-related mortality. In total, donors contributed over 1.7 million tonnes of cereals, pulses, oil and blended food in 2003—94% of requirements.' Particular attention had been given to keeping children alive. The report said that special feeding centres had been opened for 20,000 'severely malnourished' children; a further 60,000 'moderately malnourished' children and pregnant and breast-feeding women received help from supplementary feeding programmes.

Alex de Waal, the most acute and a sometimes provocative researcher on Ethiopia and the Horn of Africa, led a team funded by UNICEF to examine child survival rates during the 2003 emergency.[2] They analysed data from the 2004 Ethiopia Child Survival Survey which had covered 4,816 households in drought and non-drought areas. The report concluded that 'it is remarkable that the most extensive drought in the country's modern history passed without a measurable increase in child mortality among the general population.' But it ended with this caveat: 'The Government of Ethiopia and its international partners may have succeeded in keeping many Ethiopian children alive, who would otherwise have died during the 2002/03 crisis, but those children still have unacceptably poor life chances.' UNICEF figures showed that an Ethiopian child was still thirty times more likely to die before reaching his or her fifth birthday than a child in western Europe.

High-profile media attention for the events of 2003—or non-events as British television executives saw them—was limited

---

[2] Alex de Waal et al., 'Child Survival during the 2002–2003 Drought in Ethiopia', *Global Public Health* (June 2006).

to the coincidence of the emergency occurring around the twentieth anniversary of the last great famine. Meles Zenawi, who had now been prime minister of Ethiopia for a decade, had, after all, promised there would be no more famines in Ethiopia once the Derg had been removed.

Michael Buerk, the BBC journalist responsible for those first compelling news reports from the famine zone in 1984, returned to Ethiopia at the height of the 2003 emergency to prepare a documentary for the anniversary. He was discouraged by what he saw and reached uncomfortable and, for Ethiopian officials, most unwelcome conclusions. 'It's a story of betrayal,' he reported. 'Twice as many Ethiopians are hungry now as there were then. Twenty years on I wonder if all we've done is create a nation of half-starved beggars.'[3]

Other formal evaluations of the 2003 emergency praised the response, but also issued bleak warnings for the future, even if they were less colourfully expressed than Buerk's. 'The emergency is not over for 7.8 million people who remain food insecure in 2004,' said a report in which the government itself participated, 'and there is a high probability that more emergencies with increased frequency will occur, perhaps much larger than the 2002–03 emergency.' It then added: 'There is no guarantee that the high level of donor assistance will be repeated in future crises.'[4]

The magnitude of the crisis and the likelihood of it happening again led government and donors to look for new ways out. 'Never again' had very nearly happened, and should surely not

---

[3] 'Ethiopia: A Journey with Michael Buerk', *This World*, BBC 2, 11 January 2004.
[4] 'Evaluation of the Response to the 2002–3 Emergency in Ethiopia', Steering Committee for the Evaluation of the Joint Government and Humanitarian Partners Response, October 2004.

do so again. As the chief provider of food aid to the world's poor, the United States itself emphasized that neither the quantity nor promptness of shipments could be assured in future. In a foreword to a 2004 USAID appraisal of famine prevention in Ethiopia 'Breaking the Cycle of Food Crises', its administrator Andrew Natsios stated bluntly: 'I commissioned this work because USAID and the donor community cannot sustain the levels of food aid required in Ethiopia.'

In 2003 Ethiopia had had a lucky break. United Nations officials in Addis Ababa told me that as the emergency unfolded, the Americans had thousands of containers full of Texan wheat on board ships in the Gulf of Aden in anticipation of a prolonged humanitarian breakdown in Iraq. It turned out that President George W. Bush's war there began well enough, and so the food could be diverted to ward off a famine in Ethiopia. But US military interventions could hardly be relied on in this fashion, and there would have to be fresh initiatives on Ethiopia's own part.

Meles Zenawi took up the challenge and began shaping a new 'Coalition for Food Security in Ethiopia'. It was 'never again' all over again. Meles was asked by Michael Buerk in the documentary whether the country could really be free from aid dependency and hunger in his lifetime, and his reply was that there was no other option. 'It's either going down the drain of a failed state or moving up and we don't have much time. We will have to see a significant change over a period of five years or the window of opportunity will begin to close.' The prime minister's chosen five-year time span ran through to the Ethiopian millennium year of 2007–8. This would indeed be a period of optimism born of economic growth, but the pains of shortage would never disappear.

The government's strategy to extricate Ethiopia from hunger had several components. There would be fresh emphasis on agricultural advances as Meles and his party kept faith with the peasantry. At a cost of $3 billion over five years to be borne by government (one-third) and international donors (two-thirds), there would also be a new approach to the poorest sections of the rural community. The idea was expressed in medical terminology and distinguished between the 'chronically food insecure' and the 'acutely food insecure'. The 'chronic' group would receive consistent support until they emerged from the poverty trap in a hoped-for five years (a so-called 'safety net') while the 'acute' group would receive food aid only when their livelihoods were imperilled by drought. This formulation would have the merit of appearing to reduce the embarrassingly large number of people for whom Ethiopia had to make annual 'emergency' appeals for food aid. Last and most controversially the government decided after a fifteen-year gap to revive the discredited resettlement scheme which had been the Derg's favoured response to rural distress.

The plan announced in 2003 was to resettle 440,000 households from distressed and populous areas—some 2.2 million people—in Ethiopia's western lowlands, and officials reported in 2009 that 190,000 households—1.2 million people—had so far been moved. They claimed that more than 90 per cent of them were already self-sufficient in food. Like 'famine', 'resettlement' had become a dirty word since the campaign of coercion carried out by the Derg in the 1980s. Government officials were defensive about the new programme, but insisted that it was quite different from what had gone before. Resettlement was now voluntary, they said, volunteers could change their minds and return to their land in the highlands within three years if they wanted to, and resettlement would now take place only within regions and would involve less long-distance transportation to far corners of the country.

Ethiopia's academic authorities on resettlement, quoted earlier on the Derg's programme, remained sceptical. They acknowledged that the government this time had a more liberal approach and that the scheme was better managed, but they still had doubts. How could these people be true volunteers when there was such poverty and desperation in the highlands, when farmers had been presented with such rosy views of what awaited them in the lowlands and when in some areas, it was alleged, there had been threats to cut food aid to those left behind?

'I am against resettlement,' said Dr Dessalegn Rahmato, of the Forum for Social Studies, who as a young academic had had distressing personal experience of the Derg's programme. 'There is simply no vacant land. It's either vacant for a purpose or it's being used for purposes such as grazing.' He doubted the government's claims of self-sufficiency among the new settlers and whether I would be able to conduct any sort of independent examination of the scheme. 'You'll visit one of the success stories and talk to people who will have been hand-picked.'

At one level, Dr Dessalegn was underestimating my difficulties. I was travelling on my own. I did not speak Amharic. I did not have my own interpreter. I did not have a team of researchers who could conduct a properly sampled set of interviews. My questions would yield, to use the disparaging academic term, only anecdote. Worse, I had decided to conduct my research in Amhara Region, and was dependent on the good offices of ORDA, which had close links with the government.

There was a knock on the door at dawn in my hotel in the town of Dessie, in the Wollo region of Amhara. One of my companions from ORDA had heard from his colleague in Kombolcha, down through the hills on the road to Addis, that there were buses due to leave that morning with a group of new settlers from another town still further down the road. The buses would be setting off at 9 a.m. Did I want to see the departure? We set off straightaway. I do not believe there was anything stage-managed or hand-picked about what I saw or who I spoke to that day or in any of my subsequent encounters with the new settlers.

The two buses drawn up in a backstreet off the main road resembled those 1950s charabancs for seaside outings. The list of new settlers that day had ninety-nine names on it, ninety-two male and seven female. There was one family group and three other female dependants. All the rest were young men in their late teens or twenties. By the time we arrived at 8.30 a.m. they were already sitting anxiously in their seats, ready to go. There were no roof racks on top of the buses and no one had any luggage to speak of. The settlers setting off on a two-day journey to a new life on the Sudan border had the clothes they stood up in and at most a plastic bag placed in the racks above their head. This did not appear to be the consequence of any formal restriction. The carrier bags contained their sole possessions.

Each bus had an Amharic sign on the front announcing that the group was the 'Argoba special ethnic district settlement programme to Qara' and then the year 2001, translating from the Ethiopian calendar as 2009. The 'special ethnicity' of Argoba was Moslem, part of a large and growing community founded in centuries of invasion and migration and now living in generally impressive harmony with its majority Christian neighbours.

I clambered into the back of one of the buses and young men's faces turned to look at me. Many were older sons leaving parents and siblings to make better lives for themselves. They had walked for up to eight hours to the buses that would take them to the lowlands. Many said that the family land at home was swampy, prone to flooding, and unproductive. They were not quite sure what awaited them at the other end, but they were getting 150 birr [about £10] for the journey and they would be given food on their arrival. They had heard good things about their new home because settlers who had gone before had come back and told them. 'Some are saying that they are self-sufficient,' said a 24-year-old. 'We have heard these things.'

In contrast to the quiet anxiety on board, there were two young men outside the bus in floods of tears. I asked why. One was crying because he was saying goodbye to his brother and the other because he had not been permitted to join the group. He pleaded with officials who looked again at their clipboards, and said his name was not on the list. He would have to wait until the next resettlement round. In the first year of the programme from 2004 to 2005, there had been 5,000 from this district sent to the lowlands. After two years the figure had fallen back to 1,700, and in the last full year there had been 800. 'Look,' said my guide from ORDA gesturing at the young man still crying over losing his brother to resettlement, 'he is feeling'.

The only family travelling westwards belonged to Ahmed Nuru Mohammed. At 50 he was the oldest person making the journey. His wife and daughter were already on board sitting right at the front of the first bus. Nine-year-old Kedija was dressed for her adventure in a faded green dress, a pretty necklace, and specially braided hair. Ahmed's son was staying behind to continue farming the family's land six hours' walk from the main road. 'I am a volunteer settler,' he announced with emphasis. 'I have decided to leave the area because my land is not productive.'

Ahmed had been told that the government would provide him with help for a year at the resettlement site. This would include oxen for ploughing and hand tools for other farm work. He thought there would be a hectare of land waiting for him. Ahmed had also heard good reports of the new life in the lowlands. 'The settlers who have gone before have improved their lives,' he told me. 'They have even built their own houses.' He was leaving behind two hectares of family land with his son. 'The land is OK, but there are problems due to rainfall,' he said, and then invoked the spectre of the last big famine. 'From 1984 till now we are suffering from starvation, maybe not every year but frequently. There is not enough rainfall.'

At this point I suggested I speak to Ahmed's wife Marima, a request that as usual provoked startled disbelief. Talk to the woman! What an idea! As if she would have anything to say! Marima came hesitantly out of the bus, pulled her head covering round her face so as to obscure her mouth, and then played the part which tradition had dictated by saying almost nothing. But my interest in the family prompted the revelation that Ahmed and Marima's two children were the survivors of six. This was a loss that still upset them, and when Marima got back on the bus I asked Ahmed why they had died. 'He says it was disease,' my guide from ORDA translated, 'but I didn't want to ask him more. It is difficult.'

There was no public display of emotion as the buses bumped out of the backstreets on to the main road for the two-day journey to the border at Metemma and then to the new settlement. I wanted to follow them, if not to find this group in their new surroundings, then to speak to others who had recently arrived. Some days later in Metemma I asked where I would find them. Local officials were consulted, coffee was drunk, directions were sought, and we left the border highway to plunge through a veld of bush and woodland, of distant cliffs and ravines towards the district of Qara. We scattered flocks of guinea fowl along the empty dirt road and I asked one of my ORDA companions, a forester with several European degrees, to identify extraordinary-looking trees with red and bright green bark. 'They're exotics,' he said and left it at that.

Our objective was a village 50 miles from Metemma called Merterad, where there had apparently been recent settler arrivals. We would not have found it unless we had paid a man with a gun to get into the back of the pick-up and point the way through the scrub. The first structures in Merterad were broken down straw huts apparently abandoned by previous settlers; then we passed new straw homes only just erected and then piles of fresh straw and wooden poles indicating that construction was under way. At the centre of the village was a large tent housing grain, which had been there since resettlement in Merterad started in 2005.

A crowd assembled as we pulled up and the new arrivals rapidly identified themselves. They said that more than 400 had reached here in the past fortnight. They had travelled by bus for four days from the mountains of Shoa, north of Addis Ababa. One hundred and twenty of them had started their new lives just four days ago. Most were young men who seemed remarkably upbeat considering they faced totally strange surroundings and the challenge of making a fresh life from scratch. They said they had been promised handouts of 20 kilos of wheat per month for eight months. They had each been given cooking utensils and, for some reason, a watering can. They would get hand tools for cultivation next week, but the supply of draught animals was 'unknown for the time being'. As for land, a survey of needs and availability had to be conducted before there could be any distribution.

Everyone crowded into the shade of a partially built office to continue the conversation. Those who did not come in through the door frame simply stepped through the straw walls. I picked out two men at the front called Degaf and Wubie. They had been in Merterad for eight days, staying with previous settlers and giving them a share of their food rations as rent. They had already started building their own homes with the implements they had been given. Degaf had owned less than an acre of land back at home, and Wubie had none at all. They hoped to get land from the government, but had no idea how much. 'We will have a better chance in this place,' said Degaf, and his friend agreed: 'We are happy to be here because our purpose is to bring a change to our lives.'

As we prepared to leave—to a round of ragged applause from the settlers—I was approached by a man who introduced himself as the chairman of the village peasants' association. He told me that 20 per cent of those who had arrived in the past four years had already 'changed their mind' and returned to the highlands. This was a dropout rate far higher than that provided by the government, and it did not take into account the food aid that many of the settlers continued to need. The problem, said the peasants' leader, was waterlogging of the soil which made crop production a problem in all but the very best years. All the good land in the underpopulated lowlands had already been used up in previous migrations.

Getenet lived in Village Number Three near Metemma and was among the first settlers to arrive here in the aftermath of the 2002–3 famine. On his two acres in Wollo he grew wheat, teff, and sorghum, but in that awful year managed to raise nothing at all and eked out an existence on food aid and occasional work as a day-labourer. His fortunes had not yet been transformed by the new life. The problem, once again, was the waterlogging of the soil. In four years he had been able to support himself and his family for only one. For the other three, he needed handouts. 'I have requested the government to grant me better land,' Getenet told me, 'but there has been no answer.'

He would nevertheless press on in his new life. 'I may not be happy here, but it's better than Wollo,' he said. 'The problem there was the lack of land, so there were no options for me. Here there are opportunities, and there is something to try.' In fact, Getenet had demonstrated unusual ingenuity in responding to the challenges. First he had managed to hang on to his land in Wollo which was still being farmed by his sister—'It may be the law [that it would be redistributed after three years] but they haven't taken it'—and he had started using the income he received there to rent better land in the lowlands. He may also have a solution to the poor quality of the land he had been given. 'I've decided to stay here,' said Getenet, 'and I'm thinking of rice production. The ground gets so wet I think it could produce rice.'

Above all, trite as the observation is, human existence provides rewards even in the toughest of circumstance. When Getenet arrived in Metemma in June 2005, he came on his own and left his wife and little boy at home in Wollo. The following March his wife gave birth to a baby girl and the family now lives together in Village Number Three. She was christened *Kokobe*, Amharic for Star, and throughout the interview Getenet's hands rested gently on the shoulders of this 3-year-old in a ragged dress listening intently to every word that was said. 'I do have a star,' he said.

Food aid had to be the underpinning of the new resettlement programme just as it had to be the foundation of the new 'safety net' and emergency system after the 2003 famine-that-could-have-been. The 'chronically poor' would work on community projects in exchange for food and those overtaken by emergencies would receive handouts until the danger of starvation passed. For years it had been fashionable among progressives in the West to deprecate food aid on the grounds that it distorted markets in the developing world and inhibited local production. So the new arrangements moved towards meeting the objection by giving cash rather than food to the poor. This worked well enough until, as we shall see, food prices shot up in the global economic crash of 2008 and the poor were left with devalued cash. It turned out that Ethiopia simply needed a lot of foreign food.

At a roadside warehouse near the town of Hayk, in Wollo, I witnessed the cheerfully chaotic scenes at the other end of a food trail that began on the prairies of the American Midwest. This was the distribution of United States wheat, 'a gift from the American people'. Qualifying households received a 50-kilo bag as a monthly handout, and families from the interior had clubbed together to hire pack animals to come and collect. Now it was dusk and to the accompaniment of curses and shouts and dung and urine on the main road, villagers were loading up the horses, mules, and donkeys for the five-hour trek home.

USAID is Ethiopia's largest benefactor and is predominant in the North. Yet the Americans are no longer running a hands-on operation and employ private agencies to distribute the food and run the development projects. In my own local researches, I looked at projects run by the Amhara development organization ORDA and the British arm of Save the Children Fund.

Save the Children Fund first worked in Ethiopia at the time of Mussolini's war in 1936 where, they recorded, 'it simply had not occurred to the Abyssinians [Abyssinia was the historic name for Ethiopia] that their children were underfed, and once they realized the fact, they were very ready to learn.' SCF was on the ground in both the 1973 and 1984 famines, and twenty-five years later Ethiopia was the agency's biggest country programme. In fact their USAID project in the North, involving food distribution as well as development schemes, was worth an extraordinary $71 million over three years ($20 million of it in cash), the biggest value grant the agency receives anywhere in the world.

I spent two days with Save the Children's Ethiopian staff being shown a fraction of their work in northern Wollo which ranged from seed banks to irrigation schemes to weaving sheds and brave attempts to lift whole communities out of poverty. Such 'development' tours involve penetrating a forest of initials and jargon. I had for instance to seek a line-by-line translation of a document entitled 'Key Achievements of RDIR' which did not even let on what the initials stood for—'Reducing Dependency Increasing Resilience'. I discovered what a 'flume' was—a suspended irrigation channel—and was introduced to the animal hybrid 'shoat' which is development language for 'sheep and goats'.

Visits to the countryside also provided one response to a vexed academic debate as to whether aid to the Third World actually works. Viewed from ground level, the answer is that of course it does, often triumphantly. On a Sunday afternoon we bumped up a track with fields on one side and a deep river valley on the other to inspect a brand new sheet metal 'flume' bringing water over a ravine to irrigate the land of 87 farmsteads, accounting for more than 400 people. This was 'SSI'—small-scale irrigation. It cost $10,000 and was, as the notices said, 'Funded by USAID, constructed by the community and Save the Children Fund UK.'

Before the flume was constructed, these 87 households relied on rain alone—the early *Belg* rains had not come at all in 2009—and grew the basics to feed themselves. Favoured farmers with irrigation could now grow potatoes, beans, tomatoes, and cabbage to take to market as well as the grain to feed their families. They now had the security to make plans for their own and their children's lives. I stood on the edge of Bezabih's smallholding and watched him and his school-aged boys direct the day's water supply down through his three terraced fields. A neighbour walked by from further up the valley and eyed the water coursing through Bezabih's fields. 'He's a good farmer,' said the neighbour. 'I wanted to grow onions but I have no irrigated land. The rains didn't come, so now I'm sad.'

We drove on to a village weaving project and heard the creaking looms before we got to the shed. This was 'off-farm activity'— looked down upon by traditional farmers, but favoured by development agencies which want to help diminish the country's reliance on agriculture. There were twenty-five members of the village weavers' association—twenty-three men and two women—and so far they were managing to earn only a few pounds a month after costs. Part of the problem was clear. They were weaving traditional country textiles, in competition with cheap Chinese imports, and most of them were wearing western cast-offs.

The most articulate and optimistic figure in the weavers' shed was a young Moslem woman called Hadiya. Foreign aid had certainly worked for her. 'There were only two women who wanted to join, but it's changed my life,' she said. She often worked in the fields alongside her husband, but she had no doubt where their future lay. 'I want to go to the town and leave the land.' Her 11-year-old son was doing well at school, and she thought he had a bright future beyond farming. 'I'm absolutely certain he will go on to get a good education. My strong interest is to make him a respectable man with a good job who works in the town.'

These were good news stories, but the challenge of raising people out of poverty can be more daunting. It was to Save the

Children's credit that they took me on a three-hour journey to the village of Kaso Amba. We were now at 11,000 feet on a plateau in the Wollo highlands. The most prominent landmark looming out of a damp Scotch mist was a food aid warehouse. In Kaso Amba itself, I encountered the most distressed community of any I visited in my research. Their sense of desperation may have owed something that Monday morning to the fact that many of the villagers had gone off to a funeral.

Save the Children were running several food-for-work schemes around the village to create 'community assets'—hillside terracing, pond construction, and the digging of 'percolating' trenches to raise the water table. But each scheme depended for its benefits on the rain, and in the last two years there had been alternate floods and drought, even an early frost, so the 'community assets' had proved largely redundant. I was told by villagers that food payments were slow to arrive, even for construction work already completed. There had been only two emergency handouts totalling less than 20 kilos per person in the past eight months. 'In reality we have no food at all,' said a man called Misaw, huddled miserably in his shawl against the cold. He had to feed his six children. 'Every week I go to my relatives and borrow from them. We're existing on wild plants.'

The centrepiece of the Save the Children Fund programme in Kaso Ambo involved 'shoats' handed out in an ingenious 're-stocking' enterprise. The idea was that farmers would each receive five ewes and a ram, and that when they reproduced the offspring would be passed on to others and the process would continue in a virtuous developmental 'cascade'. The programme got under way in 2005 in the aftermath of the 2003 emergency, and early results were encouraging. The cascade effect began working in the second year, but then the rains faltered once, and then again, and finally in 2008 they failed altogether. There was no forage for the animals and some sickened and died of disease picked up from grazing in the dust. The consequence was that three-quarters of several thousand animals were lost and farmers were left demoralized and in debt. My SCF companions said there was little chance of an early revival of the project, and the chairman of the re-stocking committee emerged from his office to share the villagers' anxiety. 'The programme is completely failing. The deaths of the sheep were the last problem, so now we are worrying. There should be some solution. You have to communicate with the district people and SCF and tell them that it will become a very dangerous situation.'

There was better news in another highland community 100 miles along the spectacular Chinese-built mountain highway. The altitude was 1,000 feet lower and the soil more fertile than on the stony pastures of Kaso Amba. This was the district capital of Nefas Mewcha where the projects were also funded by USAID, but run by ORDA. There had been tension between Save the Children and ORDA over the way that the mighty USAID contract had been divided up. The Americans had entrusted the British agency with the lion's share of food distribution and gave them more districts to manage. ORDA complained of western favouritism. Their officials said that big western funders were persuaded in principle of the merits of entrusting development to competent nationals rather than foreign agencies, but when it came to awarding a contract, blood (and skin colour) often proved thicker than water.

The development focus around Nefas Mewcha was apples, and I ended up with pocketfuls of them. Having inspected apple rootstock and apple tree seedlings, I was taken through the fir trees to visit the farm of Tesfah Adena, a deacon in the local church, a 'graduate of the safety net' system and a recently honoured 'Development Hero'. This last distinction had been awarded by the regional agricultural bureau, and his prizes were a treadle pump and a transistor radio.

Tesfah Adena owned a hectare of land on which he supported his wife and four children, but never quite managed to make ends meet. He once grew wheat and potatoes, but in the lean years he relied on 'safety net' food. Now on a hillside in the sunshine he showed off his sizeable apple orchard and reeled off the benefits of learning about new crops and modern techniques. Last year he earned £100 from his apples—sold to shops in the town or direct to Chinese and Ethiopian road contractors—and another £260 from his garlic. He thought he would do just as well this year.

'I don't want to go back to food aid,' said Adena. 'I have graduated from the "safety net" and I want to be able to help myself.' As a further money-spinner he had acquired beehives, and was now planning to rear sheep. He said he and his wife had even adopted sound family planning practices. This man had seriously 'got' development. What of his neighbours, I wondered? 'It is not only a matter of land, it is a matter of attitude,' he replied. 'Many farmers have more land than I have, but they still use traditional methods. They have to change their practices, and it will require even more effort from government to get them to change.'

This pitch-perfect rendering of the development ethic had certainly had an impact on one neighbour. Mesafint was 20, he had seen what the priest was doing and persuaded his father to give him a small patch of land so he could have a go himself. He had been growing apples and garlic for two years, and last year made £160 profit of which he spent £100 building a one-room house on stilts in the corner of his plot. Mesafint too was a 'safety net' graduate and had no intention of relying on food aid again. 'Of course these apples made some contribution, but this was my own effort.' He guided me up rickety steps into his wattle and daub home. There was bedding in one corner, but no cooking arrangements because Mesafint still went across the fields to be fed by his mother. There were three torn posters decorating one wall—one of Christ, one of an Ethiopian saint I did not recognize, and the third of the French footballer Thierry Henry in his days playing for Arsenal.

Mesafint's ambition was to stay on the land and expand into other cash-crops. His own father, who until recently had resisted such new-fangled ideas, was thinking of doing the same. I asked him why he didn't want to follow so many of his contemporaries and try and get a government job. 'I think I can earn more on the farm, so I don't want to be a civil servant in the town,' he replied.

In judging whether aid has had a decisive impact on Ethiopia's rural poor, the issue is less the heartening individual stories than the matter of scale. There have been many changes for the better in the twenty-five years since famine focused popular and political attention on some of poorest people on earth, but have their prospects been transformed? The process of evaluation is not helped by the aid-givers themselves who are more enthusiastic about telling the world what they have done—'inputs' in development language—than in assessing what has been achieved. You can often hunt in vain through official evaluations to find any reference to 'outcomes'.

After the shock of the famine-that-nearly-was in 2003, the government and the aid-givers laid down a five-year time frame for the 'safety net' programme to raise the chronically poor out of dependency. Meles Zenawi had himself said that there would have to be significant progress in five years or 'the window of opportunity will begin to close'. The new system got under way in 2005. By 2009 donors and officials were planning a second five-year programme, and the Ethiopian minister responsible told me that by 2013 all but those physically incapable of working would be standing on their own feet. The price tag for the fresh exercise would be $2 billion, but this time there were doubts among aid officials over whether the money would be found in the middle of a world recession.

The figures I collected in my travels through Wollo early in 2009 underlined the enormity of the challenge and the sometimes pitiful progress towards meeting it. In South Wollo zone, for instance, there had been 790,000 people on 'safety net' food-for-work schemes. Only 17,000 were recorded as having 'graduated' from the scheme—that is, achieved self sufficiency—in the first three years of the programme, amounting to a miserable 2.1 per cent. In the district where I met the apple farmers there were 88,000 people on 'safety net' handouts. Graduates in 2008 totalled just 102, and I had met two of them. The target figure for 2009 was still only 1,900.

In the district of Gubalafo where Save the Children operates, 51,000 people were dependent on the 'safety net'. Fewer than 1,000 of them had 'graduated', less than 2 per cent, a figure which an Ethiopian member of the Save the Children team summed up as 'too minimum'. The previous year had seen very poor harvests, his colleague added, and had 'multiplied by zero all our efforts over the past three years'.

Western food aid to the Ethiopian 'safety net' programme, the largest such scheme in Africa, is coordinated in Addis Ababa. Senior foreign aid officials there were sometimes discouraged and frustrated by the sheer intractability of the country's poverty.

Even taking national bright spots into consideration, the figure for those who have put 'safety net' dependency behind them was 3 per cent. After the first five years of the 'safety net' programme, it was back to the drawing board for a second five years. The food aid officials I spoke to argued that it was more than droughts and poor harvests delivering occasional, even regular, sharp shocks to people's capacity to support themselves. Ethiopia's agricultural economy was in a state of almost permanent crisis. Farm technology was behind the times, too few jobs were being created to persuade people to leave the land, landholdings were getting smaller and smaller, and, critically, there were more and more mouths to feed.

Chapter 7
Population Matters

'These days even women with only two children are thinking they should limit their families.'

'Lucy' was the name given to the 3.2 million-year-old hominid discovered in the Afar Region in 1974 who placed Ethiopia at the very start of the human story. 'Where it all began' was how the tourist posters saw it. From those dimmest origins to the turn of the twentieth century, the population grew to 12 million. In the course of the next sixty years it doubled to 24 million.

'It has grown even faster since then with the greatest gains occurring since the 1980s,' said three leading demographers in 2007.[1] 'The decline in mortality due to diseases (malaria, smallpox etc.) has been responsible for the rapid growth of the population since the 1960s as recent famines have caused less mortality than

---

[1] Charles H. Teller, Assefa Hailemariam, and Tesfayi Gebreselassie, 'Demographic Trends and Multi-Sectoral Factors Affecting the Rural–Urban Gap in Ethiopia', Conference on Population Growth and Poverty Linkages in Africa, Addis Ababa, 2007.

earlier ones.' Increased fertility due to more treatment for sexually transmitted diseases and the lack of contraception had contributed further to growth. Ethiopia's birth rate had steadily increased from the mid-1970s to the mid-1990s.

At a time when the famine was killing hundreds and thousands in 1984, the government was trying for the first time to discover exactly how many people there were in the country. Five months before that crisis came to the world's attention, officials had conducted the first census in Ethiopian history. The decision to hold it reflected an era's anxiety over population growth, and the data would be needed if anything was going to be done about it.

When the figures were finally published, it was clear that Ethiopia's development plans were based on a population nine million fewer than the reality.[2] The census found that the population was within a few thousands of 40 million, and the Derg came under international pressure to introduce a policy to curb future growth. With United Nations help, the government drew up a population policy which was never formally presented, let alone implemented.

The transitional government which took power after the overthrow of the military in 1991 cleared the decks for a remarkable series of detailed policy pronouncements. We have already seen how peasant agriculture was the bedrock of EPRDF's policy, and this was enshrined in 'An Economic Development Strategy for Ethiopia' in 1993. It did not mince words, referring to 'the extreme backwardness of agriculture which constitutes the backbone of the economy' and it emphasized 'the spectre of accelerating population growth'.

[2] Assefa Hailemariam and Sisay Work, 'Population Policy Implementation: Achievements and Challenges', July 2003, Addis Ababa.

Population merited an eloquent sixty-page national policy document of its own. It argued that high fertility and rapid population growth exerted 'negative influences on economic and social development' and that these influences in turn created a climate 'favouring high fertility and hence rapid population growth. Because of an unholy combination of these forces, Ethiopia finds herself in a vicious circle of failure and defeatism.'

Population policy, which had so far been 'accorded low priority', would now be put on an equal footing with agricultural development and the prime minister would take personal charge of implementing it. There would be a special population office headed by a minister attached to the office of the prime minister who would himself chair a National Population Council. This structure would be replicated in the regions and further down to district level. The last twenty pages of the document were devoted to explaining this interlocking system and there was a neat organogram to illustrate how it would all work.

Ethiopia conducted its third national census in 2007. The total was then conservatively calculated at 74 million, with Ethiopian and foreign demographers agreeing that by the twenty-fifth anniversary of the 1984 famine it had in fact exceeded 80 million— a doubling in twenty-five years, more if the loss of Eritrea's three million at independence in 1993 was taken into account.

The 1993 policy document had spelt out the consequences of failing to bring down the population growth rate. If this did not happen, it declared, there was 'not even the remotest hope of attaining the goal of food self-sufficiency any time during the first few decades of the next century'. If on the other hand there was a significant reduction in fertility levels and a corresponding increase in food production, the country could 'come close to achieving the goal sometime during the first two decades of the

21st century'. While believing the worst set of assumptions might be avoided, demographers point to the 'bulge' of young people working its way through with future generations of young families to come. The consensus among Ethiopian and foreign experts in Addis Ababa is that Ethiopia's 80 million population will probably double again in 25–30 years.

Early in 2009 I travelled south from Addis Ababa past the broad blue lakes of the Rift Valley to the grim junction town of Shashemene and then struck west to Alaba. I had last been on this road twenty-five years earlier when the Mengistu regime barred media access to the North and told the press that if they really wanted to see the impact of drought they could go south and have a look. There was hunger and distress here, enough to launch a disaster appeal on British television, but it was not on the scale of the gathering catastrophe in the North.

This time I was examining the origins and dimensions of a more recent food emergency. Alaba is in the middle of a populous rural area, and the pressure was soon apparent from a rowdy break-time visit I made to a primary school on the outskirts of town. As in most government primary schools, there had to be separate morning and afternoon sessions to accommodate all the pupils, and even then the average class size was 73. Elsewhere I was told of classes of more than 100. 'That's not a class, that's a rally,' said my Ethiopian guide.

Alaba and the surrounding country is also majority Moslem, and that lent additional pressure to family size. A local nurse midwife emphasized the point with the single word 'polygamy', uttered under her breath.

The food crisis of 2008 was supposed to be over but there was a child assessment centre still operating outside Alaba and still sending its worst cases into town to be cared for. Where were they? A call on the American evangelical charity Samaritan's Purse, which was running the nutrition project, prompted a young man on a motorcycle to lead us to the town's health centre and then round the back where two wards had been taken over for emergency feeding.

'Last year this whole compound was full,' said the woman worker mixing and heating special therapeutic milk. 'Designed for the Phase I treatment of severe malnutrition,' it said on the tin. 'We had many tents at the back here,' the woman added, 'and even then we couldn't help everyone because there were so many.' Samaritan's Purse had intended to close the feeding centre long ago, but a steady trickle of desperately hungry children kept coming.

Of the dozen or so little family groups sitting on beds or squatting on blankets on the floor, I spoke to two. The reason for selecting them was simply that the women looked particularly wretched. Each had forlorn sunken eyes, and their skin was sallow with hunger and exhaustion. Their children shared the same dull complexion and forlorn manner. As we talked, a flock of weaver birds building nests in the acacia tree outside chattered noisily to each other.

Barate Ahmed thought she was 30 years old, but had no real idea. She had had to scrape together two pounds for transport to reach the assessment centre on the main road, and now stood in front of me with the two children she had brought with her, the younger one at her breast. At home, the family existed entirely on food handouts. They had no income and had not managed to grow anything the previous year.

What surprised my Ethiopian companions and shocked me were the answers to straightforward questions about the family back at home. Barate had six children and was her husband's second wife. The first wife had nine children. Her husband had just taken a third wife, but she had no children as yet. The husband therefore had a total of fifteen children, with presumably more to come, and a household at present of nineteen. In a bad year they were all totally dependent on international or government-funded food handouts. Without aid many in the family, perhaps all of them, would die.

In an era when individual rights and choices have become the watchwords for aid-givers, it has not been acceptable to voice alarm at such prodigal family life nor even to direct criticism at the men involved. The response has been to urge more reproductive health interventions from government and donors. There may one day be a more robust approach towards family size and self-support.

The second woman I interviewed at the nutrition centre was called Rawda. She appeared as woebegone as Barate, and had a 2-year-old with her. It turned out that she was the widowed grandmother, not the mother of the child, and had set off to the assessment centre within a day or two of her daughter giving birth to her sixth child. Here was another family dependent on relief which had been forced to seek help for one vulnerable infant just as a new baby arrived. I asked Rawda what she thought would happen next. 'I don't know,' she said with a faint and weary grin: 'My daughter has a very young husband, and he could take another wife.'

In my travels in the South I made contact with local community organizations which were in turn supported by overseas charities. Oxfam America gives funds to an organization called Community Development Initiative in Shashemene and one morning we careered off into the countryside on a trip which introduced me to the great merits of *enset* or 'false banana'. *Enset* looks like a banana plant; it grows tall with banana-like leaves and is admirably drought resistant. It does not fruit, otherwise I suppose it would actually be a banana, but for an apparently unproductive plant it has great uses. Its leaves are used for cattle feed and food packaging, the fronds are handy as ties for roofs and walls, and it provides food for humans. In some parts of the South, it is a staple. In the food emergency of 2008, it saved lives.

Hussein Mohammed introduced himself to me as a model farmer and the first in the area to grow *enset*. The seedlings had been provided by my companions at the local community organization. Hussein then told me how to turn the fat bulbous *enset* stem into food. It was an extraordinary process which involved cutting, scraping, pulping, burying, fomenting, drying, grinding, and sieving to make flour which will be turned into porridge. It is not very nutritious but it is edible and in the lean times it means survival.

As a model farmer, Hussein gave some of his neighbours *enset* seedlings during the 2008 crisis, but was never repaid. 'I will not do that again. They will have to develop themselves.' For himself, *enset* meant that he did not take 'one single coin of relief from the government' during the food crisis and had been able to feed his own extensive family.

How many? Well, his father still had eight children on his hands, and Hussein had fed them all. His own family? Two wives and fourteen children—all of them last year dependent on *enset*. A sizeable crowd had gathered to listen to our interview in Hussein's *enset* patch. He had already introduced me to his father Mohammed, but I had not immediately appreciated that the crowd around us consisted almost entirely of his immediate family.

Oxfam America also supports the Rift Valley Children and Women Development Association which has brought education to pastoral communities whose needs can only be met by making big adjustments to the school day and the school year. If their children were ever to go to school term times had to conform with seasonal grazing patterns, not the calendar, and daily time-tables had to fit in with children's duties as animal herders, not the convenience of teachers.

The changes demanded were far too radical for Ethiopia's education bureaucrats who resisted them for years. But by dint of practical demonstration and effective campaigning the development association won the argument and won the day. The government finally took over these informal 'under-tree' schools and Ethiopia's fine record in rural education owes much to such charitable initiatives.

At a village called Gubata off the main Addis Ababa road, I was led to the giant acacia tree in whose shade the local primary school began in 1997 with twenty-six pupils. Banged into the bark just above head height was the nail on which attendance sheets had been pinned in those early days. In 2001 the government built a new school within 100 metres of the old acacia tree and there are now 647 pupils receiving a formal classroom education. Fourteen have already graduated from the open air to university.

I was told all this by Mamiru Hayato, chairman of the parent–teacher association and the man responsible for starting up the school with the help of the Rift Valley development association. Apart from the timetable not favouring pastoralists, Mamiru said the other problem was that the nearest school was four miles away. An eight-mile walk every day was fine for boys and girls in their teens, he said, but it was too far for the smaller ones. 'If they are only able to start school at 14 or 15, it is embarrassing for them to sit with little children. They are adults by then and ready to be married.'

Out of nothing more than curiosity I asked Mamiru how many children he had. To the merriment of the crowd that had as usual gathered under the tree with us, he replied rather sheepishly that he had sixteen. No fewer than twelve of them had been through the school he started, and he added with a father's pride that one of his daughters was away at college studying nursing. I asked him how many wives he had. With a grin he raised two fingers.

Dr Assefa Hailemariam, associate professor at the Institute of Population Studies at Addis Ababa University, whose work I have already quoted, recalled a survey conducted in 1990 showing that 14 per cent of Moslem men in Ethiopia had taken two wives. There had been no such survey since, but I asked him what he thought the figure would be today. 'Not less than 10 per cent,' he replied. That at least would suggest that the number of very large families may be diminishing, and there are other heartening signs.

One of the most inspiring encounters in all my Ethiopian travels took place in the family planning unit at the health centre in Alaba, more easily found than the wards for severely malnourished children pushed out of sight at the back of the complex. Old-fashioned condoms and contraceptive pills were available from the unit, but there were also more sophisticated interventions on offer. The most popular was a six-month injectible contraceptive, and the unit offered three-year and five-year contraceptive implants as well. Two local women who were just leaving the unit as I arrived had had injections that afternoon. All the services on offer, including the regular collection of condoms, appeared to depend entirely on the initiative of women, not the responsibility of men.

The two staff members I met were the middle-aged sister on the unit, a Christian called Mesay, and a slender young Moslem nurse-midwife called Beida who wore the *hijab* and a white coat right down to her ankles. Beida was born near Alaba, but had gone away to college for her three-year diploma in midwifery. This was her first job since graduating, and she was thrilled with it. 'I feel I am becoming a strong and valuable person. I believe I am giving service to the community, and I shall be happy to stay here.'

I broached the subject of contraception in the Moslem community, doubting I would get far. I was quite wrong. 'In the Moslem faith, contraception is not allowed,' Beida began, 'but these days many women are taking it because having more than six children can have an effect on health. They fear the health consequences of having more children and they also ask how they can afford more children. This is not allowed through our community, but these days even women with only two children are thinking they should limit their families.'

At this point the Christian nursing sister joined in. 'There was an earlier assumption that having more children was good, especially among the Protestants,' said Mesay, referring to the poverty and overpopulation of the nearby Wolaita area. She searched for the biblical phrase to illustrate her point and my Ethiopian companion searched for the English translation. It was Noah's command after the flood to 'Go forth and multiply.' And Mesay added, 'Generally nowadays many women accept spacing and have one child every six years.'

I took the risk of asking Baida about her personal attitude towards contraception. 'In my religion it is not allowed,' she said for the second time, 'but I will take them because of my health and the economy of the country.' I reflected on how awkward it might be in a hospital in the West for a male reporter to conduct an interview with a committed Christian woman and a committed Moslem on the theme of religion and birth control.

My expert companions in the field were staff members of the Family Guidance Association of Ethiopia, the oldest and biggest independent family planning body in the country. The FGAE began life in 1966 when Ethiopia's population was about 25 million—less than a third of the total it reached in 2010—and it managed to run just one clinic in Addis Ababa on two afternoons a week. Even that required the personal say-so of the emperor.

A group of Ethiopian health professionals and sociologists, some recently returned from studying in India, where population growth was an important concern, went to see Haile Selassie who agreed to their proposal, but told them to 'go quietly'. Out of respect for church and state, the clinic operated under cover of providing only 'health services' and they called themselves the 'Family Guidance Association of Ethiopia' for fear of upsetting the authorities by using the offensive phrase 'family planning'.

The fixing of boundaries for family planning work had always been sensitive, but it took the US administration of George W. Bush to plunge the FGAE into crisis. Under what the critics called the 'Global Gag Rule' designed to stop US federal funds supporting organizations with any links to abortion, the independent family planners of Ethiopia faced the loss of almost a fifth of their income. Their own abortion services were non-existent, but they did refer patients to international agencies which both advised on and carried out abortions. They also objected to subscribing to the US ban on the grounds of upholding women's rights. 'The FGAE couldn't sign these terms and so we were criminalized,' said Desfa Kebede, its programme director. 'There was no way in which we could work with any United States institution or those organizations which were supported by US funds.'

The association was forced to sack thirty members of staff and cut back on clinic services and training. They faced a worse shutdown if no official aid agencies could be found to fill the financial gap of several million dollars. They appealed to the big donors in Addis Ababa, including the British, and for a time it was touch and go. The Dutch government finally came to the rescue with more than $3 million, and with additional assistance from UN bodies and private American institutions the FGAE programme survived. One of the first actions of the incoming administration of President Barack Obama in 2009 was to rescind the 'Global Gag Rule'.

The FGAE clinic in Awassa, capital of Ethiopia's southern region, provides the best reproductive health facilities in the city. 'Government officials send their own wives here because of our good reputation,' said Mengistu Kassa, the clinic head. 'We are better than the government hospitals and we are better than the private clinics.' It was in the corridor as I was being shown around the clinic's well-stocked pharmacy and well-equipped consulting rooms that Mengistu introduced me to Sudare Worom who had just accompanied a woman with labour complications to the clinic.

In the elaborate designations of the development world, Sudare is a TTBA, a trained traditional birth attendant, and Mengistu embraced her warmly as an old friend of the clinic. Sudare is a grandmother and reckons she has assisted in more than 1,000 deliveries. She had no formal qualifications, but had been on two training courses and is now a star in the network of care that the family guidance association extends to the countryside around Awassa.

A few days later I drove out of the city past hot springs into the hills to reach Sudare's village. In the yard at the back of her house there were twenty women waiting to meet me and she had given pride of place to the three whose sterilizations she had arranged at the FGAE clinic. The conversation that morning had to be three-way. My English-speaking guide was a nurse-midwife from the FGAE. She translated my questions into Amharic for the government health worker who in turn translated them into the local Sidama language for the village women. Then the answers travelled all the way back again.

Sudare said she started doing this work after she had delivered several of her own grandchildren. The local farmers' association wanted her to help other women in the village, and she was sent off on a health authority course where she learnt about normal and abnormal pregnancy, normal and abnormal presentation, signs of labour, and many other things. 'This was very helpful,' she said. 'Before I was working almost blindly, but then I became confident.'

She received more training from the FGAE, and they had the means to give her practical support as well as instruction. These were 'useful things', said Sudare, such as surgical gloves, surgical blades, umbilical cord ties, even bleach and toilet soap which were not available in the village. Best of all they had provided her with a mobile phone—a brilliant scheme funded by the British charity Safehands for Mothers—which enabled her to summon the FGAE ambulance from Awassa in an emergency. 'When mothers bleed, the ambulance comes straightaway,' said Sudare, 'so lives are saved.'

Sudare also takes her family planning responsibilities very seriously. Forty-five days after each delivery she tells women of their contraceptive options ranging from tubal ligation to the pill, from implants to injections. She herself had had four children, which she considered quite enough, although one of her daughters had so far had seven and the other was on five.

What did the group of women in Sudare's back yard regard as the ideal family size? There was a long discussion centring on whether five or six was better. I pointed out that this was above the target figure in the national population policy, and so some agreed that four was indeed a good number. Did anyone favour having fewer than four children? No one. Were they quite sure? They were sure.

Ethiopia's 1993 population policy noted that the national fertility rate had increased in two decades from 5.8 to 7.7 children per woman. The objective was to reduce that to four children per woman by 2015. The current official figure is 5.4 although the demographer Dr Assefa argues that on consistent calculations it is in fact higher than that. These statistics are based in any event not on head counts, but on doorstep surveys. Only the women are asked how many children they have had, so the findings do not necessarily reflect family size. My own survey in Sudare's back yard, conducted among women exposed to effective family planning instruction, indicated that achieving a fertility rate of four children per woman by 2015 would still be a struggle.

At national level and beginning in the rural areas, there has been an impressive new emphasis on bringing basic health services to the people. The Ministry of Health has sent an army of 30,000 trained health workers, two per village, into the countryside with a brief which concentrates on the welfare of mothers and infants. Family planning is a critical part of the initiative, and most of the health posts I visited were well enough stocked with a range of modern contraceptives.

By far the best of the health extension workers I met when I turned up in villages were themselves young women—educated, committed, and with a very clear idea of what they were trying to achieve. Under a bold initiative launched in 2009, no fewer than 15,000 of these health workers were to receive training in performing contraceptive implants to insure that women would be guaranteed to avoid pregnancy for several years. Family planning techniques have come a long way since condoms were simply handed out on the doorstep or at the clinic, and Ethiopia had taken the lead.

Yet the need is immense and growing. According to Ethiopia's last Demographic Health Survey conducted in 2005, more than 34 per cent of married women wanted family planning services but had no access to them. This figure took no account of the demands of unmarried women nor the implications of a youthful population 'bulge'. Future surveys are expected to record real achievements in contraceptive availability, but 'unmet needs' will continue to present a yawning gap.

There are also doubts as to whether the top leadership in Ethiopia and those in the rich world who fix the aid priorities have given clear emphasis to the importance of population growth in undermining the prospects of the poor. Survival, better health, and longer lives are all fundamentally important, but so too is the corresponding need to ensure that survival and self-sufficiency are likely in the long run.

In the post-colonial 'development' decades, the 'population explosion' worried the rich world sick. For many of the big aid agencies, particularly in the United States, this anxiety became their focus and *raison d'être*. It was 'birth control' before it became 'family planning' and long before it transmogrified into 'reproductive health'. It was in the 1970s that the world's outlook changed. China's one-child policy and the excesses of India's sterilization drive undermined the international consensus around an emphasis on the merits of birth control. At the United Nations and among the aid-givers 'development' itself was declared the best contraceptive.

As one development fashion has succeeded another in the decades of big aid flows, attention to the critical issue of birth control has not faded away entirely, but it has been consistently overshadowed by the emphasis given to matters of gender, the environment, governance, and latterly to climate change. The sharp equation that Ethiopia's population policy drew in 1993 between rural poverty and the birth rate—a formulation officially maintained at a policy level—has become internationally unfashionable and has been downplayed domestically. Family planning was nowhere mentioned when the United Nations drew up the Millennium Development Goals aimed at halving world poverty by 2015.

In the twenty-first century it was the AIDS disaster that deflected the international focus away from population growth. After its last major conference, AIDS and not family planning became the overwhelming financial preoccupation of the United Nations Commission on Population and Development. A report for the commission in 2009 said that such a large percentage of the funds was now going to AIDS that 'the lack of adequate funding for both family planning and reproductive health will undermine efforts to prevent unintended pregnancies and reduce maternal and infant mortality'.[3]

---

[3] United Nations Economic and Social Council, 'Flow of Financial Resources for Assisting the Implementation of the Programme of Action of the International Conference on Population and Development', 21 January 2009.

The report was carried out for the United Nations Population Fund (UNFPA) and traced expenditure under the four so-called 'population' categories of family planning, reproductive health, HIV/AIDS, and research, and said there were fears that the share of funding going to AIDS was distracting from the needs of the other three areas. 'This is especially evident in the case of funding for family planning, where absolute dollar amounts are lower than they were in 1995. If not reversed, the trend towards less funding for family planning will have serious implications for the ability of countries to address unmet need for such services,' the report said.

Family planning's share of total funding for all these 'population activities' had decreased from 40 per cent in 1997 to a pitiful 5 per cent in 2007, the report said. It projected that for 2010 the direct costs of family planning in Sub-Saharan Africa would be $414 million, about one-fifth of the direct costs of maternal health and a fraction of the billions being spent on AIDS. The total projected costs for HIV/AIDS were almost $16 billion, some $6 billion more than family planning, reproductive health, and non-HIV sexually transmitted diseases all put together.

It was clear that family planning, a core programme in the early decades of development, had become the Third World's Cinderella service. The donors had created a dangerous imbalance between their commitment to saving lives and their relative lack of interest in sustaining those lives in the longer term.

Ethiopia seems to have taken its cue from the development community at large—that patience and the development process itself will bring about significant falls in the birth rate and so stabilize population growth. Prime Minister Meles Zenawi and his health minister Dr Tedros Adhanom articulate the approach more persuasively than most overseas professionals. 'In our government we believe in teaching the community, convincing the community, trying to get them to see the benefits of doing it, trying to internalize it,' said Dr Tedros. 'If they can do that, really internalize it and understand its benefits, that's how you can scale up fast.' The key lies in his army of 30,000 health extension workers. With them, he said, all the targets for contraceptive use will be met.

Meles acknowledged that he and his ministers had faced challenges that got in the way of dealing with the population issue. In the early years, they had first to hold the country together after nearly two decades of civil war. Then they had to determine the country's overall development strategy. There had been the war with Eritrea. But in more recent years, he said the development structures had been put in place, and the key to progress would be girls' education. 'Education for women would be much more effective than even family planning. Increasing opportunity for women, and for working men and women, would be the best way of convincing them that it is better for them and for their child to have fewer, sturdier, more educated children than was the case in the past.'

The question remained whether the government had acted robustly enough in tackling the twin elements of its original analysis that population growth and agricultural backwardness were equally responsible for the country's poverty. Ethiopia is given to strong national campaigns, and in the course of my own few months there the prime minister travelled to no fewer than four farmers' rallies. I attended two of them myself. In the same period it was reported he had carpeted officials and teachers for failing to improve education services. However he gave no corresponding leadership on the population issue nor was he under any pressure from the aid community to do so. He had once used the expression 'population explosion', I was told. He did not do so any more.

The organizational structure laid out in the national policy document to tackle the population crisis was never created. There is no office of population in the prime minister's secretariat and the prime minister does not chair a National Population Council. Instead the population office has been downgraded from its place at the centre of power to the status of department in the Ministry of Finance and Economic Development. The planned structures at regional level are even less apparent, and at district level they are non-existent. With backing from the aid-givers, the government has energetically deployed its health workers to the villages, and it puts its faith in the magic of development.

Some of Ethiopia's own experts are convinced this may not be enough. In an echo of Emperor Haile Selassie's response to the country's first family planning initiative in the 1960s—'Do it, but do it quietly'—one leading Ethiopian demographer told me: 'The government are doing things, but they are doing them silently. If they were to do it aggressively, the population might not double in the next twenty-five years. If they don't act aggressively, it definitely will.'

III

NOW

Chapter 8
2005 and All That

'The good lady apparently does not know her Ethiopian history.'

May 15, 2005, was Election Day in Ethiopia. They were the most important elections in Ethiopian history. In fact they were the first fully competitive elections the country had ever held. Opposition parties took to the field and the media geared up to report on a new political era. National radio and television staged vehement public debates between government and opposition, and partisan newspapers flourished. This was going to be a proper election.

For many Ethiopians away from the big cities, the drama of the political contest was profoundly unsettling. There had been elections to parliament under Emperor Haile Selassie, but party organization was frowned upon then and almost non-existent. Under the Derg, there had also been elections, but they were exclusively one-party affairs. The EPRDF had staged two general elections since it came to power, but the opposition barely figured. Now there was to be a choice and the arrival in the villages of campaigners from the Coalition for Unity and Democracy (CUD) 'aroused terror and amazement', according to a French journalist who researched the process on the ground.[1]

René LeFort conducted some fifty interviews with villagers, each lasting between one and three hours, across two communities some hours walk from the main north road through Amhara Region. What emerged was people's anxiety over the challenge these 'free' elections posed to their view of authority—*mengist* in Amharic—and the power it held over their lives. LeFort reported: 'The question they ask themselves is: "with which candidate do I stand the least risk of reducing my chances of survival?" The answer is obvious: the one who will win at national level, or at least, in my own community.' As the vote approached, the journalist was implored by villagers to tell them who would win, since he evidently had the education and insight to predict the outcome.

Villagers were alarmed that 'militants of the opposition party dare to criticize the *mengist* in front of the offices of the administration!' The contest risked armed confrontation, LeFort was told. 'In our history, it isn't possible to have two *mengist* at the same time.' Had anyone listened to the radio debates between government and opposition? A few farmers had radios with charged batteries, but they had wisely 'forgotten it all' except for this revelation: 'This government is so weak it must sit with its enemies.'

LeFort saw the story of the national elections unfold at village level. For months the ruling party assumed it would be handed victory by a grateful electorate, and campaigned little or not at all. Only late in the day, far too late for its smooth re-election, did it mount a political counter-attack.

---

[1] René LeFort, 'Powers—*Mengist*—and Peasants in Rural Ethiopia: The May 2005 Elections', *Journal of Modern African Studies*, 45/2 (2007).

Official election observers witnessed the degeneration of the campaign during the final weeks and collated the evidence of violence and intimidation. The Carter Center, founded by former US president Jimmy Carter, drew attention to what it called 'ethnic "hate speech".' This referred to how both sides, government as much as opposition, used crude scare tactics to frighten voters into toeing their line. The European Union election mission said that the ruling party warned people that if they brought the CUD to power, there would be massacres along the lines of the 1994 genocide in Rwanda. 'Let us not give a chance to the *Interahamwe*', said an EPRDF banner, aligning opposition parties with Hutu killers. The ruling party evoked memories of the 1988 Derg massacre of civilians in the town of Hawzien as a further forecast of what the CUD had in store.

In the local polling that LeFort witnessed, opposition support varied from 63 per cent up to 84 per cent, with as many as 40 per cent prudently failing to vote at all. He attributed the result in large part to the 'swaying power of the towns' which had turned against the government. In the council elections in Addis Ababa, where campaigning had been at its most exciting and where the polls had been most closely monitored, the opposition dropped only one seat in sweeping the board, and that through a technical error on the candidate's part.

The Ethiopian elections of 2005 were certainly flawed. It would be surprising, given the country's fierce autocratic tradition and its slow pace of development, if they had not been. The Carter Center and the European Union tried to look on the bright side— 'significant advances in Ethiopia's democratisation process,' said Carter. 'Significant development towards democracy...an inspiration for the future,' said the EU. But both detailed their shortcomings. Carter concluded mildly that the 'post-election period was disappointing', but the EU underlined the counting irregularities, an ineffective appeals procedure, and human rights abuses in declaring that the election 'fell short of international principles for genuine democratic elections'.

Government and opposition each promptly announced it had won. The government could quote as proof the final tally of parliamentary seats—declared four months after the election— which gave them 327 seats to the combined opposition's 198. Their opponents said the election was stolen, and they quoted the European Union observer mission in their support. Who was right? The minds of the politicians are closed to further analysis. Events after the polls so enraged some of the election monitors that they too may no longer be dispassionate observers. The whole truth will never be ascertained, but two experienced foreign witnesses presented me with more measured testimony.

'My view is that the government probably won it, but they didn't win it immediately,' said one of these election experts. 'They got so scared that they held back and delayed publication of the results to make sure they won it. We saw the counting process slowing down, we saw it going dry, and that implies some sort of fiddling. But the opposition needed to have a paper trail to prove the point, and they weren't allowed proper access, so I never saw anything that contested the election outcome. There was no alternative data.'

Another observer, no admirer of the EPRDF, catalogued the extent of government intimidation and malpractice before and after the election in one part of Amhara Region, but added: 'I don't think the opposition won, by the way. I don't believe the election was stolen, but it *was* unfair.' Many of the results may have been unsound, but there was not the evidence to support rigging on the scale required to reverse the outcome.

The disputes over election figures soon led to a more deadly contest between government and opposition. Election Day ended with Prime Minister Meles announcing a one-month ban on demonstrations in the capital, and the lines were then drawn for confrontation.

Trouble began on the campus at Addis Ababa University. Anti-government demonstrators took to the streets, and the security forces opened fire. Thirty-six protestors were killed, scores more injured, and thousands of young people across the country were rounded up and detained. Government officials were blunt about these tactics—to crack down so hard that the momentum of protest would be halted. One source surprisingly close to government went further. He told me that security forces had opened fire on the demonstrators 'quite deliberately to show who was in charge'.

I followed the story of the strife in 2005 through one of the best sources available—the pages of Addis Ababa's most independent-minded English language newspaper, *The Reporter*. The banner headline in early June read 'Unrest in Addis' and the front page carried pictures of bloodied heads, soldiers wielding clubs, and a coffin being borne away. 'On Tuesday the view of the campus reminds one of a deserted military camp in the Hollywood movies,' its journalist reported, adding that calls for a return to studies had gone unheeded. Two days later he noted: 'The campus looked like an occupied and conquered territory on Thursday too.'

The opposition's conviction that it had been robbed of victory was based in large measure on the findings of the European Union's election observation mission. There is nothing in any of the EU's formal reports that would justify such a conclusion, but opposition leaders are nevertheless adamant. 'Oh, there's no question about that,' said Dr Berhanu Nega, the CUD leader now in exile in America. 'It's not my conclusion. The observers have concluded that. Look at the EU report.'

The report that Dr Berhanu had primarily in mind appears to be the EU mission's earliest sampling of results in the twenty-four hours after the polls closed. This showed an urban bias which necessarily tended to favour the opposition, but this reasoning was rejected by Dr Berhanu. 'This is the other mistake people committed,' he told me. 'They thought this was an urban thing. That's what the government is trying to persuade people. No! They were rejected in the rural areas. That's why they started completely stealing the boxes. They sent in the army and simply took the boxes! So the rejection is complete, and the EPRDF government realized that it is.'

I have spoken to members of the European observer mission who believe it was a mistake even to commission this survey before the official count had got properly under way. It provided only premature projections and it should not have been under-taken so early in a complex results process. But what happened next was worse. Within days of the election Brussels had drawn up and circulated an internal report based on these results and concluded that the opposition had won. The victory was sub-stantial, the EU said, even in such EPRDF strongholds as Tigray. This report was then leaked.

The political fire that the European Union had lit was ener-getically stoked by Ana Gomes, the mission's chief observer and a Member of the European Parliament for the Portuguese Socialist Party. Ms Gomes is an outspoken advocate of human rights around the world, and has since led EU election observer mis-sions to Angola and East Timor. She was a diplomat for more than twenty years before entering the European Parliament, but diplomacy did not figure greatly in her relations with the government of Ethiopia.

The first thing that Ana Gomes said to me about the 2005 elections was this: 'Fifteen days before the election, I was thinking, something is wrong, they are lying and cheating.' She went on to record how exciting Election Day had been in Addis Ababa and how her office had asked the National Election Board to keep the polls open in the city past dusk at 6 o'clock. 'At 10.30 in the evening there were still people voting in Addis. It was marvellous what happened that day.'

But Ms Gomes had no confidence at all in the neutrality of the election machinery outside the capital. She declared the judge in charge of the National Election Board to be 'just a puppet' and said that when the counting began her observers around the country had been prevented from monitoring it. 'The next day the government announced victories everywhere to compensate for Addis. There they didn't even dare to cheat.'

Ms Gomes said that her mission had more information from outside the capital than the election board. The results were being 'absolutely fabricated by the regime'. This was where the EU results sample came in. 'It showed that with few exceptions the opposition was winning. Everything was cooked up, obviously,' she said.

And what of the leaking of the EU's early report on the results? 'It could have been someone in our team. Or it could have been from one of the [European] embassies in Addis. Or it could have been the government itself. They were definitely bugging us.'

Did she accept that the leaking of the report had contributed to popular agitation against the government and thus to the outbreak of violence in June? 'It was going to happen anyway. But the leaking of the report gave the regime the chance to turn against us and blame us for the agitation—that's why I don't exclude the government being responsible [for the leak].'

Ms Gomes was not in Ethiopia when the EU report was leaked, but returned soon afterwards, on the eve of the government's crackdown on opposition demonstrators. She recalled there were military vehicles on patrol on the night she arrived back in Addis Ababa, but no one else was on the streets. Opposition figures feared for their safety, and the EU election mission's anxiety for them was to provoke further controversy.

Ana Gomes admired Dr Berhanu, the opposition leader, as much as she distrusted the prime minister. 'He really impressed me. He caught the imagination of the people. He was the one who emerged with a strategy, a vision, a coherence.' She found on her return to Addis Ababa that Berhanu had sought refuge at the EU residence, but this arrangement had angered the government and he would have to leave.

'We feared for their lives,' said Ms Gomes, and had then conceived the idea of swapping beds with the opposition leader. She would move to the EU residency while Dr Berhanu and his wife would move into the room booked for her at the Sheraton, the capital's most expensive hotel. 'In the hotel, they wouldn't possibly dare,' said Ms Gomes of any government move against Dr Berhanu.

Ana Gomes was at a meeting of European ambassadors the next day when news came through of the shootings at the university. 'I go immediately to the hospital and see people in absolute stress, including the doctors and nurses who were in total shock at what was happening.' Later in the day she met Bereket Simon, information minister and key figure in the government, 'and I have the most difficult meeting of them all when [he] levels at us the most aggressive accusation—that we have provoked them, we have caused the massacre by the leaking of our report.'

'I totally rejected this,' she said. ' "It's your people who are shooting the people in the streets. It's not us, it's not our report. This is ridiculous." And I put out a statement condemning the human rights violations that had occurred. They are absolutely furious. I write to [prime minister] Meles saying, "You accuse the others of violating the constitution. *You* are the one who is violating the constitution." They were absolutely furious with my statement on human rights violations, denouncing the massacre. They didn't expect that.' Ms Gomes laughed at the recollection. In fact in its statement of 8 June the EU election mission stopped just short of describing the crackdown as a massacre, but it told the government 'to ensure that the security forces refrain from excessive or unnecessary violence and reminds them that looking after the well-being of their co-nationals is their paramount duty'.

Ana Gomes returned once again to Ethiopia in August after elections had been rerun in a number of the disputed constituencies and after the troubled Somali Region had gone to the polls. She was unimpressed by the process, to put it mildly, and drafted a long statement cataloguing fresh electoral irregularities and human rights abuses. But by now the argument between ministers and the MEP was personal. 'She is angry and talking about it,' said the headline in *The Reporter,* summing up the press conference she gave at the end of the month.

The government had prepared for the event by planting an absurd story in the state-owned *Ethiopian Herald* that Ms Gomes stood to gain a cut of the election funds collected by opposition parties from overseas Ethiopians. At the press conference itself, a reporter also asked her about the sleeping arrangements made with the opposition leader Dr Berhanu Nega at the time of the

June violence. 'Mr Nega slept in your room,' is how she recalled the offensive suggestion put to her.

The prime minister then publicly entered the fray. It would have taken him several days to compose his letter to the editor of the *Ethiopian Herald*. It ran to an extraordinary 13,000 words, so long that the newspaper had to clear whole pages to accommodate it and even then had to run it over three days. The purpose of the letter was vehemently to dispute Ana Gomes's complaints about the elections in the EU's statement, but he did not trouble to hide his personal contempt for her. References by Meles to his female antagonists as 'the good lady' or 'that lady' are always signs of trouble.

Meles's real charge against Ana Gomes was not apparent until the last few hundred of the 13,000-word letter. It said he was letting readers in 'on another little secret'—that the EU observer had been 'peddling' the idea of a government of national unity and that the EPRDF should give up its exclusive hold on power and share it with the opposition. The government had rejected these ideas, he wrote, but she had persisted with them up until the eve of her press conference.

'The good lady apparently does not know her Ethiopian history, or her EPRDF's,' said Meles. She did not appreciate that 'merely bad ideas' would become unthinkable when 'tainted by association with an election observer turned self-appointed colonial viceroy...' In a further anti-colonialist flourish, the prime minister added, 'The good lady can apparently not take NO for an answer from the natives.'

Many considered the personal nature of the attack undignified. The opposition stalwart Prof. Mesfin Wolde-Mariam described it as 'unbecoming of a prime minister and an Ethiopian gentleman'. Ana Gomes herself reminded me, perhaps unnecessarily, that she was a politician. 'At some point someone had to come out and say the truth. The question is, am I going to fail the people who have shown their commitment to democracy, who have shown their belief in the elections . . . just for the sake of protecting a government that acts so miserably in repressing its own people? The choice to me was clear.'

Ms Gomes's confrontation with the Ethiopian government divided the European Union. EU aid officials wanted her to tone down her criticisms. Ethiopia was 'one of their biggest clients', she said. Ethiopia is in fact the largest recipient of EU aid to Africa. 'They wanted business as usual, and they didn't want me to spill the beans.' EU officials with responsibility for human rights backed her, though even here she complained that senior figures in the Commission continued to receive the Ethiopian prime minister warmly in private while denouncing his government in public.

One public illustration of the strains created within the European Commission was the emphatic disclaimer it placed on the final election mission report. It seemed to be washing its hands of the whole process. 'These views have not been adopted or in any way approved,' it said. 'The European Commission does not guarantee the accuracy of the data included in this report, nor does it accept responsibility for any use made thereof.'

European ambassadors in Addis Ababa were similarly divided—some in favour of Ms Gomes's outspokenness, others opposed to it, and some in the middle—but she told me she received the shortest shrift from the administration of President George W. Bush. She travelled to Washington to warn officials of more killings to come. 'They couldn't care less. They were totally dismissive of my warnings. By that time, they were seeing Meles as a big ally.'

The impact abroad of the 2005 killings and detentions was magnified by the build-up to the G8 summit at Gleneagles, in Scotland, which the British prime minister, Tony Blair, intended as the climax of his 'Year of Africa'. Prime Minister Meles Zenawi had been one of the select few African politicians on Blair's 'Commission for Africa' which made recommendations on tackling the continent's poverty.

The year 2005 was also the twentieth anniversary of Live Aid—global concerts were planned to maximize pressure on the G8—and the year of 'Make Poverty History', perhaps a final assault on still unresolved problems. The pop singer Bob Geldof, driving force behind so many popular aid initiatives, was also a member of Blair's Africa commission, and had what he described as a 'joshing and direct relationship' with the Ethiopian prime minister.

Channel 4 News asked Geldof for his comments on the violence in Ethiopia. 'I despair,' he said, 'I really despair.' He thought he would now get a briefing from the Ethiopian embassy in London disputing the facts, and went on, 'Grow up, they make me puke.' He turned on Meles—'a seriously clever man'—and demanded to know what he was doing 'closing down radio stations, and journalists and that. It's a disgrace. Behave!'

Geldof has a way of talking disarmingly and at length when asked questions that others might find awkward. 'I would still hold to that,' he said when I taxed him on the appropriateness of telling Ethiopians to grow up and their prime minister to behave. 'We are talking about a very smart person who fully understands the progressive dynamic within Africa, and outside, and for him to nullify the election results, gains or otherwise, and have his forces open fire in the market place on students and oppositionists is beyond the pale—and that has to be stated at all times. Bob

Geldof's disapproval is meaningless...he couldn't care less, quite rightly, but it had to be said. It sounds ridiculous to say I was cruelly disappointed, because "Who the fuck are you?" is the response. Correct again! But I was, I was.'

The British were the first to take action against Ethiopia. Hilary Benn, the international development secretary, arrived in Addis Ababa just a week after the killings in June, saw Prime Minister Meles, and then announced that he was holding back £20 million of direct support to the government. This was news to Meles who had not understood from the meeting that the British were planning to penalize the Ethiopian government in this way.

Meles and Benn had not seen eye to eye during the minister's first official visit to Ethiopia in 2004. It was at the dessert stage of an official dinner that Mr Benn brought up the 'governance' issue and the need to encourage 'civil society' organizations in public and political life. This was now a priority in the British aid programme. He described the contribution of such civil society organizations in Britain. Meles countered with his view that in Ethiopia they were little more than the 'opposition in disguise'. There were further exchanges along these lines, according to British officials present, until the minister made reference to his parliamentary constituency in the North of England. 'In Leeds...' he began, but the prime minister cut him off. 'This is not Leeds,' said Meles.

According to Meles, differences arose with Mr Benn in 2005 because of media and charity pressure on Britain to respond to the June violence. He told the minister that he understood the importance of the Blair agenda to help Africa, 'If we are standing in the way, we would perfectly understand why you have to sacrifice Ethiopia in the interests of helping the whole continent.'

But he did not accept media accusations of election fraud. 'I told him I would not agree with you if you are going to cut development assistance because we have stolen the election, because we didn't.'

These exchanges, Meles told me, 'sort of created the wrong mood' with the British. It improved only after he next met Tony Blair. 'Prime Minister Blair was the only prime minister in Europe who said publicly, "These guys, they didn't steal the elections. My view is that these guys over-reacted after the elections." While I did not agree with him on the over-reaction, nevertheless he was very blunt and frank about what he knew to be the truth.'

In its 5 November issue, *The Reporter* returned to its banner headline of June—'Unrest in Addis'—but this time the front page was bordered in black. 'Shoot to Kill! Wound by Mistake!' said another headline, 'Peaceful Struggle Turning into Outright Violence,' said a third. The country's most important opposition leaders were boycotting the new parliament, and as the trouble escalated they were arrested and imprisoned. 'By all accounts,' said *The Reporter*, 'Wednesday's riot broke out as a result of public outrage against the imprisonment of the CUD's Dr Berhanu Nega.'

The violence lasted for many days and the government, backed by some independent observers, claimed that much of it was organized. Meles Zenawi described it as 'an insurrectionary attempt' and, in my interview with him, claimed that the opposition had been prepared 'to use all means necessary to remove the current constitutional order, not just the party'. In addition to the arrests, more than 150 civilians were killed and some 600 wounded. Six policemen died and more than 60 were injured.

Fresh outrage in the West forced the government to set up a commission of inquiry to establish whether the security forces had used 'excessive force' to suppress the disorder. When the inquiry report was finally published later in 2006, it acknowledged there had been 'human rights violations', but reached the predictable conclusion that government actions had been appropriate 'in the light of budding democracy'. This was by no means the whole story.

Of the original eleven members appointed to the inquiry commission, four resigned on grounds of ill-health before it had even met. Its chairman stood down at the most critical time in the commission's deliberations and the deputy chairman, Judge Woldemichael Meshesha, fled into exile in Europe from where he subsequently gave evidence to a US congressional inquiry in Washington.

The judge told Congress that the commission had originally concluded by ten votes to two that the authorities had used excessive force in the June and November clashes, but its members had then been subjected to a campaign of extraordinary pressure, including being personally carpeted by the prime minister, to reverse its findings. The publication deadline passed, more key inquiry members fell by the wayside and it took another four months to publish a version of the report which exonerated the government and, in the words of Judge Woldemichael, 'accused victims [of] their own sufferings'.

The opposition leaders who were thrown into jail had been charged meanwhile with a mesmerizing array of offences including genocide, high treason, armed uprising and civil war, and outrages against the constitution. The net extended beyond party politicians. Journalists were locked up, and so too were members of the aid community in Addis Ababa.

One of them was Daniel Bekele, a precise, quietly spoken lawyer with degrees from Addis Ababa and Oxford. In the run-up to the 2005 elections he was in charge of policy research and advocacy for Action Aid in Ethiopia. The charity's motto is 'End Poverty Together', which it defines as campaigning for human rights as much as providing the poor with food and income. For Action Aid and many others in the modern development movement, hunger is an abuse of people's rights, and they must be mobilized to demand them.

Free elections play an important part in this 'rights-based' approach to ending poverty. 'Representative democracy', Action Aid said in a recent document, 'is a necessary but insufficient condition to promote human rights...people need freedom of information and participation, action and decision-making.'[2] It was this commitment which brought the agency into direct conflict with the Ethiopian government.

Working in partnership with the local agency Organization for Social Justice in Ethiopia and its founder Netsanet Demessie, Daniel Bekele and Action Aid were involved at every juncture in the unfolding drama of the 2005 elections. They promoted 'voter education' before the elections, they helped stage debates during the campaign, they fought and won a court battle to be able to monitor the elections, and they tried to bring peace between the warring parties in the disorder that followed.

Daniel said they had pressed opposition members to join the new parliament, not to boycott it. 'We pleaded with them to take their seats and continue to be part of the democratic process. The boycott was a big, big mistake.' Such even-handedness did not help him.

He had just dropped his girlfriend off one evening in October when he was stopped by two armed men in civilian clothes. 'Who

---

[2] *Human Rights-Based Approaches to Poverty Eradication and Development* (Action Aid, June 2008).

was I to criticize the EPRDF?' were some of the few words spoken. Daniel was badly beaten, and nearly lost the sight of an eye. A few weeks later he was arrested, without a warrant, and joined opposition leaders and others, including his activist colleague Netsanet, in Kality prison, on the outskirts of the capital. He was charged with outrages against the constitution and conspiracy to overthrow the government.

Court proceedings got under way, and after some twenty months all the detainees—politicians, journalists, and aid activists—faced life imprisonment for 'outrages against the constitution'. At this stage an outside deal was brokered involving an admission of 'mistakes' on the part of the detainees in exchange for a pardon. The politicians all signed and were released. Some in the leadership, including Dr Berhanu, left promptly for the United States where they met supporters among the vocal Ethiopian community. But Daniel and Netsanet were determined to see the court proceedings through and refused to do a deal.

Once again, Daniel was critical of opposition leaders for leaving the country, in the case of Dr Berhanu for long-term exile in the United States and for concluding that violence was the only option. 'That was their second mistake,' said Daniel. 'In spite of everything, we have no option but to work peacefully within Ethiopia.'

In the view of many attending the court case Daniel and Netsanet convincingly refuted charges of seeking to overthrow the government. It was not very difficult to do. They cross-examined witnesses who had been patently rehearsed and exposed documents that were obviously fake. But there was a price to pay for these successes. On the day they appeared to have demolished the government's case, they were driven back to prison and placed in solitary confinement in airless sea containers with no daylight.

As the final judgement was read out in court, some for a time thought that Daniel and Netsanet were being cited for an award. The judges agreed that their activities had been peaceful and that they made a 'courageous and heroic contribution' to trying to resolve the disputes between government and opposition. They had 'lived up to their professional responsibility as lawyers and good citizens'.

The court found the defendants not guilty of trying to overthrow the government. The presiding judge declared that they should go free because there was no case against them. But by a majority verdict the court declared them guilty of incitement—'acts of preparation'. They appealed—and were once again sent to the 'dirty part of the jail'—and the government counter-appealed to the Supreme Court, this time demanding the death penalty.

Daniel and Netsanet, the Action Aid 'governance' activists, had now been in jail for more than two years. Even if they were released, there was the all-too-real prospect that they would be re-arrested at the gates of the jail. At this point they were presented once more with the 'pardon' document and this time they signed and withdrew their appeal to the Supreme Court. The two of them were released in March 2008 and travelled to Britain, Netsanet for a Masters degree at London University and Daniel for a doctorate in international law at Oxford.

The escalation in street violence at the end of 2005 once again put aid-givers on the spot. It was inconceivable that the West would reduce its aid commitments to Ethiopia and jeopardize the interests of the poor. At the same time 'governance', the catch-all term for good clean government and the observance of human rights, was moving centre-stage in the search for the element that would bring about social and economic development. By any reckoning, the events in Ethiopia in 2005 had not been a healthy exhibition of 'governance'.

This dilemma was particularly acute for Britain's Department for International Development, widely seen as the most innovative of the major official aid agencies. Tony Blair had by 2005 more than doubled Britain's overall aid budget in the years New Labour had been in power, and Ethiopia had been a favoured recipient. In those eight years aid to Ethiopia had risen from £8 million a year to £62 million, an eightfold increase. That figure had trebled again by 2009.

Hilary Benn, secretary of state, arrived in Addis Ababa in January 2006, with opposition leaders in jail and clashes continuing in schools and colleges between students and the security forces. He met the private agencies and singled out Action Aid for attention. But what was he going to do about aid? He denied reports that he intended to cut the budget or reallocate the funds to the private charities or the United Nations. The decision he took was to punish Ethiopia by taking the money away from central government—'Direct Budgetary Support'—and have it administered instead in the regions.

Meles Zenawi gave me this account of 'direct budget support', with which the British had replaced project-by-project aid as their budget grew and they bore down on administrative costs. 'Once we agreed on the fundamental strategy, they would give us the money and we would spend it in accordance with our budget,' said Meles. 'They would control whether we were pilfering the money or not. They would not micro-manage how we used the money. That was the approach.'

This would now change for the British and many other donors, including the World Bank and the European Commission. In a real rush, and with significant disruption to the flow of aid money, the Department for International Development (DFID) abandoned direct budget support and switched its support to the 'Protection of Basic Services', to be monitored at regional and district level. The problem, as some researchers have pointed out, is that local government officials are no more independent of dictates from the centre than their central government colleagues. Others concluded that a process of local accountability had the effect of reducing donors' influence over the Ethiopian government. But the British and others had been seen to do something.

The larger question was whether British assistance for 'governance', which had trebled in four years, was really transforming the quality of Ethiopia's official response to people's aspirations as well as their material needs. A DFID evaluation of its Ethiopian programme published in 2009 summed up the doubts. It said it was difficult to judge progress on 'governance' because measurements relied on 'anecdotal evidence, perception indices and/or proxy indicators'. It added, 'There is little evidence yet that donor support has permanently and significantly helped to strengthen good governance in the country.'[3]

Opponents of the Ethiopian government were certain that western pressure had achieved very little in the aftermath of the 2005 elections. Dr Berhanu Nega, opposition leader in exile, said that the response of western governments had been 'a very, very serious disappointment. These are not countries which are serious about liberty, which are serious about freedom. They have their own little geo-political, strategic interests.' But the elections had nevertheless changed things. 'People have seen for the first time what it means to be free, and you are not going to box them in.'

---

[3] 'Country Programme Evaluation: Ethiopia', DFID, April 2009.

Chapter 9
Down with Democracy?

'I would have been better off running a beer house.'

The Reporter newspaper in Addis Ababa first drew attention to the threat to press freedom in Ethiopia with a sketch of a quill pen on its front page and the legend 'Free Press, Free Speech, Free Spirit'. Then it started using an evocative silhouette showing a woman being led blindfold to the gallows by a man in army boots with a gun. Around it in English and Amharic were the words 'Rescue Press freedom from the hangman!!'

In 2005 the silhouette was promoted to the newspaper's masthead. There were two subsequent changes to it over the months. First the blindfolded figure representing press freedom was shown with the noose around her neck. Then the man with the gun and army boots was seen to have kicked away the stool on which she stood.

The Reporter is owned and edited by Amare Aregawi, a stocky and ebullient figure who swept into the office for our interview in a natty brown suit and elevated heels. As well as heading a media group that struggles to report and publish the news, Amare runs the Horn of Africa Press Institute ('Supporting the journalist, strengthening the media, building a flourishing region!'). He is also a most aggravating thorn in the government's flesh.

Amare is Tigrayan and the same age as Meles Zenawi. They were boys together at General Wingate School in Addis Ababa. For many years their careers followed a similar path. Amare spent a year in prison during the 'Red Terror' before joining Meles and others in the bush. One of his roles was to run the guerrillas' underground radio station, work rewarded when they came to power and put him in charge of Ethiopian Television.

Amare's approach of 'Free Speech, Free Spirit' did not commend him to government for long. In 1995 he fell out with the EPRDF and went off to found *The Reporter*. Meles Zenawi and Amare Aregawi were no longer close.

As I followed news reports of events surrounding the 2005 elections through the bound files of *The Reporter,* I was struck by the even-handedness of the editorials which Amare wrote as the trouble intensified. This was not the work of an agitator. They seemed to me to be the earnest writings of a patriot committed to seeking a positive outcome to the crisis and to achieving something quite foreign to Ethiopian politics—a compromise.

'As we have said time and time again,' said an editorial in August as the opposition contemplated a political boycott, 'since we all have to pursue the lawful and peaceful avenue, we urge opposition parties to carefully think that the best option is to join parliament.' Later that month, in the edition which detailed the snarling breakdown between the government and the European Union observer mission, Amare persisted in his view that the election represented progress. The public had begun, he wrote, 'to stand up for its rights' and 'the other great victory is that a multiparty political order is taking root in Ethiopia.' By November 2005 his hopes of compromise had diminished. As violence swirled again around the streets and his newspaper was published with a black border, the Amare editorial said simply 'Enough is Enough.'

Looking back on the elections in 2009, the editor denounced each one of the key players in turn. 'Stupid government actions! Stupid opposition with no strategy! Stupid, irresponsible EU! I am saying that of course the government is responsible, but not only the government.'

Amare Aregawi's biggest immediate problem was with the government over press freedom. He recalled that it had all started out so well in those heady days after the EPRDF victory. The constitution, as drafted, was an extraordinarily benign document, devoting article after article to democratic rights and importing wholesale the provisions of the Universal Declaration of Human Rights. Everyone had the right to hold opinions and express them; press and media freedom were guaranteed; censorship was prohibited; even the state-run media would invite diverse views.

'We were very proud of ourselves,' said Amare. 'We thought we could compare ourselves to the United States. Then things began to change a bit, and we said, "Well, at least we have the press freedoms of South Africa and Ghana." Now? It's not even that. It's the press freedom of a Somalia.'

A mass media law promulgated in 2008—one of a series of measures adopted since 2005 aimed at 'closing down political space', according to the government's critics—upheld press freedom in principle, but ended up restricting and harrying journalists in practice. A number of them had been swept up in the arrests that followed the post-election violence.

Amare said he had been charged seventeen times with defamation and libel (criminal offences in Ethiopia) and these provisions
were being strengthened. He was regularly pursued through the
courts by senior government officials. I texted him one morning
to confirm an appointment later that day. 'I have a court case,
charged with defamation,' he texted back. 'I don't think I can make
it today.'

New registration arrangements meant that a shareholder in
a newspaper could neither edit nor write for it. He had to give
up one or the other. 'If I did that, I'm sure there would be a new
regulation saying that "any person under 1.5 metres [about five
feet] shall not be allowed to write for the newspaper,' said Amare,
who, as I have observed, is on the short side.

'I am committed to journalism and to press freedom. But as a
business this is the wrong one to be in. I would have been better
off owning a beer house—and a good deal more respected.'

Prime Minister Meles tried to assure me that the exclusive
purpose of any restrictions on the privately owned press was to
crack down on funding from abroad. This was another front in
Ethiopia's resistance to the West's 'governance' agenda. Rich governments and non-government aid agencies were increasing their
funding for activist 'civil society' organizations, and Ethiopia was
determined to counter it. 'No one can survive on the basis of their
income,' Meles said of the private newspapers. 'We believe they are
getting their funding from non-commercial sources, all of them.
These newspapers are funded from the same sources as the CSOs
[Ethiopian Civil Society Organizations whose fate we deal with in
the next chapter].'

I said that I had found Amare Aregawi to be an even-handed
and independent journalist and I asked the prime minister
whether he believed *The Reporter* was being funded in this way.

He replied, 'Funding is coming from external sources—some embassies, they are providing the funding.'

When I put the prime minister's allegation to Amare that he was taking foreign money to fund the paper, he positively bristled. 'On a factual basis, this is absolutely wrong. I will say it again and again, I will underline it and I will say it loud, that *The Reporter* has never, ever brought any help from any embassy. And we have never asked for it. Or any foreign source. What about that?' He then added for good measure, 'Not any foreign source, not any Ethiopian source, either.'

As denials go, that seemed pretty emphatic. And he was not quite finished. 'So from a factual point of view, this is wrong, and I am ashamed my prime minister's facts are like this. God save Ethiopia from other policies that depend on wrong facts.'

Beyond the technicalities and the sanctions of the press laws, life as a journalist in Ethiopia can be hazardous. Halfway through our first meeting, Amare began attending to his mobile phone. I paused. It turned out he was not checking his diary or his missed calls. He wanted to show me a picture of himself taken five months earlier. It showed his swollen and bloody face a few hours after he had been attacked in the street by two men armed with bricks. He had taken the photograph himself lying in his hospital bed.

Amare was picking up his children from school when he was assaulted. The attack came just after *The Reporter* had alleged government links with corrupt building contracts. His two assailants were in turn overwhelmed by parents and bystanders at the school gates. What would happen now? 'I never take the dogs to court, I take their owners,' he replied. 'Anything could have happened. The murders have started.'

Also in 2008 Amare was arrested and jailed after his paper reported cases of wrongful dismissal at a brewery with ruling party links in the old imperial city of Gondar. Management was so incensed by the stories that it arranged to have a policeman sent by company car to detain the editor in his Addis Ababa office 500 miles away. Amare was driven back to Gondar where he appeared in court, was refused bail, and let out after a week. He believed the police had been bribed to move against him and he was taking the case to the government's own Human Rights Commission. The chairman of the board, he reminded me, was Bereket Simon, the government's communications affairs minister.

When I met Bereket Simon for the first time, we discussed Ethiopia's progress towards eliminating hunger. 'Famine has become history in Ethiopia,' he said. It was certainly true that under the EPRDF the country had not suffered the mass death from starvation witnessed in 1984 when a brutal and beleaguered military regime presided over prolonged drought and an intense civil war. It was also the case that many in the rural areas were better off, with many farmers even very well off, compared to twenty-five years ago. As a one-time Marxist–Leninist, Bereket referred smilingly to how the government was creating a class of *kulaks*, the rich Russian peasants murdered in great numbers in the early years of the Soviet Union.

But has famine been eliminated? Here the minister staked a claim to Ethiopia's political transformation under the EPRDF. 'Famine is not a lack of food, it is a lack of good governance,' he said, adding a reference to the governments of Haile Selassie and the Derg: 'It is the lack of a receptive government. When your people are suffering it is irresponsible to hide famine. In an open democratic society, famine must be seen. There are droughts in Australia, the United States and the European Union, but there is no famine.'

Whatever Ethiopia's official claims to 'good governance', progress was certainly no settled matter in the eyes of the world or of many Ethiopians. Sympathetic observers viewed 'good governance' as a genuine aspiration being pursued by the government, the critics saw it as a semantic exercise to keep the aid-givers sweet. As for famine and 'good governance', we have still to examine the official record in the severe drought of 2008, but in making this connection Bereket Simon was endorsing a modern article of faith for the development community.

Bereket was making reference to the work of Amartya Sen, the distinguished Indian economist and winner of the 1998 Nobel Prize who is most popularly associated with studies into the relationship between democracy and famine. 'It is not surprising that no famine has ever taken place in the history of the world in a functioning democracy,' Sen wrote in *Development as Freedom*, adding: 'I would argue that a free press and an active political opposition constitute the best early warning system a country threatened by famine can have.'[1]

It was reasoning such as this which influenced a generation of western aid strategists to adopt a new approach to the challenges of hunger and poverty. In the hands of the big western donors, the approach became, to use their favoured expression, another 'aid conditionality'.

In my first interview with Meles Zenawi, we covered the government's protracted arguments with the aid-givers over the free market reforms that they expected Ethiopia to adopt and which Ethiopia on the whole resisted. This was the first of the 'aid conditionalities'. Seven weeks later I was back in the surreal quiet of the prime minister's secretariat. This time we started on

[1] Amartya Sen, *Development as Freedom* (Oxford University Press, 2001).

'governance'—the second 'conditionality'—which Meles regarded as another unwelcome neoliberal imposition. 'We believe that democracy, good governance and transparency and fighting corruption are good objectives for every country, particularly for developing countries,' he began.

> In the case of Ethiopia we go beyond that and say unless the country successfully democratizes, it will inevitably disintegrate . . . where we had our differences with the so-called neoliberal paradigm is first on the perception that this can be imposed from outside. We do not believe that is possible. . . . So this concept of the external environment imposing a certain set of governance rules is in our view impractical, and could be counter-productive . . . Internalization of accountability is central to democratization . . . the state has to be accountable to the citizens, and not some embassy or foreign actor.

What then of the argument that the eradication of poverty required better 'governance' and that Ethiopians would be much better off if 'governance' were more rigorously applied in tackling it? For a start, and however strong the evidence to the contrary, Meles simply did not accept that he was presiding over a period of harsh new restrictions. Then he gave me something of a tutorial on the 'developmental state', one of the themes of his thesis for the university in Rotterdam.

The most substantial excerpt posted on the Internet came from a chapter entitled 'Democracy, Developmental State and Development'. In it he first reviews the evidence for democracy getting in the way of development. There is the 'hustle of democracy', and the burden of government having 'to deal with democratic legitimisation of its rule'. Politicians are able to think no further than the next election. 'It is argued therefore that the developmental state will have to be undemocratic in order to stay in power long enough to carry out successful development.'

These concerns are not to be lightly dismissed, but there is a way round them, he writes. He points to the broad coalitions that kept stable democratic governments in power for long periods in Scandinavia and Japan, the 'so-called dominant party democracies'. Unsurprisingly, this is the option that Meles the politician appears to favour in his role as academic analyst. The rural population, he goes on, can be 'the solid base for a stable developmental coalition in a developing country'. There, too, analysis appears conveniently to fit in with political practicality in Ethiopia. 'The most likely scenario for a state that is both democratic and developmental to emerge is in the form of a dominant party or dominant coalition democracy.'

In the final paragraph of the excerpt, Meles adds a telling qualification. A democratic outcome is never guaranteed in the developing world, but in the right conditions 'there is a reasonable chance for a developmental and democratic state to emerge'.

Meles's quarrel with the big donors centred on their use of aid as a lever to propel the country along the democratic path at their pace, not his. They needed guarantees, timetables, and performance indicators. He had his academic studies to inform him, and he offered only 'a reasonable chance' of democracy. 'Some in the neoliberal world seem to believe that economic development and growth and good governance and democratization are inseparable,' he said.

> That is not validated by historical facts. Theoretically, there is no reason to believe that democratization is a precondition of economic development. The reverse—that democratization can be the result of a certain level of economic development—appears to

be more robust than the other way round, but even that in our view is not a proven fact. Germany was the most advanced economy in Europe prior to the Second World War. It never had much success in democratization—a brief interlude in the Weimar Republic, and even that was a very problematic period.

As in the case of the 'first conditionality' relating to free market reforms, Meles said that Ethiopia had paid a price for not subscribing to the donors' 'governance' agenda.

They have been quite frank with us, and we have been quite frank with them and in the end we came to an understanding—we get less aid, but we get more space. They get more delivery with less money.... Nevertheless the fact remains that we are to some extent externally accountable. There is some level of externalization of accountability, even here in Ethiopia. It comes with the territory.

He gave as an example relations between government and opposition in the violent aftermath of the disputed 2005 elections. Meles argued that such disputes in Europe would be addressed by the parties themselves or taken to court. 'That is not what happens in Ethiopia,' he said. 'If we have disagreements, sometimes the embassies know of them before some of us have become aware that there are these disagreements.' Yet the government did itself on occasions seek the donors' intervention to try and resolve such differences, and Meles saw that as 'a very clear indication of the externalization of accountability. That retards the maturation process of the institutions of democratic governance in Ethiopia.'

The fault line in this argument, surely, lay in the idea that political dialogue or court processes offered the opposition any prospect of redress when scores of their supporters had been shot dead and when their leadership had been thrown into jail facing charges of genocide.

In circumstances wholly transformed from the 2005 polls, the build-up began to the next national elections of 2010. The opposition leadership had emerged into the daylight in July 2007, but key figures left soon afterwards for North America and Europe. The party at home was splintered, dispersed, and disorganized. Elected members who decided to take up their seats split apart again once they got into parliament. The main faction stuck to its boycott, but lost its 'V' sign election symbol and even the right to call itself the Coalition for Unity and Democracy.

One opposition leader alone enhanced her stature in this period, and did so from solitary confinement in prison. She was Birtukan Mideksa, a lawyer and judge still in her thirties. She too had travelled abroad after being released, and in the course of a public meeting in Sweden spoke of the deal involving a signed acknowledgement of guilt in exchange for a pardon which had led to her release. It was not clear whether she questioned the legality of the arrangement or was merely scornful of the political fix that it surely was. Either way, the government was furious with her for discussing the deal and, when she returned home, demanded she retract the statement. She refused and her pardon was revoked.

Birtukan, leader by now of the most prominent opposition group in the country, was arrested in December 2008 after a meeting with the Ethiopian church minister who was trying to restore peace between government and opposition. She had been begged to reiterate her original appeal for clemency, but was having none of it. There were scuffles outside the intermediary's office and it was then that a security man cracked the elderly and redoubtable figure of Professor Mesfin Wolde-Mariam with his rifle butt. Birtukan herself was driven off to resume her life sentence.

The defence offered by the prime minister for her re-arrest was first of all legalistic—since she would not stand by the terms of her pardon, she had to resume her sentence—but he also presented it as a demonstration that Ethiopia would not respond to outside interventions in its affairs. 'If we were to succumb to external pressure and release her, we would simply be re-affirming her understanding of how politics is played here, "Never mind the law of the land, if you have the right constituency abroad, if you are a real big wig with big wig friends capable of making a lot of noise, you can get away with murder."'

In the months afterwards, Birtukan became a focus for national and international opposition to the government. The prime minister had certainly made his point, but at further cost to his claims to be building democracy in Ethiopia. In the traditional Ethiopian manner, the government would give no quarter to its enemies. The government's own Human Rights Commission was specifically banned from investigating her case.

Whenever he referred to her, Meles displayed the same icy courtesy that he showed towards Ana Gomes, the EU election observer and another woman who had dared to take him on. Here perhaps was the evidence that Birtukan had got under his skin and threatened smooth progress towards the election. Not once during our exchanges did he refer to her by name. 'My starting point is that this lady is not an idiot,' was how he began and then acknowledged her throughout as 'this lady' and once as 'this intelligent young lady'.

Like the female figure facing the hangman on the masthead of *The Reporter*, Birtukan came to symbolize the trampled political opposition at home. For weeks on end in early 2009 her Unity for Democracy and Justice party tried to stage a demonstration in protest at her imprisonment. They appeared to have Article 30 of

Ethiopia's constitution 'The Right of Assembly, Demonstration and Petition' on their side. Dates were provided, permission was sought, and for weeks on end it was denied. 'Planned public protest impossible: Government,' said the headline on a story explaining that a demonstration could not occur because Birtukan's case had already been dealt with by the courts.

Since I could not see the party leader, I fixed an appointment with her deputy Dr Hailu Araya, a linguistics lecturer once sacked by the government from his university job and also jailed in the post-election crackdown. We met at a terrace café in the middle of Addis Ababa where a comically inept eavesdropper listened to every word we said. The eavesdropper wore a beard, wire spectacles, and a baggy brown suit. Clamped to one ear was a mobile phone which was not turned on. At one point he leant so far back to catch what we were saying that he could easily have joined in the conversation. Dr Hailu turned to stare at him. 'This happens all the time,' he said.

Dr Hailu took me through the splits and divisions which had added to the opposition's woes after months of assault from the government. There was a key difference between the groups. Dr Hailu, Prof. Mesfin, Birtukan Mideksa, and other prominent members of the opposition still in the country but not in parliament were committed to the peaceful conduct of politics. Some outside the country were not, and Ethiopian history was not necessarily on Dr Hailu's side.

When I met Dr Berhanu Nega as he travelled Europe on his mission to promote the opposition in exile, he rejected any idea that his place was back in Ethiopia with suitably American emphasis. 'The so-called legal opposition which is inside, my former friends, we know and they know they can't achieve shit—literally. If you're inside you can only play by their rules. There is no other way of playing. They cannot meet in [public] halls. They have to have ID cards to demonstrate. That's a complete joke, and they know it. So the real political struggle is no more in Ethiopia. If it is, it is clandestine, it is underground, and that's what we are doing.'

At the terrace café in Addis Ababa, Dr Hailu was pained and regretful in his response. 'We say No—only a peaceful struggle will bring a lasting solution to our problems. It may take time. We have seen armed struggles in the past and the consequences, and we are determined to break that cycle. We and I cannot accept a repeat of what we saw before—an educated generation was wiped out!' said the former university teacher.

But he was not optimistic. 'After the elections [of 2010] people like me who believe in peaceful means will be reduced. The dark clouds are gathering and the rains will come down.'

Chapter 10
Free Association

'The foot soldiers of neoliberalism.'

The road out of Shashemene, in southern Ethiopia, takes you down a slight incline and across a kilometre or so of low-lying ground before climbing again and continuing westwards. On most journeys the only thing you notice is the nondescript roadside village you pass through in the dip. Nothing appeared different on this occasion until the vehicle slowed.

There was mud on the road and standing water by the side of it. Villagers had brought their possessions from wattle and daub houses to dry out, and milled around with the aimlessness which comes with shock. 'There was flooding here,' said my companion, and I remembered the BBC World weather before I left Addis Ababa with its reference to 'just a few showers across Ethiopia, mainly in the North,' as if the weatherman was talking about the English Home Counties. We stopped.

'When it rains it pours' applies in Ethiopia with damaging consequences. The deluge had come thirty-six hours earlier and flood waters had coursed through the village undermining some of the mud houses and drowning twenty to thirty livestock. It was a small disaster for one small community, and in my focused western fashion I rather wanted to press on with the afternoon's programme of visits to development projects. My companions from a local community organization showed more humanity.

We got out of the vehicle and were surrounded by clamorous villagers. A bench was found for us and an instant village meeting was convened under an old acacia tree. Angry speeches were made about all the village's woes—the most eloquent and tearful from the chair of the women's association who stood in front of us with an armful of muddy files and folders—and it seemed that my friends from Community Development Initiative were getting the blame for the indifference of local council officers.

The community workers promised they would return to the village the next day with officials in tow and we resumed our journey after a forty-five-minute delay. Only later did I feel ashamed of my impatience. My companions had done what community workers should do, and had sensibly ignored the journalist's timetable.

Community Development Initiative is funded by Oxfam America. It is a small civil society organization (CSO), also known as a non-government organization (NGO). Once they were all called charities. Oxfam America spent around $10 million in Ethiopia in 2009, and works exclusively through CSOs. Oxfam GB spent a similar sum (£4.6 million) and is operational itself in water and sanitation projects as well as also working through a score of local partners.

This whole sector of charitable endeavour in Ethiopia, national and international, was pitched into crisis in the course of 2008 by the determination of the Ethiopian government to run its own affairs.

Anyone who doubts the extent of the boom in the modern aid business should consider figures produced for Ethiopia's Christian Relief and Development Association. The CRDA was formed in 1973 as an umbrella organization for the dozen or so international charities active during the famine that year. Research at the time of the 1984 famine found that when that emergency began there were still fewer than twenty foreign NGOs in the country. By the end of 1985 there were more than sixty.[1] The imperial government and the military regime of Colonel Mengistu needed, and just about tolerated, international charities, but neither government allowed independent local organizations to operate. That changed with the arrival of the EPRDF.

According to the CRDA-commissioned research, there were forty-six foreign and twenty-four Ethiopian NGOs in 1994, three years after the overthrow of the Derg.[2] By 2007 there had been a fivefold increase in international charities to 234 and an extraordinary seventy-fold increase in Ethiopian NGOs to 1,742. This last figure was likely to be a major underestimate because it took account only of NGOs registered centrally, not those registered in the provinces. 'It is thus safe to suggest that there are close to 3,000 CSOs/NGOs working throughout the country,' the paper said. Estimates in 2009 put the figure even higher at 4,700 NGOs, an almost 200-fold increase in fifteen years.

What was additionally remarkable about the growth of the charity sector in Ethiopia, as in the rest of Sub-Saharan Africa, was its economic muscle. It comfortably outperformed all the country's other foreign exchange earners with the single exception

[1] Peter V. Cutler, 'The Development of the 1983–5 Famine in Northern Ethiopia', Ph.D. thesis, London School of Hygiene and Tropical Medicine, 1988.
[2] Dessalegn Rahmato, Akalewold Bantirgu, and Yoseph Endeshaw, 'CSOs/NGOs in Ethiopia', Ad Hoc CSO/NGO Task Force, CRDA, Addis Ababa, 2008.

of cash transfers from Ethiopians living abroad. In 2006–7 international NGOs brought in $537 million in foreign exchange, $100 million more than coffee, which is Ethiopia's largest export earner, and $160 million more than the next three export commodities combined. The report said that investment from NGOs was now 'equivalent to 25% of the government's annual budget'.

There was then the matter of how the money was spent. Along with their phenomenal growth came a change of focus for both international and local NGOs. 'The establishment and active engagement of organisations concerned with governance, human rights and advocacy', said the CRDA report, 'is a result of liberalization of the enabling environment since the fall of the Derg.' The international charity movement was implementing the West's current commitment to 'good governance' and better human rights as the means finally to pick the lock of extreme poverty.

The extraordinary growth of Ethiopian NGOs, with most of them adopting a 'rights-based' approach to development, mirrored that of the big international charities in the aid boom. The two big British charities at the centre of the famine of 1984 were Oxfam and Save the Children. They then commanded a similar annual income (£19 million for SCF and £24 million for Oxfam) and after TV galvanized public generosity towards Ethiopia they doubled it (£45 million in the case of SCF, £51 million for Oxfam). They were evenly matched at the time and decorous rivals. 'It was a bit competitive, like a husband and wife in a marriage,' said Tony Vaux, a senior member of Oxfam's disasters team. 'In fact it turned into exactly that on several occasions.'

Since then the charities have grown steadily weightier, but they have also grown apart. There is now a marked income disparity between the two (Oxfam's £300 million in 2008 compared with

SCF's £160 million), with the difference attributed by SCF to Oxfam's shops expansion in the 1990s and such pioneering fund-raising initiatives as monthly giving. But the biggest difference between them lay in Oxfam's political stance—a growing emphasis on political campaigning in the development field and an intimate relationship with the government of the day.

Oxfam had long been close to Labour. Frank Judd, later Lord Judd, was minister for overseas development in the Labour government of the 1970s. For six years from the mid-1980s he was Director of Oxfam. After New Labour came to power in 1997, proximity became something of a revolving door. At a technical level, the new Department for International Development recruited Oxfam staff to work in areas such as conflict and humanitarian aid. At a political and official level, Oxfam's influence in the corridors of power grew enormously.

Justin Forsyth, Oxfam's director of policy, was recruited by Blair to mastermind Downing Street's approach to Africa and did the same job for Gordon Brown. His immediate Oxfam predecessor as policy director, Dianna Melrose, went on to the Foreign Office and DFID, and later became British Ambassador in Cuba. When Forsyth was promoted to become director of strategic communications in Downing Street, his job as Africa adviser was taken by Brendan Cox, also formerly at Oxfam. At DFID, both the head of communications and the special adviser to Douglas Alexander, the secretary of state, were in 2009 former Oxfam members of staff.

The intimacy between Oxfam and the Labour government was defended on both sides. It had contributed to Britain's strong leadership in the struggle against global poverty, exemplified by the trebling of the UK's foreign aid budget in a decade. This was British 'soft power' at work. Tony Blair had watched the original

Live Aid concert in 1985, and the Live Aid generation was now in power. There was the Blair commission for Africa and the orchestrated pressure on G8 leaders to sign up to African priorities at the Gleneagles summit in 2005. An impressive national consensus was built in Britain around the merits of aid which after decades of scepticism was endorsed by the Conservative party of David Cameron. When Cameron launched his party's plans for development in 2009, however, he chose to do so not at Oxfam, but in the offices of Save the Children.

Oxfam's dramatic growth over the years had been in part the result of direct government funding. When I first wrote about the charity, it was to study its work in the 1960s, the first 'development decade' of half a century ago.[3] At that time, Oxfam took no money at all from government and I made my calculations on the basis of private donations (very large), Christmas cards (modest), and legacies and covenants (sizeable). I recall the amazement of African politicians when I told them how much Oxfam collected through shaking tins in pubs and workplaces and on street corners.

In 2007/8 Oxfam's 'total charitable expenditure' amounted to £145 million to which the British government contributed £18 million and the European Union £20 million—one quarter of the total. With funding from other governments taken into account, Oxfam relied for a third of its charitable expenditure on official sources.

Internal limits on permissible levels of government funding 'to protect independence from undue donor interference in its programme' have been relaxed over the years. A change in 2005 enabled the charity to accept up to 20 per cent rather than 10 per cent of its charitable expenditure from a single official source.

---

[3] Peter Gill, *Drops in the Ocean* (Macdonald Unit 75, 1970).

That was later changed back again, although significant areas of British official funding were now left out of account. At the same time some Oxfam staff chafed at the restrictions imposed by government funding and complained that their freedom of action had been compromised.

There were differences within Oxfam's international network, as there are throughout the Third World charity movement, as to which government funds are acceptable and which are not. Official funding from the United States government is predictably controversial, and many charities will not take it. Oxfam GB accepts money from USAID, but imposes a finely calculated upper limit of 20 per cent of Oxfam America's annual income. Oxfam America itself, however, refuses to accept any money at all from its own government. It raised $73 million in 2008, but received nothing from any official source.

Tony Vaux, an Oxfam staff member for more than twenty years, complained that the British charity had adopted a progressively more corporate approach through the 1990s which had snuffed out the individualism of earlier decades. He spoke of branded T-shirts and baseball caps and the need to follow the party line. In Third World emergencies he said that headquarters' media specialists would be sent out from Oxford to take over from experienced field directors for the TV cameras.

'Up to the point when New Labour came in, the aid agencies were seen to be almost the natural critics of government,' said Tony Vaux. 'From 1997 onwards they became their natural allies. Oxfam and New Labour were singing from the same hymn sheet. It seemed to me that Oxfam was endorsing New Labour.'

There was also unease over Oxfam's ubiquitous role as a leading international campaigner for development. Criticism could be anticipated from Rony Brauman, for twelve years the president of Médecins Sans Frontières, an organization still focused on medical emergencies and depending very little indeed on official money from any source. 'Oxfam has a very wide portfolio,' Brauman said. 'It's a multi-mandated world shadow cabinet, giving opinions on how many cocoa beans in commercial chocolate, the land reform issue, European agricultural policy—incredible!'

Within Oxfam itself I was told that there was a danger that the organization was becoming too much of a 'Think Tank' and that many of its campaigning and policy papers owed more to research at home in Oxford than experience in the field. 'Our spin is very good,' said one senior member of staff, 'but there is a serious risk that we will expose ourselves.'

It was the campaigning role of the charities within developing countries which began to court controversy, and it was the Ethiopian authorities which offered serious resistance. A backlash had begun against the West's 'governance' agenda, described by one scholar as 'the latest philosopher's stone of official aid agencies'.[4] Ethiopia's response to the use of official aid as a means of promoting 'governance' was described in the last chapter. The proliferation of non-government organizations represented a far greater political threat to the government—'the opposition in disguise,' as Prime Minister Meles had described them. Most of these organizations were funded by international agencies to pursue a 'rights-based' approach to development, and for the EPRDF that amounted to political interference.

The measure which passed through the Ethiopian parliament in 2008 is called the 'Charities and Societies Proclamation', and I queued up at the government stationery office in Addis Ababa

---

[4] Roger C. Riddell in *Does Foreign Aid Really Work?* (Oxford University Press, 2007).

after it was promulgated in 2009 to acquire a copy. It cost a pound. Among its provisions, the measure restricts the amount which charities can spend on administration to 30 per cent of the budget, a limit that many would find reasonable. The real challenges, however, came in the act's definition of an Ethiopian charity—one that acquired no more than 10 per cent of its funds from foreign sources—and the provision that only an Ethiopian charity could take part in activities such as 'the advancement of human and democratic rights' and 'the promotion of the rights of the disabled and children's rights'. In just a few phrases, the government had struck at the foundations of the modern aid movement whose objective was to 'empower' the poor, not just to help them. Even the law's sharpest critics accepted that it was an innovative and sophisticated piece of work.

Official justifications for the crackdown on NGOs ranged from the highly analytical to the highly political. One member of the EPRDF politburo, himself the head of a respected semi-official development agency, described foreign charities to me as 'the foot soldiers of neoliberalism'. In this account, western powers had sought to control developing countries through the use of aid and the imposition of 'conditionalities'. They had failed in their efforts to impose free market reforms on Ethiopia, but they were trying again to exercise control through demands for 'good governance' and human rights reforms. One study of the case for the new law referred to official suspicions that the international charities were 'working through local CSOs to foment unrest, and, ultimately, regime change'.[5]

At a more popular level in Ethiopia, the western charities and the organizations they fund in the field are not always seen as they

---

[5] Sue Lautze, Angela Raven-Roberts, and Teshome Erkineh, 'Humanitarian Governance in the New Millennium: An Ethiopian Case Study', Overseas Development Institute, 2009.

are at home—incontrovertibly the 'good guys'. This has less to do with all the four-wheel drive vehicles and their big foreign agency logos than with suspicions of corruption within local NGOs. 'You ask Mr X what he does, and he says he owns his own NGO,' said Tamrat Giorghis, managing editor of *Fortune* newspaper in Addis Ababa. 'The barber shuts up shop one day, and goes off to form his own NGO. There are lots of clever students in school and all they want to do is to get into an NGO—either that or an embassy job or the UN.'

As a newspaper editor, Tamrat had been struck by the contrast in the international response to the charities bill and the press regulation bill which the government had brought forward at about the same time. 'Both were controversial, but the media bill didn't have Congressmen writing letters to the Ethiopian prime minister, or have all the western ambassadors lining up or the European Union sending in its commissioner to protest. There were no initiatives, no interest or support for a free press. Surely freedom of expression is fundamental. The West gave its attention to something that wasn't fundamental. The NGOs are financed by the West and they're subservient to the West.'

Tamrat argued that the real issue was NGO accountability, a point that Prime Minister Meles was to amplify. Were the charities accountable to the Ethiopians they were seeking to help or were they accountable to their foreign funders? 'At no point did the NGOs enter into that debate. There was no public debate at all. There are some good people in the NGOs, but this issue was simply not addressed.'

It was those 'good people' of the local NGO movement whom I interviewed at length and with whom I travelled in the countryside. For them, the charities law was a disaster. In a country where government regulations are often harshly enforced, there was no option but to try and work within the new law—or close down. Wherever I went, I encountered community organizations having to rewrite their articles of association to expunge references to people's rights and stress instead their commitment to 'service delivery', the acceptable development phrase for material help. The pressure appeared most acute in areas of the South which did not have the advantage of the big well-connected development organizations operating in the North. These regions are critically dependent on community-level organizations and their international backers to provide basic services, certainly, but also to fight for people's rights.

The Rift Valley Children and Women Development Association is a case in point. This was the organization, supported by Oxfam America and others, which had brought primary education to pastoralists by setting up schools that accommodated their lifestyle rather than demanding that they fit in with a conventional school timetable. 'We were illiterate and we watched other communities being able to help their families,' said Mamiru Hayato, chairman of the local parent–teacher association. 'We didn't want to watch others. We wanted a school ourselves. The problem of illiteracy should not continue for another generation.'

The association grew from a modest Ethiopian church initiative running summer literacy camps for pastoralist children to become the big provider of informal education it is today. Its director Berhanu Geleto described to me how they had to fight every step of the way with local and national education bureaucrats. 'We don't accept this, this is not legal,' they kept telling him. 'We need to supervise everything.'

Berhanu and his colleagues persisted and won. When he began seeking foreign funds for his work in 1994, the Rift Valley association was teaching 160 children at one centre. Fifteen years later there were more than 12,000 children in 62 centres, and Ethiopia's progress towards the Millennium Development Goal of universal primary education was being credited in large measure to such initiatives. One of the government's own surveys concluded that children educated under trees did better in some subjects than those in the formal sector.

The new charities law had severe implications for the Rift Valley association, and its director declared himself to be 'one hundred per cent worried about it'. His organization did indeed deliver a service, which the government would continue to welcome, but his task was now to complement not to pressurize government, an approach which Berhanu rejected. 'My organization does not exist just to fill gaps, but because people have rights.'

In the shade of the acacia tree where one of the very first schools opened, the chairman of its parent–teacher association and father of many children endorsed Berhanu's point. 'There is prejudice against nomads, against pastoralists,' said Mamiru, 'but that is no reason not to provide us with education. People have a right to education, and you have to work with people's lifestyle.'

And what would happen if a community organization such as the Rift Valley association was to take up an issue such as the abuse of children? What of campaigns against those dreadful 'traditional' practices which impact worst of all on girls? They include female circumcision ('female genital mutilation' is the approved term) which is widespread in Ethiopia. Local charities dependent on foreign funds are specifically prohibited in the new act from promoting children's rights. 'I think the law has forced us to lose hope as a citizen,' said Berhanu.

Beyond the sophisticated legal draughtsmanship, there is concern that the new law could be used as cover by ruling party 'cadres' to hinder independence of action and to harass those who promote it. 'If you are an Oromo and an activist, you will be accused of being OLF,' said Berhanu in reference to the Oromo Liberation Front which is engaged in one of Ethiopia's regional revolts. In his career as a community organizer, this mild-mannered man told me he had been regularly accused of being 'aligned' with the OLF; had once been advised to leave the country; and in 2004 was imprisoned for ten days for running 'a cell working against the government'.

Many community-based organizations can try and remain within the law by concentrating on their role as 'service providers'. This will not be an option for organizations such as the Ethiopian Human Rights Council founded after the fall of the Derg in 1991. The council's only purpose has been the advancement of human and democratic rights—a task specifically reserved under the new law for Ethiopian-funded charities—and it has relied on European and North American funds for 95 per cent of its $400,000 annual income.

In the words of Yoseph Mulugeta, its general secretary, the human rights council will have 'to adapt or close'. When I met him, he was struggling with an 'adaptation strategy' involving the drastic cutting back of its activities, the closing of almost all its branches, and the sacking of most of its staff. It would have to keep going on the income of its 1,000 fee-paying members.

From the beginning there was no love lost between the human rights council and the EPRDF. The government refused to receive its reports, let alone respond to them; it froze the council's bank account and sometimes detained its members. Pressure intensified in the violent aftermath to the 2005 elections. Several of the council's investigators were picked up after the June violence, and after the November violence there were formal arrest warrants issued. One of those wanted was abroad and stayed there. Two of them fled into exile. 'In total we lost four investigating team members, and that really was a huge blow to the investigation capacity we had,' said Yoseph. 'They had huge experience.'

Yoseph Mulugeta is a serious-minded young man with law degrees from Addis Ababa and Pretoria, South Africa. Before taking charge of the council, he worked as a human rights officer for the British embassy and the European Union. For all his experiences, including the possible closure of the council he runs, I did not expect the measured eloquence of his assessment of the EPRDF. 'Nobody in their sane minds would want to challenge the achievements of the EPRDF on the rural front,' he said, 'but the promotion of human rights and rural development are not mutually exclusive. They can go hand in hand. What is development without people having their rights recognized, without the opportunity to assess those rights and ask questions about the way they are governed? It is not just food we are hungry for.'

It was the 2005 election which had again proved pivotal in assessing Ethiopia's domestic political evolution. If civil society was 'the opposition in disguise', then its activities would simply be reined in. One of the country's foremost academics saw the connection as cause and effect. Dr Dessalegn Rahmato feared that the Forum for Social Studies which he had founded would have to close because it could not receive foreign money to promote independent social science research. I have already referred to Dr Dessalegn's important work at the time of the 1984 famine, including his experience of the Derg's resettlement programme, and have quoted his 2008 study on the growth and importance of the NGO movement in Ethiopia.

This is how Dr Dessalegn characterized the genesis of the 2009 charities act:

> The government was very angry in 2005 and they blamed (wrongly in my view) civil society organizations for playing a role in the elections. There is no evidence at all of this. Civil society organizations did not go round telling people how to vote. There were a small number of voter registration organizations, but they were accredited by the National Election Board. Government had a grudge because they felt it was all the doing of civil society. Government always wants a scapegoat when something bad happens. They don't say 'we weren't open.' They always say it was someone else. Civil society was a convenient scapegoat.

My efforts to understand the government's case began, not at all promisingly, with the minister of justice, Berhan Hailu. We met at the ministry where he assured me that their own data showed that fewer than 3 per cent of NGOs would be affected by the legislation and that they could easily shift from a concern for people's rights to 'where we do believe there is a great gap—in service delivery for the disabled, service delivery for the children, service delivery for the youth and for the others. That is open to them.'

When I asked him what were the worst examples of NGO misbehaviour, we were back to the 2005 elections. The following exchange then took place, which I have substantially abbreviated.

Minister: 'They were funding political parties.'

PG: 'Who was?'

Minister: 'I couldn't tell you.'

PG: 'Do you have the evidence?'

Minister: 'Yes, a lot of evidence regarding this. Why don't you talk to the opposition parties in Parliament? They are not afraid to tell you they were supported by civil society in the last election.'

PG: 'Which party, the CUD?'

Minister: 'The CUD, and many others. When we had public hearings on the civil society law, they were openly telling the audience about the support they had got from civil society.'

PG: 'Can you name a single opposition official?'

Minister: 'Jima [a senior ministry official] can tell you the name of the guy who was talking on this issue during the public hearings. They were openly telling the audience that they had been receiving funding from civil societies.'

PG: 'Who do you mean? The International NGOs? Oxfam, Save the Children, the EU?'

Minister: 'He didn't specify.'

PG: 'What was the name of the opposition official?'

Minister: 'I'm told it was the CUD.'

PG: 'Which official?'

Minister: 'I don't remember his name.'

Jima Dilbo is a senior official in the attorney general's office with responsibility for registering NGOs and CSOs. I was taken to his office, and the scale of the bureaucratic problem faced by the government became clear. As the charity sector boomed and organizations proliferated, the unit in charge of them remained almost entirely in the pre-computer age. Jima had a small clerical staff which kept the register up to date by hand. The government thought it knew how many national and international charities there were in the country and could break the figure down between, say, adoption agencies and development organizations. But that was about it.

'We receive annual activity reports and we attach them to the file,' Jima said. 'We have no way of assuring ourselves what they are doing, whether they are operating entirely in line with government development policy and where the money is coming from. This is the real problem we have.' A powerful new charities agency would change that. 'It must be staffed by professionals and it will need a big budget,' said Jima, adding that western aid-givers had so far shown no interest in helping with the administration of the charity sector.

It turned out that the minister was not correct in saying that an opposition party had admitted taking foreign funds during the election. Jima believed that a member of an Oromo opposition group had in fact claimed that Ethiopia as a country would lose money from abroad as a result of the new charity law. A rather different matter, and certainly true.

The brains behind the new legislation, the prime minister himself, began his defence of the measure with some post-colonial history. 'These NGOs were initially seen as an antidote to what was said to be the main problem in Africa—the bloated state. This was supposed to be an alternative. You reduce the role of the state, including your social services, and you encourage NGOs to provide as much of the public services as possible.

'In the end we argue that the NGOs have turned out to be alternative networks of patronage. The smaller state in Africa has not ceased to be a network of patronage. It has become a smaller network of patronage. NGOs have not provided an alternative good governance network. They have become alternative networks of patronage.'

After that account of Africa in the development era, Meles returned to his theme of accountability. The West's 'governance' agenda and the use of aid to pursue it, sometimes as a condition of funding, had had the effect of reducing, not enhancing local accountability. Real accountability lay in Ethiopian institutions, not with foreign actors.

In the case of foreign-funded civil society organizations, their 'leadership is accountable to whoever is providing the money, not to the membership. The membership are beneficiaries, so whoever can write a proper report or whoever has the connection with sources of funding effectively becomes the leader of some civil society organization, irrespective of the acceptability to the membership of the leadership. The leadership is seen to be delivering goods and are the benefactors of the membership. What you have is a quasi-feudal relationship of inequality in the membership and that cannot be a democratic relationship.'

One flaw in this argument lay, once again, in the disputed elections and the impact they have on a government's accountability to its people. For all the EPRDF's intolerance of dissent, however, the Meles thesis finds significant support among western academics. In the fast-growing field of humanitarian studies, there is surprisingly little comfort to be found for the international NGO movement.

In essays published under the title *Humanitarianism in Question*, Professor Janice Gross Stein of Toronto University observed, 'A discussion of accountability has not been easier within the humanitarian community than a conversation about power... There is almost a sense of moral outrage among some humanitarians when the subject is raised.'[6] The editor of these studies, Professor Michael Barnett of the University of Minnesota, linked charitable aid agencies to western governments and continued, 'As aid agencies allied themselves with states and

---

[6] Michael Barnett and Thomas G. Weiss (eds.), *Humanitarianism in Question* (Cornell University Press, 2008).

donors, they made compromises that slowly corroded their core values and beliefs.' Prof. Barnett then quoted the alarming call to arms issued by Colin Powell, US secretary of state at the time of the US attacks on Afghanistan in October 2001, who told a conference of NGO leaders, 'Just as surely as our diplomats and military, American NGOs are out there serving and sacrificing on the frontline of freedom. NGOs are such a force multiplier for us, such an important part of our combat team.'

Closer to home, Professor Mark Duffield, once an Oxfam field director in the Horn of Africa and already quoted in this book, has written of the 'petty sovereign power that NGOs had asserted among the world of people' which he described as being 'part of the strategic designs and policy preferences of effective western states'.[7] When I interviewed him at Bristol University, he spoke of aid being 'the biggest industry in the world, an industry of people getting paid to help others'. No figures were available, he said, but in countries such as Ethiopia and Sudan he believed aid agencies were the biggest employers outside the capital cities.

Yet the 'aid industry' remained invisible. Prof. Duffield said he was not talking in terms of 'plots' to account for the growth of NGO power, but since the Ethiopian famine of 1984 there had been 'end to end emergencies' and the level of employment in aid agencies had gone up and up. As in the famous observation about the British Empire, Duffield said, this humanitarian trusteeship over poor people in the developing world had been acquired in a fit of absent mindedness.

There is some concern within the agencies themselves on the issue of NGO accountability. Marc Dubois, head of Médecins Sans Frontières in Britain, told me flatly that aid was 'the one

---

[7] Mark Duffield, *Development, Security and Unending War* (Polity Press, 2007).

business where the customers don't have any influence at all'. Beverley Jones, former head of the Catholic development agency CAFOD in Ethiopia, told a civil society conference in The Hague, 'Some staff within national NGOs are becoming more reflective about the legitimacy of NGOs to hold Government to account when they are not yet modelling exemplary accountability in their own delivery of services to communities.'[8]

A final part of the defence offered by Prime Minister Meles for the charities law was the evolutionary argument. He had made the same point about the West's commitment to spreading—and sometimes imposing—democracy. After taking me through a century of British history from the Great Reform Act to votes for women, Meles said of Ethiopia, 'We started with the whole cloth of universal suffrage, so the evolution of democracy here has to be one of quality rather than quantity.'

He broadened his point in his references to the growth of non-governmental organizations. 'In the developed countries, civil society organizations developed organically, and were not financed from abroad. Even now the practice in all these developed countries is to prevent foreign funding of any activities that are political. Actually the US is the largest source of voluntary giving by individuals, and is unlikely to be inundated by money coming from Ethiopia, Somalia and Chad and so on.'

Restrictions on charitable funding from abroad are rarely applied in the rich world and would be redundant in practice. Certainly there is no such ban in Britain, although the interpretation of charity law towards political campaigning has changed markedly over the years. In the early 1990s, for instance, the

[8] Beverley Jones, 'Leading Civil Society up the Governance Path', INTRAC, The Hague, December 2008.

Charity Commission took the view that Oxfam's campaign for sanctions against apartheid South Africa was 'inconsistent with its charity status' and the references had to be dropped. Back in the 1960s the commission had even questioned whether it was strictly charitable for Oxfam to deliver 'development aid' and whether it should not confine itself to relief and welfare.[9]

Ethiopia's challenge to western NGOs followed in the footsteps of government crackdowns elsewhere in the world. A range of restrictions on NGO activities had been imposed in Russia, several of the former Soviet republics, and in the Middle East. Very few countries in Sub-Saharan Africa, heavily dependent as they are on official and charitable aid from the West, have made any such move, but several were paying close attention to the Ethiopian initiative.

[9] Maggie Black, *A Cause for Our Times* (Oxfam, 1992).

Chapter 11
Pastoral Affairs

'Since we are Moslems, we have to believe in God and that life will get better.'

Western journalists are not especially welcome in the Somali Region of Ethiopia, but I was a guest of the government. My visit was arranged by the minister for communications in Addis Ababa, and I was received by senior officials in the region. I was driven everywhere in government vehicles, and interpretation was provided by my hosts. The arrangement was not ideal, but it suited me well enough. I had not expected in three days to understand the intricacies of Somali clan politics or meet rebels of the Ogaden National Liberation Front (ONLF) who are conducting Ethiopia's most serious revolt. My interest lay in seeing something of one of the world's worst—and least reported—humanitarian emergencies.

The early morning flight brought me first to Dire Dawa and then over grey fields waiting for rain to Jijiga, the Somali regional capital. There, for the much of the day, I sat in comfortable isolation in the government guest house while senior regional officials presented themselves for interview. The next morning I flew on over this vast territory as smudges of green gave way to yellowing, featureless scrub. My destination was Gode, another important stop on Ethiopia's famine trail.

In the year 2000 there was a great hunger in Somali Region as there was to be again later in the decade. A research team from Save the Children Fund USA, backed by UNICEF and the US Centers for Disease Control and Prevention, did an unusually thorough job of investigating it. No such thing was to happen later in the decade. The team looked at 'excess mortality' in Gode district—that is, they surveyed the difference between the expected number of deaths and the number dying during the emergency—and concluded there had been more than 6,000 'excess deaths' in the district in the first eight months of 2000.[1]

'Excess mortality' for Gode district was then extrapolated for Gode zone (there are nine zones in Somali Region) and the conclusion reached that 20,000 may have died in the emergency. The researchers did not stop there. Extrapolated further to the five worst affected zones, it was said that around 100,000 may have died. By any reckoning this was a famine. The suffering was immense and it served as an evil portent for the new century.

Ethiopia was at war with its northern neighbour Eritrea in the build-up to the southern famine, and there is little doubt that the government in Addis Ababa failed its Somali citizens dismally during the crisis. Indifference to the human suffering was compounded by the distrust or worse of many northern officials for their Somali compatriots. A number of western academic

---

[1] Peter Salama et al., 'Malnutrition, Measles, Mortality and the Humanitarian Response During a Famine in Ethiopia', *Journal of the American Medical Association* (August 2001).

commentaries, however, concentrated their fire on another aspect of a negligence that kills—that of the aid donors.

The conflict between Ethiopia and Eritrea from 1998 to 2000 cost tens of thousands of lives, and was likened by outsiders to two bald men scrapping over a comb. Without showing too much interest in the rights and wrongs of the war, the aid-givers simply disapproved and wanted it stopped. Britain's Department for International Development, by then emerging as politically the most influential of government donors, led other European agencies in freezing development aid to Ethiopia. 'I do not believe that anyone in the UK believes we should be providing long-term assistance to a country which is increasing its spending on arms year on year,' said Clare Short, the secretary of state.[2] Prime Minister Meles Zenawi countered: 'In Ethiopia, we do not wait to have a full tummy to protect our sovereignty.'[3]

As in the West's shocking response to the Ethiopian famine in 1984–5, governments sought to draw a distinction between development aid (apparently subject to donor policy preferences) and humanitarian assistance which should never be denied. As in the 1980s, the distinction did not really wash. In the Mengistu era, the West punished the starving for being ruled by Cold War communists. During the Ethiopia–Eritrea conflict, hungry Somalis suffered because their government had chosen to go to war on a distant northern frontier.

Development analysts concluded that the war in the North had certainly impacted on aid to Somali Region. 'Off the record many field staff of donor agencies were willing to suggest that

---

[2] *Guardian* Unlimited (2000) quoted in Joanna Crichton, *The Politics of Donor Response to the 1998–2000 Food Crisis in Ethiopia* (Save the Children Fund, 2002).

[3] Quoted in Laura Hammond and Daniel Maxwell, *The Ethiopian Crisis of 1999–2000: Lessons Learned, Questions Unanswered* (Disasters, Overseas Development Institute, 2002).

political and diplomatic considerations had a lot to do with the slow response to the worsening situation in 1999,' one research paper reported.[4] 'Though no one in the donor community would admit it publicly in 1999–2000, pressure on Ethiopia and Eritrea to settle their conflict peacefully contributed to at least the delay, if not denial, of humanitarian assistance,' said another study, adding 'there is little to celebrate in this latest chapter of the politicisation of humanitarian response'.[5]

There was another echo of the mid-1980s in the role played by the media. By the time the unblinking eye of BBC television finally saw people starving in the Somali Region, it was already too late for many thousands. Then, and only then, did the aid begin to flow—just as the crisis peaked—and the politicians settled into their familiar ritual of finger-pointing. The Ethiopian government, still smarting over the West's linkage of aid to the Eritrean war, shrugged off its own responsibility for the disaster. 'This is Africa,' said the foreign minister, Seyoum Mesfin, 'and the situation in Africa always gets a response from Europe or the international community when people start to see skeletons on screens.'

My trip to Gode in April 2009 coincided with the height of the piracy crisis off the coast of Somalia, another part of the vast Somali homeland which the imperial powers, Ethiopia included, carved up a century ago. Twenty ships were already being held when pirates attacked several American vessels, and the US Navy sailed into Somali waters. Two of the US ships were carrying American food aid, with one cargo due for United Nations

---

[4] Ibid.
[5] Sue Lautze and Daniel Maxwell, 'Why do Famines Persist in the Horn of Africa? Ethiopia, 1999–2003', in Stephen Devereux (ed.), *The New Famines* (Routledge 2007).

distribution in Ethiopia itself. As well as being in the middle of an ugly local war, civilians in Somali Region were caught in the reverberations of a conflict across the border between Somali jihadists and an Ethiopian army backed by the West's anti-terrorist coalition.

I was met at Gode airport by Abdinasir Mohammed, the zonal administrator, and we finalized the plan for the day over breakfast of goat stew. I wanted to meet Somali pastoralists for whom the social consequences of famine are as grave as the personal suffering. They lose their children to hunger, they lose their animals to hunger, they lose their future livelihoods, and they forfeit their nomadic culture. I also wanted to see food distribution in action. The World Food Programme (WFP) of the United Nations had been accused of allowing the Ethiopian army to control where international relief went and thus withholding it from civilians suspected of being supporters of the ONLF. 'Your eyes will be your witness today,' said Abdinasir with a poetic flourish.

We headed out of Gode in a plume of white dust. Standing in the back of the pick-up were four policemen with rifles slung across their backs. I wondered then which provided the greater security— an armed escort or one of the stickers fixed to aid agency vehicles in the Somali Region which show a no-entry sign superimposed on a machine gun and the message (in English) 'No Weapons On Board'. We drove 30 miles to the village of Hadhawe where the bleached bones of dead animals littered the dusty roads and WFP staff members in smart baseball caps and T-shirts prepared to distribute the monthly rations.

In response to a protracted environmental crisis compounded by conflict, the United Nations had been shipping 20,000 tonnes of food a month into Somali Region and feeding some 1.7 million people, almost half the population. In the worst-affected zones two-thirds of the people were dependent on relief.

For supplies to get no further than those communities whose loyalty to the government was assured—and not to reach the hungry wherever they were—was intolerable. Yet it took the UN a year to negotiate arrangements where government gave up their control over distribution. As a result it would now no longer be drivers from northern Ethiopia dumping food where the army told them, but Somali drivers from local trucking companies taking the food where a committee of UN personnel, civilian agencies, *and* the army decided. WFP noted that they were no longer being denounced on ONLF websites for incompetence and partiality, and concluded that the new system had to be working well.

There was no mystery at the WFP distribution point in Hadhawe as to where the food came from because donors stamp their names all over the bags. 'Gift of Saudi Arabia', 'USAID—from the American people', 'Donation of the European Union'. The chairman of the village council, shading himself from the sun under an umbrella, told me that 1,803 of Hadhawe's 3,800 residents were dependent on these monthly handouts, a little over half.

The talk among the men in the aid queue was of the terrible price of food in the market, and of how recent drought years compared. The present one was bad, they said, 'because we've already lost our livestock in previous droughts'. Then there was 2003. But 2000 was surely the worst. It was the women, firmly holding their own in this Moslem community, who gave fuller accounts of how family life had been turned upside down by failures of the rain. They wore long batik shifts which covered their hair and framed their faces in perfectly beautiful ovals in the Somali fashion.

Namun Kilas and her family had lost 20 cattle and 250 sheep and goats in the famine of 2000. 'We even lost our donkey carts because the donkeys died,' she said. With poor rains this year, there was no chance of growing anything, and the nearest irrigated land was at the river 30 miles away. The only chance Namun had to earn a few pence was through collecting firewood in the bush and the wild gum used as incense. Even if the climate changed, aid could scarcely begin to finance the wholesale re-stocking of herds for destitute pastoral communities. Namun told me that the only animal the family had received from the aid-givers was a gift from the British charity Islamic Relief. That was a goat for slaughter during the last Eid celebrations at the end of Ramadan—a generous gesture, but hardly developmental.

'It is a very hard life just collecting firewood,' she said. 'Without this food relief we could not live.' In answer to my absurd reporter's question about summing up the last decade and her family's future prospects, she replied: 'Since we are Moslems, we have to believe in God and that life will get better.'

As we left the crowd around the WFP distribution point, I noticed three women struggling to heave 50-kilo bags of grain on to a donkey cart. I thought at first they might be three generations of one family—they all looked elegant enough to be relations of a western supermodel—but it turned out that three families had contributed a pound each to rent the cart and bring their rations home. While the youngest woman held the donkey, I spoke to the older two.

Nasi Weyrah was 45 and her family's fortune had been wiped out by the 2000 famine. They lost 20 cattle and 400 sheep and goats. 'We did not sell them for money, they died,' she said, emphasizing the point for the foreigner's benefit. Far worse, Nasi lost three of her eight children—boys aged 6, 3, and 2.

Yet, incredibly, she had real hope for the future, a hope founded on a simple faith in the power of education.

As pastoralists following their animals through the bush, Nasi's family had never had access to schooling. Then came the destruction of livelihoods through famine and a sedentary existence had been forced on them. Her five surviving children were all now going to the government school and receiving extra Koranic instruction. 'My children are learning and we don't want to go back to the old life,' said Nasi. 'They could be merchants or get a government job—or work for an NGO.'

Asha Ma'alim was 73 and the grandmother in the group. 'Town life is much better,' she agreed, and thought for a moment. 'We get oil for cooking from the relief. We don't want to go back to the bush.' She believed her fifteen grandchildren (none had died in the 2000 famine) would have a better life than she had. 'My grandchildren are learning in the school and then there is the religious school. They are bringing a new road here, so they will be able to become merchants.' A modern world of shopkeeping and maybe an NGO salary in the family beckoned in the dry and dusty wastes of Somali Region.

When we drove the 30 miles back to Gode our armed police escort was nowhere to be seen. It had probably been provided in the first place as much out of courtesy to me as a serious security precaution. This was, after all, a 'low intensity conflict', suggesting we would be unlucky to be seriously inconvenienced. My host, the zone administrator, certainly seemed unconcerned in the journeys we made together, and Gode was considered a trouble spot. The regional government acknowledged an ONLF presence in a third of its territory, but took the official Addis Ababa line that the threat had diminished since the ferocious clashes of two years before.

With backing from the US administration of George W. Bush in its 'War on Terror', Ethiopia had launched a full-scale invasion of neighbouring Somalia late in 2006. The Somali Region was the take-off point, and in April 2007 ONLF guerrillas struck a murderous blow of their own against the Ethiopian government. They attacked a Chinese oil exploration camp in the town of Abole, overpowered the troops guarding it, and gunned down seventy-four civilians including nine Chinese workers. Another six Chinese were kidnapped. The Zhongyan Petroleum Exploration Bureau pulled out of Ethiopia and did not return. It sustains operations through Malaysian and other sub-contractors.[6]

What happened next, in the words of one aid official, was that 'the gloves came off'. Ethiopia's counter-insurgency operation was fierce, prolonged, and cruel, and it took place in a region where access could easily be denied to journalists, relief agencies, and human rights groups. The fullest account to emerge of the crackdown came a year later from Human Rights Watch which condemned the ONLF for conducting 'summary executions', but was unsparing in its judgement of Ethiopia's security forces. A horrific catalogue of executions, 'demonstration killings', including by strangulation, torture, expulsions, the torching of villages, and the rupture of trading links amounted, said Human Rights Watch, to 'war crimes and crimes against humanity'. These crimes were being 'committed with total impunity, on the thinnest of pretexts'.

The relative calm I encountered in Somali Region in 2009 may have been the consequence of the violent repression two years before. But the crackdown had strained to breaking point Ethiopia's

---

[6] Monika Thakur, *Building on Progress? Chinese Engagement in Ethiopia* (South African Institute of International Affairs, 2009).

relations with two of the world's boldest humanitarian organizations, the International Committee of the Red Cross and Médecins Sans Frontières. In crucial respects this was the 1980s all over again, except this time round it was innocent Somalis who were suffering instead of innocent Tigrayans under the Derg.

I admit to unqualified personal admiration for the International Committee of the Red Cross (ICRC). It springs from a number of encounters over the years, including in Ethiopia, and in particular from an incident in southern Sudan where a small group of journalists got caught in a landmine explosion, a television colleague was killed, and ICRC personnel displayed a combination of undemonstrative efficiency and courage in helping us out.

The ICRC had been engaged for years in the Somali Region when the Chinese oil facility was attacked in April 2007. It helped gain the release of kidnapped Chinese and Ethiopian civilians. When government counter-insurgency operations got under way the next month, the ICRC was in a position to monitor troop behaviour towards civilians and document allegations of abuse. Ethiopia rejected all these allegations. Within a matter of weeks the organization was told it had seven days to pack up and leave the region.

As guardian of the Geneva Conventions, the ICRC has a unique status among international humanitarian organizations. Its presence in Ethiopia, as in other countries, is governed by formal agreement, although that had not prevented its summary removal from the border when war broke out with Eritrea in 1998. That was a war across an international border and the ICRC did at least return at the end of hostilities. It was in areas of internal conflict where the ICRC had sought to extend what is called its 'soft mandate' that Ethiopia most resented the intrusion.

The Ethiopian authorities gave me their account of the reasons for the expulsion. There was formal diplomatic talk of 'serious dismay and continuing concern', of a 'breach of trust', and more directly of 'political interference repeatedly committed in the name of the ICRC under the pretext of humanitarian activity'. There followed a litany of specific charges—ICRC offices being used for Ogaden National Liberation Front meetings; ONLF personnel travelling in ICRC vehicles; food and medicine being given to the rebels; handing over state-of-the-art radio equipment to the ONLF; and finally the 'grave misconduct' of the ICRC delegate posted to the region in allowing all this to happen. The ICRC had hastily removed him from the country, the government complained, and he was wanted back for questioning.

'The regional authorities had every reason to believe that the [ICRC] office was rather involved in undermining the security of that region,' I was told at the Ministry of Foreign Affairs in Addis Ababa. 'So their office had to be closed within seven days and they had to clear out.'

The ICRC tried to provide an explanation or a context for the charges levelled at them. They had never hosted ONLF meetings—it was possible that ONLF supporters had come to their offices; the ICRC had brought wounded ONLF guerrillas to hospital—'it is a right they have'; radio equipment had been stolen by a Somali jihadist group during a kidnapping—its theft had been officially reported; the delegate in Somali Region had been routinely transferred from Ethiopia several months before any complaint was made about his conduct.

More than two years after its abrupt expulsion, the ICRC remained barred from playing its unique role in the humanitarian crisis in Somali Region. The government would not allow the organization back until the issues the ministry had raised in

2007 were resolved. To do that it said it needed to conduct a full investigation into the incidents and it wanted the transferred ICRC delegate brought back to Ethiopia for interview. He was described as a 'suspect'. The ICRC refused to produce him and offered the Ethiopians a meeting in Geneva instead. There the matter stuck. The ICRC was no longer able to operate in the region and that may have suited the government perfectly well.

The ICRC's 'soft mandate' activities—in which its 'conventional mandate' in international conflicts was extended to internal affairs—had proved increasingly irksome to the Ethiopians. There had been resistance, for example, when the ICRC sought access after the 2005 post-election violence to the prisons and military camps where opposition detainees were held. This is a trend not confined to Ethiopia or the Horn of Africa. Objections to the neutral role of the ICRC have been recorded elsewhere in the world.

At the time of the 1984–5 famine the ICRC had been the first organization to denounce the Derg for withholding food from Tigrayan civilians and for its enforced resettlement programme. Only the existence of the ICRC's 'special status' agreement with the Ethiopian government, I wrote at the time, may have saved it from expulsion.[7] Now domestic circumstances were sharply reversed in Ethiopia, with Tigrayans predominant in government, and the ICRC appeared to be operating more on sufferance than ever before.

Médecins Sans Frontières, which ranks with the ICRC in its focus and single-mindedness, posed a still greater challenge to the Ethiopian authorities. Founded by a group of French doctors and now truly international, here was an agency with a well-defined sense

[7] Peter Gill, *A Year in the Death of Africa.*

of mission—giving medical aid to people close to death—and a huge popular constituency that owed almost nothing to governments of any stripe. Unlike the major American and British agencies, MSF relied on voluntary contributions for almost all its income. When Ethiopia took on MSF, one government official said to me, they felt they were not just taking on the French government, but a far more formidable force—the people of France.

MSF sprang from the same tradition as the ICRC, but wanted to bear witness—*témoignage*—as well as provide medical assistance in the worst of crises. It was an awkward, sometimes intolerable combination for governments. The very name 'Doctors without Borders' struck alarm in bureaucratic hearts. An Ethiopian Foreign Ministry official told me of an Amharic saying—*sim yimeral, tuaf yaberal*—which translates as 'the name shines a candle on the purpose', or 'the name gives the game away'.

Here in Ethiopia was a government trying to put down a rebel group, and here was an agency that simply would not heed the frontiers between security forces and insurgents. 'MSF says they have to deal with both sides in the conflict,' said the official. 'OK, but if the ONLF does not have to worry about its medical needs, they will be a good fighting force! MSF would be trying to sustain them when the Ethiopian side was trying to kill the terrorists! It's an absolute conflict.'

The radicalism of MSF's origins in the aftermath of the Biafra war was reinforced by the arrival in influential positions of the 1968 generation from the streets of Paris, and that spirit also endured. Academic critics of the modern humanitarian movement often make an exception of Médecins Sans Frontières. One of them, Professor Michael Barnett of the University of Minnesota, observed that MSF believed in 'a more rebellious and rowdy humanitarianism'[8] and on another occasion that 'being a curmudgeon' had helped preserve 'MSF's impartiality and thus its moral standing'.[9]

The point was neatly made by one senior MSF official who provided a personal account of the anxious reaction in some parts of the organization to the agency's achievement in winning the Nobel Peace Prize in 1999. In an article headed 'At our core, a resounding *Non!*' he recalled 'there were murmurs about how this would mark the end of MSF as we knew it; after all, from here on we would be *part of the establishment* [his italics].'[10]

The Ethiopian government was careful not to accuse MSF of aiding the Somali rebels directly but, as the Foreign Ministry saw it, the agency was refusing to abide by the rules. 'We need to know who is doing what,' said the official.

> MSF behaves very erratically, bypassing checkpoints and driving into the wilderness. . . . Then they object to the checkpoints and start kicking up a fuss. The regional government wanted them to operate, but they wanted transparency from them. They wanted people to respect the security arrangements laid down.

The Somali authorities were stronger in their strictures against MSF. 'Their thinking is not good, by the way,' Dawood Mohammed Ali, the regional president, told me in his office in Jijiga. 'I believe they have a hidden agenda. MSF is consulting with elders who have close ties with the ONLF and they hire staff who are ONLF sympathizers. They should collaborate with the government. We are educated persons and we are committed to develop the region. From

---

[8] Michael Barnett, *Humanitarianism in Question*.
[9] Michael Barnett, contributor, *My Sweet La Mancha* (MSF International, 2005).
[10] Michael Barnett, *My Sweet La Mancha*.

a medical emergency point of view, it's good. Our people are poor and they need help. But they are helping the anti-peace elements, and we will make them stick to the rules.'

In Addis Ababa, a decision was reached on how to respond to the MSF challenge in the Somali Region. With its international network of voluntary support, the organization proved in some ways a more formidable antagonist than the ICRC. Ethiopia certainly wanted to avoid the diplomatic and media fall-out that an expulsion would bring. 'We daren't remove them,' the official said to me with surprising candour, 'so the answer is to restrict them.'

Médecins Sans Frontières had been trying to build up its operations in Somali Region from the start of the government's 2007 counter-insurgency operation. No fewer than four separate MSF sections—Belgian, Swiss, Dutch, and Greek—were in place in different corners of the territory by early 2008. This only added to the complexity of the situation as officials tried to work out who was doing what and with what intention in the midst of a conflict with both national and international dimensions. If the government was confused, so was everyone else.

In Addis Ababa I was told that local MSF staff from the different operational centres had to attend lectures and refresher courses to remind them of the bewildering complexity of MSF's international network.[11] It is a commonplace among aid activists that more coordination is needed among the big official agencies in order to reduce aid duplication and to ease the administrative burden

---

[11] One afternoon in Addis Ababa I walked the 100 yards from the office of MSF Holland (Amsterdam Centre covers MSF Germany and MSF United Kingdom as well as MSF Holland and others) to the office of MSF Belgium (Brussels Centre covers MSFs Norway, Sweden, and Denmark as well as MSF Belgium and others). But I chose the wrong gate and found myself inside MSF Greece. There was nothing at the entrance to distinguish between MSF Greece and MSF Belgium. This was because MSF Greece had moved into the offices recently vacated by MSF Switzerland and had not yet put up their new sign.

on poorly resourced Third World governments. The argument is commonly advanced by campaigners from the NGO movement which is itself the greatest offender.

Teams from MSF Holland and MSF Switzerland were at work in two of the most troubled areas of Somali Region, and it was the Swiss section in the town of Fiq which seemed to be subject to the most oppressive restrictions. Dr Bruno Jochum, director of operations for MSF Switzerland, described them as a campaign of 'administrative harassment' that lasted from their arrival in December 2007 to their decision to pull out of the country in frustration six months later.

MSF based the decision to open its programme in Fiq on an under-fives nutrition survey, conducted in October 2007 by Save the Children Fund, itself operational in the region and subject to the same pressures as MSF. The survey found up to one in four of the children malnourished, and the problem was getting worse. MSF's own surveys in the early months of 2008 showed the rate of 'severe acute malnutrition' among young children nearly doubling over two months from one in twenty to almost one in ten.

Yet the Swiss team hardly began to address the problem. Over six months they were allowed to operate for just ten weeks in the town of Fiq and five weeks in nearby villages where needs were even greater. In that time they managed to care for just 84 malnourished children in the town and fewer than 700 people were able to reach their mobile teams in the villages. It was a sorry effort. 'We decided to get out of Fiq because we believed that the space we were given was a fiction,' Dr Jochum said. 'This had to be put on the table. We had negotiated for about six months and had not been able to remove the obstacles.'

In a briefing note on its experiences entitled 'Mission Impossible?' MSF Switzerland detailed three incidents in the course of June 2008 alone:

> June 1: Expatriate staff threatened with arrest if found delivering drugs to health posts 'where the enemy are'.
> June 8: Expatriate staff threatened with expulsion if reports on the humanitarian crisis got to the press.
> June 18: Five Ethiopian staff members arrested and detained for 19 days without charge.

The facts of the matter between the government and MSF Switzerland were not at serious issue. Officials had not expected the Swiss team to pull out and considered the withdrawal unmerited. The Swiss section had gone, they said, but MSF Belgium, MSF Holland, and MSF Greece were all still operating in Somali Region. 'MSF seems to have understood how resolved the government is to work as a partner, but not to see the flouting of the sovereignty of the country and the laws and regulations of the country,' said the ministry official. 'So maybe the message has got through to MSF, and that's why we don't have these kinds of incidents that we saw last year [2008].'

Tensions were set to escalate in Ethiopia and elsewhere between rival notions of sovereignty—national sovereignty as espoused by governments and a sovereign humanitarianism propounded by agencies such as the ICRC and MSF. It is a clash of practicality as well as principle. 'They [the Ethiopian authorities] cannot accept the fact that a humanitarian organization establishes basic links with the ONLF,' said Dr Jochum. He distinguished between 'basic' and 'direct' links, with the latter conducted only 'through representative channels' abroad, and went on:

> We consider that in a conflict situation to ensure the security of our team we should at least inform each belligerent what our

activities are, where our teams are and what we are doing, so please do not threaten them in any way. For any sovereign state, it is extremely difficult to accept an organization liaising with armed groups. But this is a founding principle of humanitarian work. Belligerents want to force us to choose sides. A channel of information is a threat to security.

Not many governments anywhere in the world would comfortably accept that 'founding principle of humanitarian work'.

As in the clashes between NGOs and government in Ethiopia in the 1980s, it was again Francophone organizations which proved difficult to bring to heel in the Somali humanitarian crisis in the 2000s. One academic commentator has likened MSF, in particular, to the Jacobins. 'For it seems to me that MSF's most fundamental ambition is to always maintain the possibility of disobedience, even to the extent of violating self-interest,' wrote Peter Redfield, of the University of North Carolina, Chapel Hill. 'MSF stands apart from more docile forms of humanitarianism in its willingness to bite.'[12] This 'awkward squad' radicalism is facilitated by financial independence of government, and contrasts with the approach of major Anglo-Saxon agencies. This less 'rowdy' approach to the humanitarian imperative is connected at one level to their relative dependence on official income and often translates itself into a greater respect for foreign governments.

But one British project did fall foul of the authorities in Somali Region and ended up being barred from operating there. The Pastoralist Communication Initiative (PCI), based in Kenya, was set up not to represent pastoralists but to promote dialogue between them and governments so that the pastoralists could

---

[12] Peter Redfield, 'Biting the Hand That Feeds You', *My Sweet La Mancha*.

represent themselves. 'It's a bit like building a telephone exchange,' said one of its founders, Alastair Scott-Villiers.

PCI arrived in Somali Region in response to the famine of 2000 and went to work under the auspices of the United Nations. The terrorist attacks of 9/11 in the United States lent political urgency to working positively with disaffected Moslem communities in the Horn of Africa, and the British Department for International Development backed PCI with more than £4 million over the following years. The Ethiopian government was similarly open-armed in the early years of the project.

Then domestic politics in Ethiopia took a decisive shift with the post-election crackdown of 2005—a shift accentuated in the Somali Region by the subsequent strife—and the government's attitude changed. The role of PCI was all the more suspect in official eyes for its championing of a pastoralist cause so readily identified with rebellion. It did not help when PCI translated into Somali a solid report from the Institute of Development Studies at Sussex University on 'the causes and consequences of livelihood vulnerability' in the region.[13] This was regarded by the authorities as a treasonable piece of work.

One short section of the report was entitled, provocatively as it turned out, 'Perceptions of political representation'. Popular attitudes were surveyed and tabulated, and the Somali interviewees did not hold back. 'These are discouraging findings for government,' said the report. 'They suggest that three-quarters of people in Somali Region feel disenfranchised (not fairly represented) and believe that government is not working effectively to serve their interests (ineffectively represented).'

[13] Stephen Devereux, *Vulnerable Livelihoods in Somali Region, Ethiopia* (Institute of Development Studies, 2006).

There then followed a series of comments from focus groups in the field of which these are typical: 'Government, government—what government are you talking about? We only see the army, if that's what you mean.' 'No one talks to us to ask what we need. The government does not exist here.' 'The government does nothing at all for us.'

The first casualty of fierce government objections to the report was not a white expatriate, but an unfortunate Kenyan researcher Abdi Umar working for PCI in the Somali Region. Umar was arrested and imprisoned in Jijiga where he remained, for all the efforts of the United Nations and PCI officials, for seven months. When he was eventually released, he was deported shoeless straight across the border into Kenya.

Next the Ministry of Foreign Affairs threw the rule book at PCI itself. Its status within the UN was quite irregular, the ministry complained, the agency had been misusing this privilege, and had failed to pay its taxes. 'OCHA [the UN's Office for the Coordination of Humanitarian Affairs] had them squatting under their roof while they were making this mess,' I was told at the ministry. 'We told Alastair [Scott-Villiers] to turn in his papers and pay back what you owe us. We are still dealing with OCHA over this.'

Staff from the Pastoralist Communication Initiative still travelled in and out of Ethiopia on short-term visas and could still work with the country's other pastoral communities, but they were barred from the Somali Region, by far their most important focus. For Ethiopian officials, they had crossed the frontier into politics. 'They go too much overboard to sensitize local communities and that should be left to the people and citizens of this country,' said the official. 'How do you think you would feel if an NGO was going into these people's area and interacting with those elements?'

In the Institute for Development Studies paper that caused so much offence, Stephen Devereux had a concluding section in which he discussed the future of Somali pastoralism in the era of climate crisis. He referred to the government's policy of 'phased voluntary sedentarisation [settlement] along the banks of the major rivers as the main direction of transforming pastoral societies' and he reflected on the range of opinion among farmers and pastoralists as to which is the better life. Like Devereux and unlike those campaigners who favour the perseveration of traditional lifestyles at all costs, I too found the same variety of perspective.

Before I flew out of the Somali Region, I visited the big farm cooperative on the banks of the Wabe Shabelle, just outside Gode town. This was the old imperial experimental farm which became a state cotton enterprise under the Derg and was then handed back to Somalis. There are now some 2,000 farmers and their families on a hectare each of irrigated land. Most of them are former pastoralists and most had been made destitute by drought. It was the same terrifyingly simple narrative each time: the rains failed one year; they failed a second year and it was serious; a third failure and a way of life collapsed.

Ahmed Abdi stood in front of me with his hoe across his back. It had been his day for the water, and he had spent it channelling the supply around his maize fields. It was a guaranteed crop, half to be eaten and a half to be sold to buy other essentials. He still needed some food aid to feed his two wives and ten children.

Year 2000 was the 'dangerous year', Ahmed said. In the poor rains over previous years he had lost two or three animals at a time. In 2000 he lost them all—40 cattle and 240 sheep and goats. I asked him whether he was sad at the loss of that previous life. 'That was a better life,' he said. 'It was good. It was what I knew. I could sell an animal and make money. Or I could kill one if I wanted to eat meat. I could drink milk. Now all I have is this farm.'

He paused, but only for a beat. 'On the other side, this life is also good. The children are learning, and in the bush they could not learn.' Another pause. 'On balance the future is brighter.'

IV

PROSPECTS

Chapter 12
Spoiling the Party

'You need purposefully to exaggerate to really get into their pockets.'

In the twenty-five years since the Ethiopian famine of 1984–5, the western world has developed ever more sophisticated techniques for predicting the onset of food emergencies. Famine early warning systems utilize satellite technology and a range of baffling earth sciences. They monitor crop production and market prices. Their forecasts are then subject to the bureaucratic and political judgements and misjudgements of the aid-givers and the aid-receivers. When a real crisis builds, it is often better to rely on good people on the ground with the eyes to see.

In April 2008 Father Yohannes Michael, a priest in the Ethiopian Catholic Church, had been in his new parish for only a matter of weeks when something troubled him at Sunday morning mass. As the congregation rose for his final blessing—'The Lord be with you'—he saw that some of his elderly parishioners had to be supported. 'Even the most faithful couldn't get up,' he said.

Outside in the sandy village streets of Ropi, in southern Ethiopia, he started looking around at the children. 'I saw that many had swollen arms and legs.' Then he began to receive little notes scrawled on scraps of paper from outlying homesteads in the parish. 'They said they were suffering.'

Fr Yohannes made contact with his Catholic secretariat in Meki, 150 miles away. 'At first my bishop did not believe me,' Fr Yohannes said, 'but then he contacted the Missionaries of Charity in Addis Ababa and he came here with those sisters. We knew then that eight people had died of hunger. One lady lost five children and she was also very weak.'

The Missionaries of Charity were founded by Mother Teresa to help the poorest of the poor in India. They came to Ethiopia in 1973 in immediate response to the terrible famine of that year and they have been in the country ever since. I remarked to Fr Yohannes what wonderful people the sisters were. 'Look,' he replied, 'they work day and night. I will never forget one of the sisters. Her name was Sister Marinella from India. She arrived one day, and all night we entered house after house, day and night. That sister got TB, and she is back in India. I am still here, thanks to God, but we have to pray for Sister Marinella.'

Fr Yohannes drove all around his parish with the sisters. 'Some people were so weak they couldn't come out of the house, so they couldn't come to us. We had to go house to house to find them.' An immense food crisis, the perverse product of floods followed by drought, was building in several southern areas. The government and the official aid-givers were slow to react, but at least the Catholics were there.

The next step was the mobilization of other parts of the Missionaries of Charity network. More sisters in their white saris with blue trim arrived in Ropi and transported the most critical cases back to their centre in the southern capital Awassa. I called in on Sister Gisela and asked her how many they had brought back. 'Many,' she said. 'How many, Sister?' 'Many,' she repeated. That exchange was typical of a number of polite but professionally unrewarding conversations I had with the Missionaries of Charity in Ethiopia, for they set very little store by press relations. The last telephone contact I had with them at their home in Addis Ababa concluded, 'I don't know what Sister Janneke will say, but certainly I could not meet you.'

In April 2008 Mother Teresa's missionaries forged another link in a humanitarian chain when they informed Médecins Sans Frontières of the extent of the suffering they had witnessed. Their initial point of contact was MSF Greece in Addis Ababa. The Greek section did a rapid assessment on the ground, and passed on the information to other groups. MSF Belgium promptly conducted its own assessment and was so alarmed by what it found that it was operational within a week. 'The position was really amazingly serious,' one of its coordinators recalled. 'The team received so many children in such a bad situation we'd almost never seen anything like it before.'

By May the Belgian group had mounted one of its largest emergency interventions of the decade. 'For us it was huge,' I was told, 'the same sort of size as the Asian tsunami.' Some sixty-five expatriates were sent to southern Ethiopia in a total staff commitment of over 100. In the careful accountancy of relief work, MSF Belgium was to treat 34,266 severely malnourished children over the following ten months along with an additional 42,616 moderately malnourished children.

Fr Yohannes handed over his church compound in Ropi to MSF Greece and the Missionaries of Charity so that they could start their emergency feeding. 'Many arrived very weak and even with treatment they died. Some returned to their homes and I think they died there also.'

As in the infamous Ethiopian famines of the past, the 2008 food emergency struck at an awkward time for the government. Ethiopia had been recording impressive 'double digit' economic growth for several years, and there was optimism among government officials and aid-givers that one of Africa's most intractably poor countries was finally turning the corner. Senior Ethiopian officials told me early in 2008 that for the first time in decades Ethiopia would require food aid for fewer than one million people (most of them in the troubled Somali Region) compared with the 14 million for whom appeals had been launched just five years earlier.

Setting the seal on this new era of hope was the carefully crafted promotion of Ethiopia's entry on its third millennium. By the Julian calendar, the country reached New Year's Day 2000 in September 2007, and instead of just a night and day of celebration its significance was marked for months. When I returned to Ethiopia eighteen months into the new century, there were still weathered millennium decorations on the streets. The talk was of an Ethiopian renaissance, and the very last thing the government, or its people, wanted was another famine spoiling the party.

As the hunger crisis intensified, the government began to acknowledge it would need more help than originally forecast. In April it appealed for food aid for 2.2 million people—more than the previous year, but still well short of an alarm call. It was also plain that officials would not welcome anyone else raising the alarm. 'If you bring journalists to this feeding centre, you will not be able to keep working here,' one Médecins Sans Frontières administrator was told as the agency's workload built up in the south. MSF chose to put discretion and duty of care before bearing witness.

'We decided to refuse to see journalists unless they were cleared by the authorities,' said the MSF Belgium coordinator on the ground at the time. 'Journalists had to be cleared by the federal authorities in Addis before they could move to the field. Then I wanted to see an extra stamp from the zonal authorities and the head of the health bureau. We didn't want to be seen always with journalists, and this was our way of avoiding jeopardizing our activities.'

Despite the lack of press access—with its acknowledged link to preventing starvation—the Ethiopian food emergency of 2008 became major international news. It also led to an angry public dispute between the government of Ethiopia and a key player in the humanitarian world. As is so often the case with the media, the story emerged by accident.

In January 2008 the United Nations children's fund, UNICEF, had a good news story to tell the world about Ethiopia. The country was said to be at the centre of a 'child survival revolution', having recorded 'dramatic achievements' in reducing under-five mortality rates by 40 per cent between 1990 and 2006. Ethiopia would be 'a beacon' for other African countries. A UNICEF press release quoted the Health Ministry as saying that Ethiopia was 'in a position to confidently deal with severe and acute malnutrition'.

One international news organization which got the message was CNN, which decided on a one-hour special programme on child survival for broadcast in the summer. A CNN crew arrived in May to film the Ethiopian section of the report. They came with the intention of covering this 'good news' story of child survival, but they too had eyes to see what was happening and they were accompanied by local UNICEF officials who were alarmed by the impact of the food crisis on young children and the lack so far of an effective response.

For months UNICEF had had a $30 million international appeal on the table, but western governments had been reluctant to fund it. Only a paltry $1 million had so far been raised. For their part, Ethiopian government officials were firmly resisting any idea that the United Nations might use their country's problems for international fund-raising purposes.

From as early as March 2008 Bjorn Ljungqvist, the well-connected UNICEF country representative, had been pressing Ethiopian ministers to take more urgent action. The minister of agriculture kept reassuring him that the seasonal rains would soon come, planting would begin, the 'hungry season' would pass, and life would go on. 'Bjorn,' ministers told him, 'if the donors haven't responded so far, why will they specifically respond now?'

When I met Ljungqvist a few months after he left Ethiopia, he recalled Prime Minister Meles saying to him, 'All you guys want to do is to create this Ethiopian famine image again so you will be able to raise money for yourselves. That might help get food for some people for the day, but it totally undermines our longer-term objective of promoting Ethiopia as a modern emerging country which is not a country of helpless starving children.'

Ljungqvist had also had a string of similar exchanges over the years with the health minister, Dr Tedros Adhanom, who was later to accuse UNICEF of lying about the 2008 emergency. The minister had once flown home to Addis Ababa on British Airways and complained afterwards about the airline's 'Change for Good' campaign where passengers are encouraged to give their spare cash to UNICEF. 'How can you do this?' the minister asked. 'You create a picture in which you drop a few coins in an envelope, and that's how to save kids! You should know better.'

Taking exception to such a charitable campaign might surprise frequent fliers on British Airways. What surprised me was Bjorn

Ljungqvist's response to the minister's complaint. 'I think he had a point. Too many donors and too many NGOs are attracting large sums of money by using Ethiopia and Ethiopian children for begging. And who benefits most but those organizations?'

The CNN crew shooting the 'child survival' special travelled with UNICEF from Addis Ababa to East Hararghe, another Ethiopian hunger zone many hundreds of miles from the Médecins Sans Frontières operation. Here they filmed the benefits of what the agency called the Enhanced Outreach Strategy put in place after the 2003 emergency to deal with the 'severe acute malnutrition' which kills so many children. In that optimistic UNICEF press release issued three months earlier, Dr Tedros, the health minister, had been quoted as saying, 'No Ethiopian child need die of preventable causes. That is the underlying principle guiding our child and maternal health programme.'

Principle proved a fine thing in 2008 when the world began to be buffeted by an economic crisis which obliged the rich to slim down and the poor to starve. In East Hararghe, as in other parts of Ethiopia, a perfect storm was brewing, compounded of rising global food prices (reducing the capacity of donors to provide their regular levels of aid) and domestic inflation which drove up the cost of food by more than 50 per cent in a year. For those very poor Ethiopians at the receiving end of the West's latest aid idea of giving handouts in cash as well as kind—thus drastically reducing what they could afford to eat at a time of rising food prices—2008 was to prove a particularly cruel year.

The UN's World Food Programme simply did not have the food to go round. Ethiopia displaced Sudan as the world's largest recipient of WFP aid in 2008, but it still did not have enough food. The authorities in East Hararghe wanted nutritional surveys conducted in every district in order to help the worst-affected children, but that would not be possible, either. The aid-givers had decided that it would be 'unethical' to survey people's needs if there was no prospect of actually feeding them. The solution adopted was food aid triage where about half the districts—those where the government had formally declared an emergency—would receive extra help and those on the regular 'safety net' programme sometimes would not. As well as recording the 'good news' story, CNN wanted, reasonably enough, to film in a district which was not getting special treatment.

'So they went randomly to the villages and asked parents if they would bring out their children,' said a UNICEF official. 'They found these kids who were severely malnourished—quite a few of them—and they asked parents if there were more malnourished children, and they were brought out as well.' Both CNN and UNICEF knew they had found the story which would show how global economic collapse was leading to starvation among the poor. Once again, wretchedly, it was happening in Ethiopia.

CNN broadcast its 'child survival' special as planned in July, but it put out the news story from East Hararghe within a week or so of leaving Ethiopia. For the Ethiopian leadership it could not have come at a more embarrassing time. When the story broke and other broadcasters scrambled to take it up, the Ethiopian health minister was in Geneva for the World Health Assembly and the prime minister was in Japan where UNICEF was launching a report entitled 'The State of African Children'.

'Tedros wakes up next morning in Geneva and sees starving Ethiopian kids again,' Bjorn Ljungqvist recalled, 'and even worse, Meles is in Japan at a meeting saying Ethiopia is ready to take off. And these bloody kids!'

However hard it tried, Ethiopia simply could not put its reputation for hunger and suffering behind it. And UNICEF was certainly not helping. Troubled by what was happening on the ground and conscious of the pictures that CNN was about to broadcast, the agency tried first to organize a visit to the hunger zone by the major official agencies, but there was no interest in such a last-minute arrangement. So it announced a trip for the media instead, and the take-up was immediate. UNICEF then caused itself even more trouble. Supposedly to clarify matters and set the food crisis in context, the agency issued a press release on 20 May.

It was the opening paragraph which did the damage. 'An estimated 126,000 children are in need of urgent therapeutic care for severe malnutrition,' it began, and then, 'UNICEF Ethiopia today cautioned that up to 6 million children under 5 years of age are living in impoverished, drought prone districts and require continuation of urgent preventive health and nutrition interventions.'

On the strength of this press release, it was not surprising that many journalists put two and two together and concluded that millions of children could starve. CNN itself had an on-screen reference to 'seven million children facing famine'. The government disputed all these figures, but the story of a fresh Ethiopian disaster was now in print and in pictures. UNICEF officials had wanted to clarify the facts and put the record straight. They accepted that the press release did not achieve this. It muddied things further.

A typical headline appeared in the *Daily Telegraph* in London in early June, 'Ethiopia facing new famine with 4.5 million children in danger of starvation'. An on-line version of the story increased the figure to six million. Other journalists were more cautious. Gavin Hewitt, the BBC's special correspondent, travelled to southern Ethiopia and thoughtfully concluded, 'What we have seen in the villages is not famine—but it is a crisis. Some say tens of thousands of children are at risk. I can believe that.'

When I met the health minister almost a year later, he was still livid with UNICEF's handling of the emergency. 'We told them not to fabricate figures,' said Dr Tedros. 'Even I told them "This is just a lie."' He accused some agencies—he did not name UNICEF specifically—of putting their funding interests before the facts. 'You can only do that by showing a desperate human face that needs support very badly and you make your donors cry so you can get more money. You need purposefully to exaggerate to really get into their pockets.'

To understand the basis of this dispute about the level and severity of child malnutrition, it is important first to recognize that there is a shocking lack of solid figures on which to base any such calculations in Ethiopia. There are no national head counts for child malnutrition or child deaths from hunger, so a rich western world ruled by statistics must fall back on assumptions and past assessments.

UNICEF told me how it had reached the figure of up to six million Ethiopian under-fives requiring 'urgent preventive health and nutrition interventions'. First it took Ethiopia's population at 80 million. Between 40 and 50 per cent of them were considered to be 'malnourished at any given time' and between 16 and 18 per cent of those malnourished children were under five. So the answer can be worked out in seconds on a calculator—six million or so.

There was a further step needed to arrive at a figure for those suffering from SAM—Severe Acute Malnutrition—and thus in immediate danger of dying of starvation. This was based on the calculation that 4 per cent of malnourished children would be suffering from 'severe acute' malnutrition and thus at immediate risk of death in the current emergency. This figure was then divided by two because UNICEF had in mind six months of therapeutic care, not a full twelve months. The answer reached by this method was indeed around 126,000.

Government officials did their sums quite differently. As far as they were concerned, there was only an emergency where they had declared one. For this they relied on the ultimately artificial distinction made after the 2003 emergency between those receiving food aid as part of the new 'safety net' arrangement and those needing emergency aid as a result of a contemporary drought and crop failure. The official view was that those on the 'safety net' were getting help anyway, and would not need more. As the CNN team discovered in Hararghe, this was a tragic fiction.

When the dispute first arose between the government and UNICEF, there were 2.2 million declared to be in need of emergency help. As the food crisis intensified during 2008, the government increased its emergency requirements first to 4.6 million and then to 6.4 million. On those calculations, the government appealed in June for help for 75,000 severely malnourished children, an increase of 35,000 in two months but still 50,000 short of UNICEF's figure a month earlier.[1]

Between these two sets of figures, no one really knew what the true number was. All that was clear was that the suffering was immense—even if it did not amount to full-scale famine, the government had underplayed the crisis, and the aid-givers had not shipped in enough food. In the months leading to the twenty-fifth anniversary of the famine of the 1980s, something else was also clear: far too many Ethiopians continued to live in the shadow of hunger. Their government had made determined efforts to improve agricultural performance and had something

[1] Government-Partners Joint Document, 'Revised Humanitarian Requirement for 2008', Addis Ababa, 12 June 2008.

to show for it in the traditional famine lands of the North. But the South and South-East had received less attention, and severe hunger there would frustrate the promise of an Ethiopian renaissance early in the new millennium.

'I do sympathize,' said Bjorn Ljungqvist about the row over numbers, 'but at the same time it is absolutely essential to be able to have a clear conversation about how many there are, where they are and so on, and what we can do to help.' He thought that the 'safety net' arrangement—'a sort of social protection'—could lead to a reduction in the sensitivities surrounding emergency appeals. 'Previously', Ljungqvist acknowledged, 'there was a tacit understanding between donors and Ethiopia that there would have to be a measure of exaggeration in their appeals.'

Well over a year after the crisis, there was still no reliable assessment of the number who may have died of hunger in 2008. Unlike earlier emergencies, there appeared to be little appetite among academic researchers (or their funders) for any project that might establish the level of 'excess mortality'. Certainly the government would not encourage such an initiative. For as soon as the millennium bunting had faded, there was the prospect of another round of national elections in 2010. Too much talk of starvation, localized or extensive, is as bad for a government's prospects at home as it is for Ethiopia's reputation abroad.

Ministers had consistently brushed aside accusations of government sloth. I was told that the assessments and appeals had all been made on time, and it was the aid-givers who had been at fault. I took the matter up with Meles Zenawi and expected a similar response. What I got instead was a remarkably frank admission. 'That was a failure on our part,' the prime minister said. 'We were late in recognizing we had an emergency on our hands.'

The reason the government had been caught 'completely by surprise' was a very unusual set of weather conditions. Too much rain at the wrong time had rotted root crops and these floods were followed by drought during the main growing season. 'This combination had not happened in the past, and we did not know that a crisis was brewing in these specific areas in the South until emaciated children began to appear.'

Meles made another significant admission in his references to southern cropping patterns. 'The South is largely dependent on root crops, and perhaps this is a reflection of the fact that some of us who are not from the South did not adequately study the diet of the South and we needed to learn the hard way.' The EPRDF is regularly characterized by its critics as a Tirgrayan minority regime foisted on the people of Ethiopia. Here after almost twenty years of focusing on agriculture was its leader saying that he and his colleagues had not quite appreciated how southern farmers survived the year.

But he did not let the aid donors off the hook. 'First they did not respond quickly. They didn't have the means to respond quickly. But they were exaggerating, and it appears to us that they were deliberately exaggerating, and there was a lot of resentment... my own interpretation of the reasons for exaggerating is because they have to shock and awe the international community in order to get money.'

When I visited the area at the heart of the 2008 food crisis in the South, I depended on local community organizations for travel and interpretation. This innocuous trip turned out to be politically the most sensitive I undertook. 'You know there is an election coming,' one of my companions said as we prepared to leave for the field. 'The best strategy is not to say you are a journalist. If you do, there will be a problem with the local cadres or the farmer cadres.' The 'cadres' were the ubiquitous EPRDF party people. We hit upon the job description of 'development researcher'.

When we stopped in town to fill up with petrol for the journey, I said I would pay. You are our guest, they said. No, I insisted, I was an independent journalist and had to pay. Remember, they said, and please do not mention that word.

We set off for Ropi where I hoped to find Fr Yohannes, the priest who first alerted the Missionaries of Charity to the terrible hunger in his parish. My travelling companions also knew the story. 'They rescued many children,' said one of them. 'The Catholics are very good people. Where there is a problem, you will always see them.'

Ropi is an over-sized village some 25 miles from the main road down rutted tracks and through farmyards fenced with living cactus. Whenever we passed a homestead excited children would rush out to the vehicle hoping we might stop. 'Last year the children were not like this,' said my companion, referring to the listlessness of malnutrition. 'They were not running here and there.'

As we got closer to Ropi, children spotted the white man in the vehicle and shouted 'Abba, Abba', 'Father, Father', hoping I was a foreign priest on his way to do something useful. It was preferable to the shouts that visitors often get in the towns of Ethiopia. 'Ferenj, Ferenj', 'Foreigner, Foreigner', or, more abruptly, 'You! You!' or, even worse, 'Give me money', 'Give me money'.

There was a village meeting going on under the trees in the middle of Ropi. A group of about twenty men, and they were all men, was considering the case of a farmer whose own mother had complained that he was planning to sell off his possessions to raise cash. Those possessions included the family's supply of grain. The mother had a simple question for her son—'What will your children eat?'—and she wanted the village meeting to prevent the sale. I interrupted proceedings to talk about the 2008 food emergency.

It was soon apparent there would be a party line in response to questions about the crisis. The lead cadre appeared readily identifiable from his loud voice and his fondness for using it. He assured me that the 'safety net' had been specially extended to the village the previous year (there had admittedly been 'some short-ages') and that the government had been aware of the situation from as early as February. Indeed it was the government which had informed the Catholic agencies of the difficulties in the area and so had been responsible for making sure that Mother Teresa's nuns, Médecins Sans Frontièries, Christian Children's Fund, and Catholic Relief Services were all on hand to help.

As is so often the case in discussing disaster, simple human truths trump carefully crafted official positions. Sitting on his haunches to my right was a man who became increasingly agi-tated as this account of official effectiveness went on. He had a riding crop in front of him and had ridden a donkey in from a nearby village. There were tears welling up in his eyes, and I asked what had happened to his family.

'There was a case of death,' was the answer. His brother had died leaving a widow and seven children. She had no farm animals and no land to cultivate. She was also not well. 'Everybody knows that he died because of hunger,' said the man.

This revelation changed the mood. There were other recollec-tions. Someone recalled four children dying in one family. Someone else volunteered that even in the relief centre in Ropi two or three were dying every day. And the man who had lost his brother had not quite finished his story. 'There were so many funerals that people stopped going to them. There were many deaths and sometimes we heard about them after four or five months.'

I did not take down any names from the group, in part because I was not supposed to be a journalist and in part because at that point one my guides said firmly, 'It is better if we stop there.' These accounts of the food emergency were in danger of breaching the party line. We had a quick walk around Ropi, looked briefly into the church compound and drove off.

On our way back to the main road, I protested that I had met no women in Ropi and I needed to hear from them. We stopped in another small village where I spotted several women selling sugar cane by the roadside. Instead of talking to them on the spot, they were instructed to follow us to another, more discreet location. We were still surrounded by a large crowd and a halting conversation began. The two women I spoke to had lost no family members during the emergency, but they had survived only because of the arrival of relief food. There was then an argument about who had been responsible for the relief effort, but this was not immediately translated.

When we were back in town, I asked what had been said. One of my companions explained that when I had asked who had provided relief for her family, one of the women gestured at me. 'These people,' she said. 'What do you mean, these people, do you mean him?' she was asked. 'Maybe not him, but his people,' she replied. The next thing was that she complained about neighbours in the crowd prodding her in the back, apparently to make her change the story, but she stood her ground. 'His people,' she repeated.

I never met Fr Yohannes, the Catholic priest in Ropi. When I visited his village, he was at a church meeting in Addis Ababa. We tried to meet a few days later on the road as he travelled home, but that did not work because he ran out of petrol. Once he was back in Ropi, I relied on the mobile telephone network, and tried scores of times to reach him. Then one evening, miraculously, I got through.

Exactly a year after the start of the 2008 crisis, he was again worried for his parishioners. 'If the rains come, with the blessing of God, that will be good. But if the rains stop, there will be the same situation.' The rains did stop in some areas and in others they barely arrived. The government maintained the distinction between the 'safety net' food aid recipients and 'emergency' recipients, but on the very anniversary of the TV revelations of the 1984 famine Ethiopia ended up with a food aid requirement in 2009 for 13.7 million people, an additional 1.6 million over 2008.

At the end of our conversation, I wished Fr Yohannes a Happy Easter by the Ethiopian calendar. 'Our history is in front of us,' he replied. 'Pray for me, and I will pray for you. Happy Easter. Ciao!'

Chapter 13

Enter the Dragon

'Sometimes some of the western countries impose. That's something we never do.'

'We have a saying,' explained Xu Chun, second secretary at the Chinese Economic and Commercial Counsellor's Office in Addis Ababa. 'If you want to get rich, you have to build a road first.' We were sitting in a large marbled reception area. Around us were a huge blue and white vase, a ping pong table and a rug depicting the Great Wall of China. 'Without communications, we cannot make money,' Mr Xu continued. 'We are helping African countries to improve their infrastructure. It is, it is,' and he paused to make sure he got the development jargon right, 'it is capacity-building'.

The Chinese in Ethiopia are certainly building roads—hundreds and hundreds of miles of them. Some are brand new; others need widening and straightening and asphalting; and some of the most important are the ones that cut across the country's grain from east to west. There has not been so much road-building since the Italian occupation of the 1930s when the invaders constructed the main north–south highway and were extravagantly praised for their work by the writer Evelyn Waugh. He was an enthusiast for the Fascist cause and imagined how 'along the roads will pass the eagles of ancient Rome, as they came to our savage ancestors in France and Britain and Germany...'[1] The Italians lasted five years in Ethiopia.

I drove westwards through the mountains on several highways being upgraded by the Chinese. One of them has always been known as 'China Road' since it was originally built by them in the 1970s. At one point in the middle of road works there appeared the sign 'High Sliding Drive' to warn us of the steep gradient ahead. A Chinese road camp in the heart of Tigray had an 80-yard frontage of coloured flags and an entrance gate strung with paper lanterns. I also counted to seven the number of times children shouted 'China, China' at me as the pale-faced foreigner. It was not as flattering as 'Abba, Father', but preferable to 'Ferenji' or 'Give me money'. It was also evidence that the world was changing.

The great Chinese project in the capital was the Addis Ababa ring road. It brought overwhelming disruption to city streets and cut off the wonderful old railway terminus from the rest of the line which now ended 100 miles short of the city. One of the ring road's key intersections was under construction and had been well nicknamed 'Confusion Square'. Traffic continued to seek a way round and through the building site as immense diggers driven by purposeful Chinese rose and fell within inches of minibuses bursting with passengers. 'This is rough road,' said my taxi driver, 'not good feeling, not comfort.'

I feared I would find out almost nothing about China's activities in Ethiopia other than what I could read on websites or see

---

[1] Evelyn Waugh, *Waugh in Abyssinia* (Longmans, Green & Co., 1936).

on the streets. Much of what I had learnt so far about the Chinese in Africa was certainly uncomplimentary. They were said to be interested only in fuelling their own industrial expansion by plundering Africa's natural resources. And they were prepared to befriend a rogue's gallery of unsavoury African dictators to achieve their ends. Behind that, it was said, lay darker strategic designs on Africa's future. I assumed I would encounter a prickly defensiveness among Chinese officials in Addis Ababa, and so I spoke first to the embassy in London to secure an introduction to their colleagues in Ethiopia. I was told I would have to approach them direct.

I began my researches with a single web page of contacts for Nori-La, Norinco-Lalibela Engineering and Construction Ltd., 'Our Motto—we build the Future.' Could I speak to Mr Feng, the general manager? Mr Feng was no longer in Ethiopia, but I could speak to his replacement Mr Lin. Mr Lin came on the line, and told me that despite its elaborate website and all its hoardings around town, his company was not a very big player. I should really speak to CRBC, China Road and Bridge Corporation, by far our biggest contractor, said Mr Lin. How should I make contact with them? Mr Lin suggested I speak to Mr Lu, the economic and commercial counsellor, and he gave me the telephone number. Mr Lu picked up the phone, listened courteously to what I had to say, and suggested I send an email explaining what I wanted. The upshot, after a few days, was that I was outside the headquarters of CRBC in Addis Ababa with an appointment to see Zhou Yongshen, the country manager.

The Chinese were consistently the most courteous and helpful foreigners I encountered in Ethiopia. They may not have strayed from the party line during interviews, but they seemed to welcome inquiries. Even quite senior officials answer their own telephones rather than hide behind Chinese walls of automated switchboards, answer machines, and voice mails, as most of the westerners and United Nations officials do.

At CRBC headquarters there was no mistaking I was at the right address. On either side of the front door were placed large whiteboards with characteristic Chinese 'denunciations' in English, one directed at a local businessman, the other at a local employee. The first was a 'warning letter' about an overpriced contract. 'That means your work very nearly seriously causes losses for the company,' said the denunciation and levied a penalty of 100 birr (about six pounds) or 'we will not give you the opportunity to work with us again'.

Solomon Abebe, a clerk in CRBC's customs clearance department, was denounced on the other side of the front door for not having turned up to work for weeks. 'Your bad behaviour will be unbearable for any company in the world. Accordingly the termination of your contract will take effect right now.'

Mr Zhou, the country manager, told me he had worked in Ethiopia for seven years, interrupted by a break back in Beijing as head of procurement for CRBC. When he first arrived in 1998 he was posted to the North as a project manager and recalled how Ethiopian children would then shout 'Japan, Japan' or sometimes 'Korea, Korea' at him as an easterner. Now he was pleased to note that everyone from the Far East—and the West, I told him—was pursued with cries of 'China, China'.

From the large board in his office and the folders he had to hand, Mr Zhou and I did a calculation on the total length of road completed by CRBC or under construction. There were 13 projects in all amounting to 1,350 kilometres—840 miles of road often through the toughest of terrain. The contract price was $615 million—£370 million at the November 2009 exchange rate.

CRBC employed 1,500 Chinese on its projects in Ethiopia and probably accounted for up to a quarter of all the Chinese in the country. One of the South African university institutes which have conducted the most thorough recent research into Chinese engagement with Africa estimated that there were between 6,000 and 8,000 Chinese in Ethiopia.[2]

The country was a non-family posting for the road-builders, whatever their seniority. They got a ticket home once a year, although they might be lucky and get back on business, said Mr Zhou. 'You can see our camps. They are very tough. To tell you the truth, the living conditions are not good. Chinese come here for work. China is developing very quickly. The Chinese worker must try his best; otherwise he will lose his job. In China there is a lot of population and so the Chinese are competitive.'

The engaging Mr Zhou was proudest of all of CRBC's work around the capital. He told me how the company had won the ring road contract in 1998 after a western firm had had trouble honouring the terms. 'They couldn't face the challenge and they escaped, so our company took on the challenge.'

The ring road was financed on very favourable terms. 'China wanted a very good relationship with Ethiopia. Maybe it was free.' There were other CRBC projects aimed squarely at winning hearts and minds. The company was at work for nothing on Revolution Square in the centre of Addis Ababa and put up the money—about £13,000—for an annual relay race in a city and a country obsessed by running prowess. There is a four-kilometre

---

[2] 'China's Engagement of Africa: Preliminary Scoping of African Case Studies', Centre of Chinese Studies, University of Stellenbosch, 2007.

'China–Ethiopia Friendship Road' also built for free, starting near the airport. 'That road is very famous', said Mr Zhou. 'We needed only 70 days to finish it. The local paper says this is a miracle.'

China's largest infrastructure commitment in Ethiopia, even bigger than the roads, is in telecommunications. The $1.5 billion Ethiopia Millennium Project financed through the Export-Import Bank of China will create a fibre-optic network across the country and expand the mobile telephone system with an estimated 8.5 million new connections.[3] For those who travel in Ethiopia, and for those who will come to rely on modern communications, this development cannot come soon enough.

By the time I reached the northern town of Woldiya on my researches, I had been without a mobile telephone connection (and therefore any means of communication) for the best part of a week. I was sitting in the hotel restaurant next to a young Chinese who was eating his Sunday lunch of fish and chips. We were watching a Kung Fu movie on TV called *House of Fury* subtitled in Arabic and broadcast on satellite from the Middle East.

He worked for ZTE, the Zhong Xing Telecommunications Equipment Company, one of China's largest undertakings. He had been in the country for eight months, and had another month to go. I told him that I had had no mobile connection at all on my 0911 number since arriving in Woldiya. 'You wait three months,' he said. 'No problem.'

The Chinese are very apparent in provincial Ethiopia, but somehow less visible than westerners. Instead of sweeping around

---

[3] *Building Bridges: China's Growing Role as Infrastructure Financier for Sub-Saharan Africa* (World Bank, 2009).

in big white four-by-fours they draw up at roadside cafes in beat-up minibuses. There is something in the official Beijing line that China too is a developing country—indeed the largest developing country of them all—and that they share a bond with Africans in their common experience of European colonialism.

I had very much wanted to encounter the Chinese at close quarters in Ethiopia and my ambition was fully realized one wet night in the town of Nefas Mewcha at 10,000 feet in the northern highlands. We had driven halfway along the old 'China Road' and squeezed past the big graders preparing for the asphalt crews which came behind them. We would complete the journey to the shores of Lake Tana the next day. In the cold and drenching rain the Yemisrach Hotel was a welcome sight, and there was one room vacant on the third floor.

'Too many Chinese,' said the hotel manager, by which he meant that there were a lot of them, not an excess. The Yemisrach was headquarters for three large Chinese infrastructure projects marching in lockstep across the Amhara highlands. As well as the 'China Road' managers, there were the men in charge of laying fibre-optic cables and others working on the mobile telephone network. Forty Chinese had been living at the hotel for several months and were due to stay at least two more years. 'Very big projects,' said the hotel manager.

I took the room for four pounds and shared a squatting lavatory and washroom along the corridor with my Chinese neighbours. Their rooms were the same size as mine, but they had installed bunks for multi-occupancy. 'Three beds on top of each other—like students,' said the hotel manager. It was a crowded floor, but night-time comfort was guaranteed by the presence in the corner of my room of a pink potty with a pop-up lid.

At 6.00 a.m. there was a blast of martial music followed half an hour later by some aggressive banging on doors. By a few minutes after 7.00 all the Chinese had left for the day dressed in blue boiler suits and wide-brimmed hats and driving uniform Mitsubishi trucks and Zhan Gi jeeps.

China's interest in creating the infrastructure of the future contrasts with how the West's priorities are sometimes seen in Ethiopia. Although the European Commission spends much more than China on infrastructure projects, there is less interest from individual countries. A research paper published by the South African Institute of International Affairs in July 2009 made this observation, 'Ethiopia has continuously asked EU [European Union] countries to help provide infrastructure development, and the EU has focused mainly on calling for more liberalisation of trade and preventing Ethiopian agricultural products from coming to European markets.'[4]

Remarks made to me on the road by Ethiopians about the Chinese were almost always appreciative. Their work rate was considered awe-inspiring, and I kept being told that the roads they built were superior to those of the Ethiopian Roads Authority. I could see no difference. Formal surveys of opinion on the Chinese in Ethiopia have reached contrasting conclusions.

A report from the Pew Research Centre in Washington showed that two-thirds of Ethiopians held a generally favourable view of China compared with less than a third unfavourable—67 to 28 per cent.[5] When Ethiopians were asked whether China's growing economic influence was a good thing or a bad thing,

---

[4] Monika Thakur, *Building on Progress? Chinese Engagement in Ethiopia*.
[5] 'Global Unease with Major World Powers', The Pew Global Attitudes Project, Washington, DC, 2007.

the balance of opinion was similar—69 per cent 'good', 25 per cent 'bad'. Perhaps the most significant finding contrasted Ethiopian views on the merits of China's influence with that of the United States, the country's strategic ally and largest aid donor. Chinese influence was considered a 'good' thing by 61 per cent and a 'bad' thing by 33 per cent. This was almost a mirror image of opinion about American influence—34 per cent 'good', but 54 per cent 'bad'.

But the survey just quoted by the South African research institute looked at Chinese-owned workplaces and painted an unsettling picture of the relationship between Chinese and Ethiopians. The Chinese were said to have brought with them 'an unsavoury and racist view of Ethiopians and Africans as "lazy"; "mentally inferior/stupid"; and "lacking discipline, commitment and hard work", factors that have led to the stagnation of both country and continent.' These findings were based on off-the-record interviews and focus groups, and the researcher concluded: 'In the long run, these attitudes could have an explosive impact and potentially create a rift between "foreigners" and "locals," especially at the local level.'

The biggest charge against the Chinese in Africa—that they are interested in the continent exclusively for its vast natural re-sources—cannot be sustained in Ethiopia. Chinese companies have indeed prospected for oil in Somali Region and Gambela in the West, but none has yet been discovered, certainly not for commercial exploitation, and Chinese workers were pulled out of the Somali field after the murderous guerrilla assault on them in 2007. They have maintained operations there, but through sub-contractors. The mountains of Ethiopia may well be full of gold—a British firm found some in 2009—along with other valuable metals, but it will be many years before Ethiopia and its partners become rich on their proceeds.

In one recent year, China was nevertheless revealed as Ethiopia's top export destination. The commodity in question was sesame seeds, of which China was suffering a great dearth in 2006 and where the export of $110 million worth benefited from China's new zero tariff policy.[6] By the following year, with its sesame crisis over, China slipped back to fifth place, Germany was once again at the top, the United States was in seventh place and Britain was nowhere in the top twelve.

In 1995, China's trade with Ethiopia was $32 million. In just over a decade it rose eighteen-fold to reach $563.5 million in 2006. Two years later it doubled again to $1.1 billion. The problem is that the balance is heavily in China's favour—by a factor of around five to one—with the Chinese sending their textiles and industrial goods in exchange for oil seeds and leather in addition to some of those valuable metals. Chinese officials told me that they have tried to reduce the imbalance through the duty free regime and incentives to importers, but accept that the problem remains. 'The principle is that just for the sake of balance we won't stop exporting,' said Gu Xiaojie, China's ambassador to Ethiopia. 'We try to strike a balance or alleviate the very huge gap between the two while at the same time we try to increase total volume.'

My meeting with the ambassador was arranged by Miss Xiao, his private secretary, who asked me when it would be convenient to call. It took place at the ambassador's residence which is part of the embassy compound on the edge of Addis Ababa. As we

---

[6] 'China's Engagement of Africa', University of Stellenbosch; Monika Thakur, *Building on Progress?*

walked from the front gate, I told Miss Xiao that the grounds were as beautiful as those of the British embassy, although maybe not as extensive as the 90 acres (including the six-hole golf course) that the British have retained for more than a century.

We began the interview by tracing the history of China's associations with Ethiopia. I said that I had read there were contacts between China and the kingdom of Axum early in the Christian era. 'This would have been the Han dynasty in China, the Eastern Han dynasty,' the ambassador replied, 'and during that period the Silk Route was very much active. People came [from] North West China and Central Asia, [via the] Persian Gulf, present-day Middle East . . . and also Mediterranean countries like Egypt—maybe to Axum.'

Ambassador Gu then made an emphatic reference to the Battle of Adwa in which the Ethiopians had seen off the Italians in 1896. 'I think we both suffered and were subjugated to colonial rule and plunder, and we both through armed struggle fought very bitter battles with the European colonial powers.' In the twentieth century much had been made of Chairman Mao's commentary in support of the Ethiopians at the time of Mussolini's invasion. 'I read it,' said the ambassador. 'At that time China was being invaded by Japanese aggressors and this country was occupied by the Italian fascists.'

During the long Tigrayan struggle against the military government of Colonel Mengistu, the Chinese stuck to their 'principle of non-interference', but noted with appreciation the serious Marxist credentials of the rebels who are the rulers of today. 'They were reading the works of Chairman Mao and they knew a lot about the Chinese struggle. Meles himself read Marxist works and adopted some of the techniques and translated them into their struggle.'

In the modern era, there has been another association—their mutual experiences of poverty. As successive governments in Ethiopia have confronted and have sometimes been overwhelmed by famine, China has been lifting people out of hunger. 'Right now I think it's 20 million people still in our calculation under the poverty line in China,' said the ambassador. 'I think ten years ago it might be 200–300 million, so a huge achievement by the Chinese government and that has been acknowledged by the international community and the United Nations.'

African countries were interested in China's experiences and they compared notes, said the ambassador. 'There's a lot more to do in this country and the population is growing and some people are still suffering from malnutrition and they need emergency relief, but I think this government is committed to lifting people out of poverty.'

The record shows that China has three times given emergency food aid to Ethiopia. In the famine years of 1984 and 1985 the Chinese gave 290,000 tons of maize to a number of African countries, including Ethiopia,[7] and Mr Xu of the Economic and Commercial Counsellor's Office said that in the 2008 emergency China had given Ethiopia $400,000 worth of food. But the aid relationship has grown dramatically in recent years.

In 2005 Tony Blair hosted the G8's 'Africa' summit at Gleneagles, the climax of Britain's 'Year of Africa'. President Hu Jintao of China was invited to Scotland, but was not apparently invited to discuss Africa.[8] It was an omission unlikely to be repeated. In 2006 in the Great Hall of the People, China held an African

---

[7] 'China's Engagement of Africa'.
[8] 'Globalisation and Global Poverty', Submission to the Shadow Cabinet, Conservative Party, London, 2007.

summit of its own with most of Africa's leadership in attendance. This was the Forum on China–Africa Cooperation (FOCAC) where Ethiopia emerged close to centre-stage.

Addis Ababa had hosted key ministerial meetings leading up to the summit, and when the time came for the 'reading-out ceremony' of the declaration in the Great Hall, Prime Minister Meles Zenawi was in the forefront on the right-hand side of President Hu. President Mubarak of Egypt was on the left.

In Chinese eyes Ethiopia is much more than the poverty-stricken basket case of Western image. Its resistance to European colonialism counts for something. So too does its role as permanent host to the African Union and the United Nations Economic Commission for Africa. It is the major strategic power in the Horn of Africa, a status dubiously confirmed by its decision to invade Somalia in 2006 with American encouragement. The country has also owed its contemporary recognition to the intellectual command of Meles Zenawi, the African leader to whom the world listened most.

At the FOCAC summit China made a number of aid pledges to Africa—to double aid by 2009; to provide $5 billion in loans and credits; to cancel debt to the poorest countries—and Ethiopia was alone in benefiting from them all.[9] It became, for instance, the first country in Africa to receive Chinese volunteers, replicating such earlier western initiatives as the US Peace Corps and the UK's Voluntary Service Overseas. More young Chinese volunteers have arrived since—doctors, teachers, and IT specialists.

'The assistance given by the Chinese government is very much limited compared to that given by western donors because China is a developing country,' said Ambassador Gu. He then sang his

---

[9] Monika Thakur, *Building on Progress?*

own hymn of praise to roads, 'Of course infrastructure is very much essential to rural development—that's our lesson. When they have their roads and infrastructure, they can ferry their harvests, they can transport what they've grown because the country is developing commercial agriculture. If you've already harvested crops or horticultural produce but don't have adequate infrastructure [Here Mr Gu raised his voice for emphasis] *how do you make money out of your harvests?*'

If roads were an answer, were there other lessons to be learnt from China's rise out of poverty? The ambassador had mentioned Ethiopia's population growth, and I asked him whether China's restrictions on childbirth were relevant here. 'What is happening in China proves it is suitable in our development,' he replied, but then repeated several times that this was a matter for the Ethiopians. 'My impression is that the government will not implement a kind of restrictive policy on population out of their cultural heritage, religious considerations, and many other factors—and of course the population policy is for the Ethiopian government to handle. It is not for somebody else from outside to comment.'

'Non-interference in each other's internal affairs' was the principle most often invoked in my conversations with Chinese officials over their role in Ethiopia. Ambassador Gu kept coming back to it. In his view it marked out the Chinese from the western approach to aid and development. 'Sometimes some of the western countries impose; that's something we never do. The big difference is that most of the time the western governments attach strings, but China never attaches any political strings to our assistance and we never say "If we provide this, then you will do this." No political strings—that is the very essential part of our assistance.'

The West's use of aid to bring 'good governance' to Ethiopia was resisted with increasing vehemence by Prime Minister Meles and China's stance fortified his position. 'Good governance can only come from inside,' he told a journalist in 2007.[10] 'It cannot be imposed from outside. That was always an illusion. What the Chinese have done is explode that illusion.'

What the Chinese also did, according to critics of the EPRDF government, was to reduce any prospect that the 'developmental state' promoted by Meles would turn out to be anything other than an 'authoritarian developmental state' in which 'economic growth trumps and is pursued at the expense of political development, democratisation and justice'.[11] That was the view of two prominent Ethiopian academics interviewed for the South African research study which I have already quoted.

One telling example of Ethiopia's official restrictiveness was the blocking of anti-government material on websites and blogs, particularly from Ethiopians in exile in the United States and Europe. The Open Net Initiative recorded in 2009 'substantial' filtering of sites covering politics, conflict, and security in Ethiopia, although the average visitor would be hard-pressed to tell the difference between a very poor dial-up service and deliberate blocking. I was told by a European 'governance' adviser that China had provided Addis Ababa with the software it used to block these sites. I was not able to confirm that.

The South African study already quoted concluded: 'Due to China's policy of non-interference, there is a possibility that the incumbent regime in Ethiopia could use Chinese assistance to avoid changes in the direction of the rule of law, democratisation,

---

[10] *Financial Times*, 6 February 2007, quoted in Deborah Brautigam, *The Dragon's Gift* (Oxford University Press, 2009).
[11] Monika Thakur, *Building on Progress?*

accountability and human rights. This has the potential of creating authoritarian stagnation, as opposed to authoritarian development.'

As the enormity of the global economic crisis struck home during 2009, Meles Zenawi was raising public alarm at its likely impact on Africa. He told fellow African leaders in February that 'the coming decade is likely to be very dark indeed for Africa', and that without additional, better-administered aid and more action on climate change 'the majority of African states could become failed or failing states'.

By November he was asking delegates at an African economic conference whether it was even 'possible to foster development when we have a whole era of economic crisis ahead of us'. Yet his analysis of how Africa should respond to the crisis had changed over the months and he appeared to have reduced his faith in western ideas of development because 'neoliberalism and the associated strategy of managing chronic poverty were largely imposed on Africa' and had 'now become thoroughly discredited...'

'For several decades now, managing chronic poverty was the name of the economic game in Africa and in recent years we had begun to do well in that regard, although there were significant and tragic exceptions to it.' Then came the global crisis that threatened 'to push our economies over the precipice'. Development aid was under pressure; foreign investment was down; and climate change threatened 'the very survival of African agriculture, the mainstay of our economies.' What was the upshot? 'The current era of economic crisis thus makes our strategy of managing chronic poverty unviable.'

There were some rays of hope, he said. The world might be serious about climate change and Africa could be the beneficiary. A better prospect lay with China, however. Rising Chinese labour costs might encourage some of their industry to relocate to Africa. More likely was that the Chinese would direct 'some of their surplus savings to infrastructural development in Africa . . . it is not only possible but also highly probable that the Chinese will take the steps that would widen the window of opportunity for Africa.'

Chapter 14
Us and Them

'Oh my God, this is the challenge of our careers.'

For a time I really did think that the village of Koraro had been overtaken by some Third World calamity—an earthquake perhaps or an aerial bombardment. We arrived there in the fierce midday sun. There was not a soul in sight. On each side of the main street there were rows of small stone houses which appeared empty. Some were just piles of rubble. Others were boarded up. Most seemed partially built—or partly destroyed. Either way, they looked abandoned.

After my friend Yohannes and I had stood for a few minutes wondering what to do next, a little girl in a green dress edged out of one of the buildings. Her hair was combed back and tightly plaited in the Tigrayan fashion. She was joined by another little girl in a red dress who looked like Olive Oyl in the Popeye cartoons. Then a young man emerged in a baseball cap with a silver cross around his neck and a transistor radio in his arm. The young man told us that some of the houses had been occupied for a time but that people had moved out because of the food shortages. He thought about three-quarters of them had gone off to the towns in search of a better living.

Koraro is one of a number of Millennium Villages around Africa chosen to show that foreign aid really can work—even in the most unpromising places. The project is the brainchild of Professor Jeffrey Sachs, director of the Earth Institute at Columbia University in New York and the leading academic advocate of the rich world making big new aid commitments to the poor. He has said that the end of poverty by 2025 is within reach.[1]

There were signs up and down the main road welcoming travellers to the Koraro Millennium Village, but nothing to tell you where to turn off. From the junction it was still another 12 miles to reach the village. Instead of fields on either side of the track the prospect was almost entirely barren. For several miles there were just hillocks of black rock and shale resembling the waste tips of coal mines.

On the last few miles of our journey the horizon was dominated by a fringe of massive sandstone cliffs and crazy sandstone towers. This is the Gheralta region of Tigray, part of what Ethiopia's tourist authorities describe as an open-air museum. High up in the clefts of these natural fortifications are exquisite medieval churches, each guarded by a resident priest. My Bradt guidebook advised that climbing up to one in particular 'should emphatically not be attempted by anybody who has doubts about their agility, or has even the mildest tendency towards vertigo'. Older guidebooks suggested obtaining ropes from the village.

When Prof. Sachs first drove through this landscape to see Koraro, he turned to one of his colleagues and said, 'This may be

---

[1] Jeffrey Sachs, Reith Lecture 4, BBC Radio, May 2007.

one village too far.' There were other aid specialists from the Earth Institute with him, and there was general consternation at what they had taken on. 'Oh my God, this is the challenge of our careers.'

We set off to the marketplace in Koraro to find someone who could show us around. We met Yehameh who worked for the Millennium Villages Project. I asked him whether he had ever met Prof. Sachs. 'I have met the owner twice,' he replied. 'Founder', I corrected him.

In academic circles there has been a debate over the eye-catching Millennium Villages Project. Does it really work? How would we know? Can it be sustained? Can it be scaled up? Many of the critics do not appear to have been to these villages or studied them on the ground. To do that would perhaps taint science with anecdote. I can report only what I saw and heard in Koraro. What emerged was a very mixed picture of the fortunate and unfortunate.

For a start I heard more about the tumbledown houses. The drought of 2008 had indeed driven people out, but the houses were freshly built in anticipation of the aid-funded good times, and these people would return. Electricity would shortly reach Koraro—supplied by government, not the aid-givers—and that would be a powerful incentive to come back. I had smelt the fresh creosote on piles of electricity poles dumped by the roadside. They would soon be erected to carry the new power lines.

Our first call was on the health post in Koraro. It turned out to be closed for a Moslem holiday, although that had not stopped health posts back along the main road being open and busy. Health staff were summoned from home to tell me about the assistance they had received from the millennium project. There was a minibus to take patients to hospital, but unfortunately the vehicle was away for repair at the moment. The health post now had running water, but the generator supplied by the project to pump it into the compound had unfortunately broken down seven months ago, so the system was not working. This meant that the new testing laboratory and its technician financed by the project were not yet functioning properly.

The Millennium Villages Project had built a new health clinic about eight miles away as it began to expand further into the neighbourhood. Solar panels to provide electricity had been installed with some fanfare, but the clinic was not yet open. The windows had not arrived and the government had yet to fulfil its part of the bargain by providing medical staff, basic equipment, and drugs.

One of the project's big investments was building a community flour mill. Whether farmers have grown their own food or in a bad year had to rely on food aid, they must pay to have the grain milled. The idea behind the community mill was to help the poor by locating it close to the middle of Koraro and to subsidize the cost so as to make it cheaper than the privately run mills.

On every rural journey I took in Ethiopia, a visit to the local flour mill was a high point. In villages without shops or post offices or pubs, the mill provides the communal focus of all three. It's a long wait for your turn at the mill and a chance to gossip. The men gather on one side of the compound, the women on the other, and the mules and donkeys are all around them. Everyone still in the queue looks quite normal. Everyone who has been through the mill has turned ghostly white.

Kahsu Assefa, the manager, emerged into the sunlight covered from the top of his head to the toe of his sandals in flour dust. As we talked, I began to understand something of the mysterious economics of the community mill. When it first opened, the two private mills in Koraro were charging farmers 12 birr per quintal (80p per 100 kg) to have their grain milled. The Millennium Villages Project decided to charge 8 birr (50p) per quintal, a saving of more than a third for the poor of Koraro.

That was the position in 2005. What were the prices in 2009? All three mills were now charging the same—20 birr per quintal (£1.30 per 100 kg). This was a 60 per cent increase for the two private mills, but an amazing 160 per cent hike for poor people who used the community mill. What was the reason? 'The price of fuel,' said Kahsu. 'Originally it was cheap because of low fuel prices.'

But what happened to the differential for the poor? Well, there was still a tiny subsidy for tiny quantities of grain. The needy widow, for instance, who had just a kilo of grain could still have it milled for a few cents less at the community mill (20 cents instead of 25), but that was all. 'In the beginning, the assumption was to provide a service at low prices to support poor people,' said Kahsu. 'But, as I've told you, they make it now a similar price.'

It took an interview with an Ethiopian professor at Columbia to resolve this mystery. Professor Awash Teklehaimanot coordinates the Ethiopian village project and is responsible for malaria and neglected tropical diseases for all the millennium villages in Africa. What had happened in Koraro, he explained, was that the community mill provided by the project had in fact now been handed over to the community. 'There is a committee run by the Women's Association,' said Prof. Awash. 'They set the prices and they use the resources for other purposes—credit schemes or hand pumps. They have seen the demand and they have seen that even if they raise the prices, they won't lose money. We don't interfere.'

The first phase of the Millennium Villages Project—'A New Approach to Fighting Poverty'—was planned to run for five years, from 2005 to 2010. Jeffrey Sachs's team at Columbia has worked closely in the field with United Nations agencies and host governments. It has had the financial support of big foundations and corporate donors. Each village has received $125,000 a year and as the Ethiopian project has expanded to other communities in the neighbourhood the commitment there has grown to $450,000.

In Koraro itself the project's greatest success has been its response to the desperate scarcity of water. Spend just a couple of hours around that village and the phrase 'water of life' takes on new meaning. It rains on occasions in Koraro, of course, as it does elsewhere in the stony hills of Tigray, and sometimes it pours. The water cascades down the gullies of those sandstone cliffs, joins streams that are carefully marked 'seasonal' on the map, and then disappears. With luck the stony fields have been properly watered and there will be food to grow. Then drought returns.

Village wells are as cheerful places as the village mills, except here only women and girls meet up to talk and wave back at passing vehicles. If they are not already at the pumps, their yellow plastic jerricans will be lined up in the queue for later in the day. The millennium project has laid down five kilometres of pipeline to bring water into Koraro and we drove to its source as afternoon shadows began to throw the sculpture of the cliffs into dramatic relief.

Up ahead was a slash of vegetation marking the ravine whose seasonal torrents had to be tapped. In partnership with the World Food Programme, the Millennium Villages Project had constructed a series of dams out of stones encased in wire (I learnt a new word 'gabion') and the run-off had been halted. The whole way back to the village more little dams, percolation ponds, and trenches were all aimed at making sure that the water went to give life and not to waste.

Right up under the cliffs irrigation ditches fed off the dams and watered steep fields of papaya trees and chillies. Here was one small community which was truly flourishing. On almost vertical ground above their heads, farmers had placed new beehives supplied by the project. Everywhere I went in the rural North there was a bee-keeping scheme—another 'cash crop' and a supplement to farm income. 'Everyone in Tigray is going to be very sweet,' said one of the Koraro managers.

Later in 2009 Professor Sachs himself visited Koraro again as part of a Millennium Villages Project annual retreat and he told me afterwards he had been very excited by what he saw. But Koraro was still a 'fraught environment. You can kind of see the pathway through but it is like threading a needle.' He spoke of the degraded environment and the water scarcity—both of which the project was trying to address—but among the 'forces of disorder' threatening the region he singled out climate change and demographic pressures.

> I feel that unless the fertility rate comes down sharply I'm running out of ideas. I can't see how to keep ahead of the kind of population growth that Ethiopia and other countries in the region are experiencing. I believe I can help to find the solution *if* the population and fertility rates are brought down very quickly and give a time path towards stabilization of the population.

I reminded him that Ethiopia's population had doubled since the famine in Tigray twenty-five years ago and could double again in the next twenty-five years.

> It is absolutely unmanageable. This landscape, this physical environment is so unforgiving and the difficulties for any society

to manage fertility rates of five, six or seven [children per woman] are beyond any of our tools right now.

Had the 'development community' dropped the ball on the population issue? 'Absolutely. This whole discussion has been suppressed by a few fundamentalists, including the United States.' Prof. Sachs was referring to the decades of Christian Right predominance in America where the critical importance of contraception was consistently downplayed. 'This has been a conscious and not a hidden conspiracy of silence.'

Turning to what I had termed the 'development community', he said he no longer believed such a community existed. 'I'm nearly giving up on our country because we don't have the honesty or stamina to do this. And what is interesting is that China is playing a much larger role. I'm truly grateful for that, I have to say, because for all the debates about China's role, the fact of the matter is that they are doing something—where we are not there at all.'

For Jeffrey Sachs to betray such pessimism is striking. This is the man who drew up the blueprint for how the United Nations Development Goals could be reached by 2015. His 2005 book *The End of Poverty* was subtitled 'How we can make it happen in our lifetime', a timeframe he subsequently revised downwards. He co-founded and heads the Millennium Promise Alliance, 'Extreme Poverty Ends Here'. He is the great prophet of 'Big Aid' and has declared himself an optimist in the past.

With the world in the grip of economic crisis, will there be enough new aid?

I think there is a very good chance it won't be forthcoming, but it has nothing to do with the economic crisis because that was true during the boom as well as the crisis . . . I've heard every explanation you can imagine as to why not to give aid. So I'm utterly, completely unimpressed with an argument about the business cycle. I've been on this issue for twenty years. It's nothing to do with the business cycle. It's just an attitude, deeply ingrained, an attitude of politics.

Looking at the rich world, Sachs said that some countries did continue to show a serious commitment to the poor world. He identified the Scandinavians as 'the ones doing the pushing'. I asked him about Britain, which has been considered a leader in development since the establishment of an independent Department for International Development in 1997. 'The British have been in the middle of the pack. They are big talkers, modest deliverers.' He said that the G8 Gleneagles summit hosted by Britain in 2005 had been the moment when the rich world made their commitment to the Millennium Development Goals and 'to doubling aid to Africa and getting the job done. After that effort was made, there was no follow-through. The British followed through a bit on their own, but not in continuing to honour what was promised under British leadership.'

Prof. Sachs concluded that the rich would now suffer from what he termed the severe consequences of a less just and more unstable world. 'I view this not as inexplicable, but as a lack of moral imagination, leadership, and awareness. We've essentially not heard a word about this from President Obama ... I know the dynamics inside the White House. They absolutely don't want to talk about this issue except when they absolutely have to. And they don't have to very often.'

The deadline for reaching the Millennium Development Goals is 2015, and Ethiopia has made some remarkable progress. The country had three times as many children in primary school as it had in 1990 and was on track to meet Goal Two by providing universal primary education by 2015. Gender equality in school enrolment was also on track with the primary school ratio rising from 7 girls to 10 boys in 1990 to 9 girls to 10 boys in 2007.

Some of the goals are so off track there is little or no hope Ethiopia will reach them. The world signed up in 2000 to reduce maternal mortality during pregnancy and childbirth by three-quarters. It is failing to deliver. The world promised to cut mortality among children under 5 by two-thirds. It is very unlikely to happen. There has been some progress in both areas in Ethiopia, but the world promised more than some progress.

Goal One was to halve extreme poverty and hunger by 2015 and for Ethiopia that has been the touchstone. Extreme poverty was defined as living on less than $1 a day. United Nations figures had it declining from 60 per cent of the population in 1995 to 39 per cent a decade later. Overall figures for hunger ('undernourishment') have shown a similarly impressive fall from 71 per cent of the population in 1991 to 46 per cent in 2004. Ethiopia was officially the hungriest country in the world in 1991, according to the Global Hunger Index. By 2009 it had risen six places, although it remained in the 'extremely alarming' category.

For western political leaders facing the future, 'it's the economy, stupid.' For an Ethiopian political leader, it's the economics of poverty. Widespread death from starvation led to the undermining and eventual destruction of the last two Ethiopian governments. In my final interview with Meles Zenawi in April 2009, I questioned him on the prospects for the people of Ethiopia, for his government and for himself.

On the Millennium Development Goals, he accepted there were problems on maternal and child mortality. But on Goal

One, he displayed a politician's emphatic optimism. 'As far as halving poverty is concerned, we will achieve it. I have no doubt about it.' He went further: 'I believe by 2025 we will be a middle income country with a per capita income of at least $1,000 [per annum] and at around that time, slightly before perhaps, we will be completely free of aid of any variety. We will not need food aid much earlier than that.'

Having reintroduced the question of aid, he reiterated his complaint that western donors had consistently used it to impose their own policy preferences on Ethiopia. 'By 2025 I am confident we will reach a stage where we do not have to externalize accountability by depending on aid.'

Complex international crises promoted Meles Zenawi to prominence on the world stage in 2009. He represented Africa at both the London and the Pittsburgh G20 summits on the global economic meltdown. In December he led Africa's delegation to the climate change summit in Copenhagen. At home the political and security chessboard presented a set of problems every bit as intricate.

National elections were due in 2010, the first since disputed polls five years earlier had ended in violence and repression. They would not be fought in the spirit that made 2005 such a landmark in Ethiopian history. Although many opposition parties would contest the polls, the most prominent grouping had been cowed and fractured by a government determined to hold the ring. Exiles argued for the government's violent removal and there were the stirrings of revolt in the countryside.

I met Dr Berhanu Nega, the opposition leader in exile, when he visited Europe to meet his supporters in June 2009. He was later condemned to death in his absence for plotting to overthrow the government. 'In the next five years a more coordinated resistance to

Meles is going to gain momentum—much before 2015—in a very, very serious way,' he told me. 'So the future is going to be dependent on his forces—how the state responds to this. But the determination to fight is now sealed. It is done. OK.'

Dr Berhanu named his 'May 15' organization after the date of the 2005 elections. 'The main part of the organization is in Ethiopia. A few symbols of the leadership are outside. We will make it impossible for them to govern while those who are armed will make it impossible for them to repress without resistance.' He said that conventional political opposition was no longer possible and that there were already 'six or seven' active guerrilla movements in the country. 'Real political struggle is no more in Ethiopia. If it is, it is clandestine, it is underground, and that's what we are doing. If not it would be the other armed movements.'

Meles and his fellow guerrillas came to power almost twenty years ago and the core policy document his party adopted in 1993 referred to a development strategy covering 'a period of up to two decades'. The prime minister himself has spoken of the need for renewal, and for several years journalists had pressed him to clarify what he meant by saying he wanted to leave office. But African leaders and their parties rarely go quietly, least of all those that came to power through the bullet.

Ten years ago, said Meles, the EPRDF declared that its biggest achievement and therefore its ultimate objective was 'to make itself redundant'. I asked him if this was still the aim. 'If it doesn't do that, it has failed absolutely—miserably failed in its objective. That is exactly the same argument for my own role.'

I asked him if the party accepted it would have to do without Meles. 'It's not just about Meles. It's about the old generation of leadership, the armed struggle leadership. There is consensus that the leadership has to go. I think there is more or less unanimity that the next five year period [2010–15] should be the transition period. Which part of the next five years is the only debate I am aware of. Sometime during the next term the whole leadership has to go—I think there is a very broad consensus.'

The years leading to 2015 could be perilous for Ethiopia. If Meles means what he says, there needs to be a period of political reopening to compensate for the recent restricting of political space. Most of those I spoke to are not sanguine. The autocratic tradition in Ethiopia is too strong; the fearfulness and insecurity that seem to lie at the heart of the Tigrayan leadership are too great.

Yet Meles has shown himself to be a brilliant tactician as well as a far-sighted leader. If he does not achieve the peaceful transition he promises, it will be in his own words an absolute and miserable failure. His personal legacy will be in question. There will be a cost to the modest but real progress that Ethiopia has made under his government. It will be borne by poor and hungry Ethiopians.

Select Bibliography

Barnett, Michael, and Weiss, Thomas G. (eds.), *Humanitarianism in Question* (Cornell University Press, 2008).

Black, Maggie, *A Cause for Our Times* (Oxfam, 1992).

Brautigam, Deborah, *The Dragon's Gift* (Oxford University Press, 2009).

Buerk, Michael, *The Road Taken* (Hutchinson, 2004).

Clapham, Christopher, *Transformation and Continuity in Revolutionary Ethiopia* (Cambridge University Press, 1988).

Collier, Paul, *The Bottom Billion* (Oxford University Press, 2007).

Davis, Mike, *Late Victorian Holocausts* (Verso, 2001).

Devereux, Stephen (ed.), *The New Famines* (Routledge, 2007).

de Waal, Alex, *Evil Days: 30 Years of War and Famine in Ethiopia* (Human Rights Watch, 1991).

—— *Famine Crimes* (James Currey, 1997).

Duffield, Mark, *Development, Security and Unending War* (Polity Press, 2007).

—— and Prendergast, John, *Without Troops and Tanks* (Red Sea Press, 1994).

Easterly, William, *The White Man's Burden* (Oxford University Press, 2006).

Geldof, Bob, *Is That It?* (Sidgwick and Jackson, 1986).

Gill, Peter, *Drops in the Ocean* (Macdonald Unit 75, 1970).

—— *A Year in the Death of Africa* (Paladin, 1986).

Henze, Paul B., *Ethiopia in Mengistu's Final Years*, vols. i and ii (Shama Books, 2007).

Jackson, Laura, *Bono, the Biography* (Judy Piatkus, 2001).

Korn, David, *Ethiopia, the U.S. and the Soviet Union* (Croom Helm, 1986).

Markakis, John, *National and Class Conflict in the Horn of Africa* (Zed Books, 1990).

Marsden, Philip, *The Chains of Heaven* (Harper Perennial, 2006).

Mockler, Anthony, *Haile Selassie's War* (Oxford University Press, 1984).

Moyo, Dambisa, *Dead Aid* (Allen Lane, 2009).

Pankhurst, Alula, *Resettlement and Famine in Ethiopia* (Manchester University Press, 1992).

Pankhurst, Richard, *The History of Famine and Epidemics in Ethiopia Prior to the Twentieth Century* (Relief and Rehabilitation Commission, Addis Ababa, 1985).

Rahmato, Dessalegn, *Agrarian Reform in Ethiopia* (Nordic Africa Institute, Uppsala, 1984).

Riddell, Roger C., *Does Foreign Aid Really Work?* (Oxford University Press, 2007).

Rieff, David, *A Bed for the Night: Humanitarianism in Crisis* (Simon & Schuster, 2002).

Sachs, Jeffrey, *The End of Poverty* (Allen Lane, 2005).

Sen, Amartya, *Development as Freedom* (Oxford University Press, 2001).

Shepherd, Jack, *The Politics of Starvation* (Carnegie Endowment for International Peace, Washington, DC, 1975).

Starving in Silence: A Report on Famine and Censorship (Article 19, April 1990).

Stiglitz, Joseph, *Globalization and its Discontents* (Penguin Books, 2002).

Terry, Fiona, *Condemned to Repeat? The Paradox of Humanitarian Action* (Cornell University Press, 2002).

Thakur, Monika, *Building on Progress? Chinese Engagement in Ethiopia* (South African Institute of International Affairs, 2009).

U2 and Neil McCormick, *U2 by U2* (HarperCollins Entertainment, 2006).

Vaux, Tony, *The Selfish Altruist* (Earthscan, 2001).

Waugh, Evelyn, *Waugh in Abyssinia* (Longmans, Green & Co., 1936).

Wolde-Giorgis, Dawit, *Red Tears: War, Famine and Revolution in Ethiopia* (Red Sea Press, 1989).

Wolde-Mariam, Mesfin, *Rural Vulnerability to Famine in Ethiopia 1958–1977* (Intermediate Technology, 1986).

Wrong, Michela, *I Didn't Do It for You* (Fourth Estate, 2005).

Young, John, *Peasant Revolution in Ethiopia* (Cambridge University Press, 1997).

Zewde, Bahru, *Pioneers of Change in Ethiopia* (James Currey, 2002).

Index

Abdinasir Mohammed 200
Action Aid 19–21, 156, 158
Addis Ababa University 24, 75,
    128, 145
Adwa 64
    battle of 248
African Union 250
Agricultural Marketing
    Corporation 56–7
aid conditionality *see*
    conditionality
AIDS 135
Albania 74–5
Alexander, Douglas 179
Amare Aregawi 161–5
Amin, Mohammed 37, 40
Article 19: 51
Assefa Hailemariam, Dr 128, 133
Awash Teklehaimanot, Prof 259
Axum, Kingdom of 1, 248

Band Aid 12–13, 52
Barnett, Prof Michael 192–3, 208
BBC 34, 36–7, 39–40, 101, 175

Benn, Hilary 153–4, 159
Bereket Simon 148–9, 166–7
Berhan Hailu 189–90
Berhanu Geleto 185–7
Berhanu Nega, Dr 95; and 2005
    elections 146, 148–50, 154,
    157; in exile 157, 160, 173,
    265–6
Biafra War 208
Birhan Woldu 21–3, 53
birth control *see* family planning
Birtukan Mideksa 171–3
Bitter Harvest 40
Blair, Tony 80, 154, 159, 179–80,
    249
Bono 13
Bowie, David 22
Bradt Guide 256
Brauman, Dr Rony 50–1, 181–2
Britain 263
    aid 153, 159, 180–1; charity
    law 194–5; trade 247; *see
    also* DFID
British Airways 226–7

British embassy 188, 248
Brown, Gordon 179
Buerk, Michael 36–7, 40, 101–2
Bush, George W 102, 130, 151; *see also* United States

CNN 225, 227–9, 231
CAFOD, Catholic Agency for Overseas Development 194
Cameron, David 180
Canadian Broadcasting Corporation 22
Carter Centre 143–4
Carter, President Jimmy 143
Catholic Relief Services 235
Channel 4 News 152
Charities and Societies Proclamation 182, 184, 189, 191, 194
Charity Commission (UK) 195
China: aid 249–51; non-interference policy 251–2; one child policy 135, 251; relations with Ethiopians 245–6; road-building 10, 115, 238–44, 251; trade 113, 247
China Road and Bridge Corporation (CRBC) 240–3
Chinese in Ethiopia 238–254; attack on 204–5, 246

Christian Aid 3
Christian Children's Fund 235
Christian Relief and Development Association (CRDA) 177–8
Christian Right 262
civil society organisations (CSOs) 153, 164, 176–8, 183, 185, 189–90, 192
climate change 253, 265
Clinton administration 81, 88
Coalition for Unity and Democracy (CUD) 142–3, 154, 171, 190
Columbia University, New York 256, 259–60
Commission for Africa 80, 180
Commission of Inquiry (election violence) 154–5
conditionality 167, 170, 183, 191, 265 *see also* governance
Community Development Initiative 125, 176
contraception *see* family planning
Copenhagen summit 265
Cox, Brendan 179
Cuban troops 56

Daily Telegraph 229
Daniel Bakele 155–8
Davis, Mike 27–8
Dawit Wolde-Giorgis 44–5
Dawood Mohammed Ali 209

de Waal, Alex 43, 48–9, 60–1, 72, 100
Demographic Health Survey 134
Department for International Development (DFID) 179, 214, 263; aid suspensions 159–60, 198; governance 160
Derg, the 36, 84, 141, 178; and 1984 famine 39, 75, 101, 166; and attack on Hawzien 61, 143; decline and fall 62, 71–2, 76, 187; military operations 33, 60–2, 73; and population 121; and resettlement 14, 54, 60, 68, 103, 188; Soviet experiments 56–8, 92, 216
Dessalegn Rahmato, Dr 47–8, 104, 188–9
Development as Freedom 167
developmental state *see* Meles Zenawi
Devereux, Stephen 216
Dimbleby, Jonathan 28–31, 33–6, 98–9
direct budget support 159–60
Disaster Prevention and Preparedness Agency 97
Dubois, Marc 193–4
Duffield, Prof Mark 69–70, 193
Dutch Interchurch Aid 68

Earth Institute 256–7
elections: 2005: 141–60, 188; post-election violence 147–8, 152, 154–5, 170, 189, 207, 266; 2010: 171, 233, 265
Emergency Relief Desk 68–9
Erasmus University, Rotterdam 79, 168
Eritrea, liberation struggle 36, 45, 68, 76
Eritrea, war with Ethiopia 79, 137, 197–9, 205
Eritrean People's Liberation Front 73
Ethiopian Airlines 84
Ethiopian Economics Association 81, 95
Ethiopian Herald 25, 149, 150
Ethiopian Human Rights Council 24, 187
Ethiopian Nutrition Institute 30
Ethiopian People's Revolutionary Democratic Front, EPRDF: achievements 183; cadres 234–5; coming to power 74–6, 85, 163, 177; and elections 141, 143–4, 146, 150, 157; and famine 166; future 266; and NGOs 182–3, 187–8; policies 66, 80, 93, 121
Ethiopian Roads Authority 245

Ethiopian Telecommunications 92
Ethiopian Television 162
Europe:
aid 69, 151, 180, 201; European Commission 151, 159, 245; European Community 11, 39, 69; European Parliament 146; European Union 184, 188, 245
European Union election observer mission 143–8, 150–1, 163
Export-Import Bank of China 243

Family Guidance Association of Ethiopia (FGAE) 130–2
family planning 16, 128–37 *see also* population
famine 27, 166; in 1958: 25–7; in 1973: 28–32, 34, 38, 98, 177, 222; in 1984: 9, 11–18, 31, 36, 42, 98–9, 166, 177, 198, 207, 221, 231, 237; in 2003, threat of 97–100, 231; in 2008, food crisis 123, 213–237; in Somali Region 197–9, 203
Finance and Economic Development, Ministry of 138

Food and Agriculture Organisation, United Nations 38
Foreign Affairs, Ministry of 206, 208, 215
Forsyth, Justin 179
Fortune newspaper 90, 184
Forum for Social Studies 188
Forum on China-Africa Cooperation (FOCAC) 250

G8 152, 180, 249, 263
G20 265
Geldof, Bob 12–13, 21, 23; and Margaret Thatcher 41–2; and 2005 elections 152–3
General Wingate School 162
Geneva Conventions 205
Germany 247
Gisela, Sister 223
Gleneagles Summit 152, 180, 249, 263
Global Gag Rule 130–1
Globalisation and its Discontents 82, 85
Gomes, Ana 146–8, 150–1, 172
Gorbachev, Mikhail 61
governance 135, 153, 158–60, 167–8, 170, 178, 182–3, 191, 252; and China, 252
Gross Stein, Prof Janice 192
Gu Xiaojie 247–8, 250–1

Haile Selassie, Emperor 1, 2, 54, 58, 130, 138, 141, 166;
and 1958 famine 25;
and 1973 famine 26, 29, 34;
downfall and murder 1, 2, 26, 33–5
Hailu Araya, Dr 173–4
Hawzien, attack on 61, 143
Heavily Indebted Poor Countries Initiative (HIPC) 90
Henry, Thierry 117
Henze, Paul 57, 71, 74–5
Hewitt, Gavin 229
HIV/AIDS see AIDS
Howard, Jim 42
Hoxha, Enver 74
Hu Jintao, President 249–50
Human Rights Commission 166, 172
Human Rights Watch 43, 48, 72, 204

Institute of Development Studies 214, 216
International Committee of the Red Cross (ICRC) 205–8, 210, 212
International Monetary Fund (IMF) 81–94, 96
Islamic Relief 202
Italian colonisers 2, 5, 27
ITV 34, 37, 39–40, 98–9

Jackson, Michael 12
Jima Dilbo 190–1
Jochum, Dr Bruno 211–13
Jones, Beverley 194
Jubilee Campaign 90
Judd, Lord 179

Kality prison 157
Kennedy, John F 3
Kenya 213, 215
Kershaw, Sir Anthony 40–1
King, Dr Kenneth 38
Kissinger, Henry 3
Korn, David 61

Labour government 179, 181
land ownership 91–6
LeFort, René 142–3
Live 8 13, 22
Live Aid 3, 13, 22, 53
Ljungqvist, Bjorn 226–8, 231
'Lucy' 120

McGuinness, Paul 13
Mackay, Col. Hugh 40
Madonna 22
Make Poverty History 3, 13, 152
Mao Tse Tung 248
Marxism, Marxist-Leninism 75

Médecins Sans Frontières
(MSF) 182, 193, 205, 207–10,
213; and 2008 food
emergency 223–4, 235; MSF
Belgium 51, 212, 223, 225;
MSF Greece 212, 223; MSF
Holland 211–12; MSF
Switzerland 211–12; and
resettlement 49–51; in
Somali Region 205, 209–11
Meesook, Oey 91
Media Law 163, 184
Meles Zenawi:
and 2003 food
emergency 102–3, 117–18;
and 2005 elections 145, 150,
153–4; and 2008 food
emergency 226, 232–3; and
Birtukan Mideksa 171; and
the Charities Law 194 *see
also* NGOs; and China 250,
252–4; and the Commission
for Africa 152; and the
constitution 59; and
democracy 168–9; and the
developmental state 85, 91,
168–9, 252; and direct budget
support 159–60; education
and studies 79–80; and
famine 4, 101; and the
future 266–7; and governance
and conditionality
164, 167–8, 170, 265; as

guerrilla leader 63–4, 66–7,
72, 74–5; and the international
financial institutions 83, 90,
93; and land ownership 93–4;
and the Millennium
Development Goals 135,
264–5; and NGOs 182,
184, 191–2, 194; and
neoliberalism 85, 90, 96, 169,
253; and population 136–7;
and the press 162, 164–5; and
the state of Africa 253; and
war with Eritrea 79, 198; and
world economic crisis 253–4
Melrose, Dianna 179
Menelik II, Emperor 28
Mengistu Haile-Mariam,
Colonel 36, 70–1, 177, 198,
248; fall of 76; and
famine 39, 43, 56; and Red
Terror 65–66; and
resettlement 43, 46, 48; and
Soviet Union 57, 61–2
Mesfin Wolde-Mariam, Prof
24–5, 31, 94, 150, 171, 1732
Millennium Development
Goals 135, 186, 262–5
Millennium Promise
Alliance 262
Millennium Villages
Project 256–61
Ministry of Foreign Affairs *see*
Foreign Affairs, Ministry of

Missionaries of Charity 222–3, 234–5
Mother Teresa 222–3, 235
Mubarak, President 250
Mugabe, Robert 76

National Election Board 147, 189
Natsios, Andrew 102
neoliberalism 81, 85, 167–9, 253
Netsanet Demessie 156–8
New Labour *see* Labour government
Newai Gebre-Ab 84–7, 92
Nobel Peace Prize 209
Non-Government Organisations (NGOs) 69–70, 176–8, 182–4, 188–91, 193–5, 203, 211, 213, 215, 227
Norinco-Lalibela Engineering and Construction 240

Obama, President 131, 263
Ogaden National Liberation Front (ONLF) 196, 200–4, 206, 209, 212
Ohashi, Ken 81
Open Net Initiative 252
Open University 79
Organisation for the Relief and Rehabilitation of Amhara (ORDA) 31–2, 54, 104–8, 111, 115

Organisation for Social Justice in Ethiopia 156
Oromo Liberation Front (OLF) 187
Oxfam 12, 42–3, 69, 176, 179–82, 190, 193, 195; and New Labour 179–80; and resettlement 48–52
Oxfam America 125, 127, 176, 181, 185

Pankhurst, Dr Alula 46–7
Pankhurst, Prof Richard 27, 46
Pastoralist Communication Initiative (PCI) 213–15
Peace Corps 250
Petros Gyorgis 5
Pew Research Centre 245
population 120–38, 251, 261–235, 254–5; policy 122–3, 135, 137–8, 251; *see also* family planning
Portuguese Socialist party 146
Powell, Colin 193
privatisation 91–2
Protection of Basic Services, PBS 160

Raison, Sir Timothy 40
Reagan, President 38
Red Terror 36, 65, 162
Redfield, Peter 213

Relief and Rehabilitation
    Commission 38, 43–4
Relief Society of Tigray
    (REST) 66–67
Resettlement: and the
    Derg 45–55, 188; and the
    EPRDF 103–7
Rift Valley Children and Women
    Development Association
    127, 185–6
Ritchie, Lionel 12
Rwanda genocide 143

Sachs, Prof Jeffrey 256–7, 260–3
Safehands for Mothers 132
safety net programme 103, 110,
    118–9, 228, 231–2, 235, 230
Samaritans Purse 124
Save the Children Fund (SCF) 31,
    37, 178–80, 190, 211; 1984
    famine 37; 40–2; early
    associations 111–12;
    resettlement 48, 51–2; present
    day operations 111–15
Save the Children Fund USA
    197
Scott-Villiers, Alastair 214–15
Seeds of Despair 37–8, 42
Sen, Amartya 167
Seyoum Mesfin 199
Shepherd, Jack 29–30
Short, Clare 80, 198

Somalia 199, 200, 204
South African Institute of
    International Affairs 199,
    200, 204
Soviet Union 74, 166; abandons
    Derg 61–2, 74; alliance with
    Derg 40, 69; military
    supplies 56, 73
state farms 57–8
Stern, Lord 80
Stewart, Brian 22–3
Stiglitz, Joseph 81–3,
    88–91, 96
Sudan 68, 193, 205, 227
Swedish Red Cross 30

Tamrat Giorghis 184
Tedros Adhanom, Dr 136–7;
    and 2008 food emergency
    226–8, 230
Tefari Wossen 34
Teodoros, Emperor 28, 66
Teshome Erkineh 98
Thatcher, Margaret 40–2
The End of Poverty 262
The Hidden Hunger 35
The Reporter 145, 149, 154, 161–2,
    164–5, 172
The Unknown Famine 28–30,
    34–6, 98–9
Tigray Development
    Association 16

Tigrayan People's Liberation Front, TPLF 45, 63, 65–8, 70, 73–5
Tsadkan Gebre-Tensae, Lt Gen 64–7, 72, 75

Umar, Abdi 215
United Nations 31, 38, 121, 135, 159, 200, 214–15, 260
United Nations Children's Fund (UNICEF) 13; and 1973 famine 30; and 2003 emergency 100, 197; and 2008 emergency 225–31
United Nations Commission on Population and Development 135
United Nations Economic Commission for Africa 250
United Nations Office for Coordination of Humanitarian Affairs, OCHA 215
United Nations Population Fund, UNFPA 136
United States 44, 74, 95, 131, 134, 181, 214, 246, 247, 252, 262; and 1984 famine 39; administration of George W Bush 130–1, 151, 193, 204; and food aid 26, 69, 102, 111, 199

USAID 39, 102, 111–12, 115, 181, 210
United States Centers for Disease Control and Prevention 197
United States Congress 155
Universal Declaration of Human Rights 183
USA for Africa 12

Vaux, Tony 42–3, 50–1, 178, 181
villagisation 57
Voluntary Service Overseas 250

'War on Terror' 204
Waugh, Evelyn 2, 239
Willemse, Jacques 68
Wolde-Mariam, Prof Mesfin, see Mesfin Wolde-Mariam, Prof
Woldemichael Mehesha, Judge 155
Wolfensohn, James 91
Workers Party of Ethiopia 39, 47–8, 61–2
World Bank 81–4, 88–94, 159
World Food Council 3
World Food Programme, WFP 200–2, 227, 260
World Health Assembly 228
Wrong, Michela 56

Xu Chun 238, 249

Yohannes, Emperor 53
Yohannes Michael, Father 221–4, 234, 236–7
Yoseph Mulugeta 187–8

Zenawi, Meles, *see* Meles Zenawi

Zhong Xing Telecommunications Equipment, ZTE 243
Zhongyan Petroleum Exploration Bureau 204
Zhou Yongshen 240–3
Zimbabwe 76